MAKING
CONNECTIONS

MAKING CONNECTIONS

Wade Rowland

GAGE PUBLISHING LIMITED
Toronto, Vancouver, Calgary, Montreal

Designed by Mario Carvajal
Cover Design by Brant Cowie

Canadian Cataloguing in Publication Data

Rowland, Wade, 1944-
Making Connections
ISBN 0-7715-9442-9
1. Connections (Television program)
2. Television – Canada – Production and direction – Case studies.
3. Television broadcasting of news – Canada.
I. Title.

PN1992.75.R69   791.45'7   C79-094729-3

Printed in Canada
1 2 3 4 HR 82 81 80 79

Contents

For my wife Chris and her violet light

Connections: The Underworld Cast

ROME →

Domenic Barbino
Mafia Member and Cousin to the Late Paolo Violi

TORONTO

Paul Volpe
Toronto Mafia Boss
Raymond "Squeaker" Greco
Toronto Enforcer
Angelo Pucci
Real Estate Speculator and Volpe Associate
Mike Racco
Toronto Mafia Leader
Domenic Racco
Son of Mike Racco
Dave McGoran
Toronto Mob Associate
Remo Commisso
Toronto Mafia Leader

MONTREAL

Paolo Violi
Late Mafia boss of Montreal
Vic Cotroni
Godfather, Montreal Mafia
Frank Cotroni
Brother of Vic Cotroni
Joe DiMaulo
Lieutenant to Vic Cotroni
Nicola Dilorio
Lieutenant to Vic Cotroni
Hell's Angels
Bikers
Claude Dubois
Head of the Dubois Gang
Pierre McSween
Ex-gangster

NEW YORK

Carmine Galente
Late U.S. Mafia Boss

ATLANTIC CITY

Bonnie
Local Real Estate Agent, Associate of Angelo Pucci

HAMILTON

John Papalia
Toronto/Hamilton Mafia Boss
Giacomo Luppino
Godfather Toronto/Hamilton Mafia Family

BUFFALO

Stefano Magaddino
Late Buffalo Mafia Leader

MIAMI

Meyer Lansky
U.S. Mafia Associate, Specializing in Laundering of Money

CALGARY

The Grim Reapers
Calgary Motorcycle Gang

VANCOUVER

Joe Romano
Vancouver Mob Associate
Carlo Gallo
Vancouver Mafioso
Pasquale Calabrese
Aliases: **Pat Cala**
Frank Angelo
Former U.S. Mafioso and Undercover Police Investigator
Joe Gentile
Vancouver Mafia Leader
Frank Magasono
Vancouver Mafioso

SAN JOSE

Bill Bonnano
Son of Joe Bonnano
Angelo Marino
California Mafia Leader

ARIZONA

Joe Bonnano
U.S. Mafia Boss

VENEZUELA

Nick Rizzuto
Former Montreal Mafioso

viii

Prologue

Investigative journalism, like trout fishing, demands as much patience as it does skill. First you wade out hip-deep in icy water. Then you set the bait, wait, freshen the bait, wait some more and, with a little luck and a good deal of perseverance, you might catch something. This kind of journalism is usually associated with print reporters on the big metropolitan dailies: the Woodwards and Bernsteins of the seventies and the dashing press-card-in-fedora scoop artists that Hollywood dished out in the thirties and forties. (''Hello sweetheart, get me rewrite!'') Print reporters travel light, burdened only by a notebook and pencil, but even on newspapers a good investigative journalist requires months, not hours, to do a job well.

Investigative journalism on television has always suffered by the medium's cumbersome technology. It is as if the trout fisherman first had to find his way to a secluded stream in an armoured personnel carrier accompanied by tactical air support, and then somehow entice the fish onto his hook while flares explode and sirens wail over the water. The technology is so unwieldly and expensive – the two-ton pencil, they call it – that television has, by and large, simply ignored investigative journalism and concentrated its resources on the coverage of spot news and news analysis.

There have been some notable exceptions to this rule, and this book is about one of them.

On Sunday, June 12, 1977, at 9:30 p.m., the first of two, ninety-minute programs on organized crime in Canada appeared on the Canadian Broadcasting Corporation TV network and caused an instant sensation. All the underworld figures we'd read about – Paolo Violi, John Papalia, Paul Volpe, Vic Cotroni, Carmine Galente – were there on the screen. We saw them outside ice cream parlours, beside highways, on church steps, in real estate offices and in back yards. We saw them eating, meeting on street corners and whispering to each other at funerals. Sometimes we could even hear what they were saying.

The second ninety-minute program appeared at the same time the next night. The reaction across Canada was one of stunned fascination, not so much for what was revealed as for how it was revealed.

"The most staggering, shocking and revelatory documentary ever made," gasped the Winnipeg *Tribune*. "The biggest and most daring TV exposé ever undertaken into organized crime," said the *Goderich Star* (Ontario). "Perhaps the finest thing the CBC has ever done," said the *Toronto Sun*. "The CBC has done a valuable job for the community," intoned the Toronto *Globe and Mail*.

It was like watching the first televised moon walks: one was fascinated by the scenery, but even more staggered by the fact that it was there to be seen on the TV screen.

The two programs, called *Connections*, took three years and more than half a million dollars to make. If the investigative journalists on the *Connections* team didn't travel as lightly as the print reporters, they learned some new tricks of their own. They used camera equipment developed for military use in Vietnam – a lens capable of multiplying available light 80,000 times. They used film so fast that it could only be processed in a special New York laboratory. They used camouflaged surveillance vehicles and relayed instructions to one another *sotto voce* over sophisticated walkie-talkies. They used hidden body-pack tape recorders the size of pocket books and concealed microphones smaller than an olive pit. They used informers, decoys and renegade mob members.

None of the members of the team had much conventional journalistic experience, and none knew much about organized crime when the investigation began. Therefore, they began by asking the most basic questions, and they invented unorthodox approaches to getting the answers on the air.

Television is a medium plagued by personality conflicts. *Connections* endured its share of these. Sometimes they led to a kind of creative ferment, and sometimes they were simply exhausting and destructive. In both cases, they played an important part in shaping the programs.

When it was all over, the producers were unanimous in vowing "never again." But then there were the rave reviews, and offers of lavish budgets from the CBC (and even, perhaps, a nagging call to duty) . . . and nearly two years later, in March, 1979, three sequels were aired under the title: *Connections – The Second*

Series. And in many ways the second series, though flawed, was even more fascinating than the first. The investigative techniques had been refined and polished, and some significant new wrinkles added. Once again, critics were lavish in their praise.

I was asked to write this book late in December, 1978, three months before the second series went to air. The manuscript was completed in mid-April. It was an extremely hectic period for the men and women responsible for *Connections*, and yet they were always willing to take time to talk about the series and to answer my many questions. I am especially indebted in this regard to the three prime movers of the project: producers Bill Macadam and Martyn Burke, and research chief Jim Dubro, and to executive producer Dick Nielsen.

I hope that the story as I have recorded it in the following pages does justice to their remarkable achievement in conceiving, re-searching and producing those five estimable television programs.

Part I

Connections
An investigation into organized crime in Canada
A CBC/Norfolk Communications Ltd. co-production

The Credits

Co-producer: William Macadam
Co-producer: Martyn Burke
Research Director: James Dubro
Researchers: Michel Auger
              Jean-Pierre Charbonneau
              Craig Taylor
              John Sham
              Andrea Kolchinsky
              Kevin Sinclair
Camera: Francis Granger
Sound: John Crawford
Editors: Names withheld by request
Sound and Music Editor: Bruce Nyznik
Unit Manager: Kim Hester
Service Producer: Alf Norris
Facilities Co-ordinator: Casey Kollontay
Production Assistants: Clarissa MacNair
                      Seven names withheld by request
Graphics: Name withheld by request
Sound Consultant: Name withheld by request
Narrator: Name withheld by request
Executive Producer: Richard Nielsen

Innocents Abroad

"You would fold your arms and everybody would fold them along with you and then they would give you the official words for the ceremony . . . you would kiss everybody, write your name in the book and it's over."

Toronto mobster describing his initiation into the Mafia

December, 1974. Had I not been expecting Jim Dubro and Bill Macadam, I could have sworn when I greeted the two men at my front door that they were either Mormon missionaries or Bible salesmen. I don't think I have ever seen two more unlikely-looking crime reporters. I watched while they removed their galoshes (which they had both buckled all the way to the top), and then ushered them into my small study. While they were busy extracting pencils and notepads from jacket pockets, I sized them up.

Dubro, hopelessly natty in Harris tweed, bearing a slim and expensive leather briefcase, exuded Ivy League charm and spoke with the laconic precision of a lecturer in eighteenth-century literature. He sounded a lot like a young Ogden Nash. A wedge of wiry blond hair protruding like a sports car cap over his forehead, a large beak of a nose, a prominent Adam's apple and a tendency to project his face far in front of his body as he squinted myopically from under a heavy brow – all these combined to give him an odd, streamlined look. He had a large pocket watch which he wore on a fob attached to his belt. His shortsightedness forced him to bend almost in half to get close enough to see the dial when he wanted to check the time. Apparently it had never occurred to him to put it on a longer chain. He seemed an affable sort, possessed of a sincere but slightly clumsy charm.

And Macadam – a few years Dubro's senior at thirty-six, and

3

slightly stooped; wispy, wind-whipped blond hair, aviator's glasses, a threadbare grey flannel suit that looked like it had been dry-cleaned once too often, and a horrible, narrow little Ralph Nader tie. I caught a glimpse of initials hand-embroidered on his shirt pocket and a family signet ring, as he reached for his pencil. His briefcase was of the workaholic's miniature suitcase variety, and from the way he lugged it across the room it must have weighed at least twenty-five pounds. He had a slight stammer which I later discovered could vanish completely when there was no advantage to be gained from using it. Macadam, too, was a charmer, although it did not seem to me to come as naturally to him as it did to Dubro – he had to work at it and you could see that he was a little uncomfortable at not being completely in charge of the situation.

They had come to talk to me that afternoon because I had once reported on organized crime for the old Toronto *Telegram* and had thus been included by Dubro on a long list of people-to-be-talked-to, a list he had compiled in the first days of research. The three of us spent a couple of hours discussing organized crime in general terms . . . where it had come from and where it was headed. I did what I could to try to counter what seemed to me to be a blithely naive enthusiasm for the subject with a description of some of the headaches and frustrations that print journalists had encountered in trying to cover it. It seemed to me that trying to do the job on television, with the added burden of ungainly technology, was a virtually hopeless task. But I gave them the names of a few useful police contacts and one or two other sources I had used and wished them good luck, hiding my skepticism as best I could.

I have a distinct memory of saying to a friend later that day, "Those poor saps . . . they don't know what they're getting into."

Apart from two or three well-lubricated get-togethers over dinner at Noodles, a classy Italian restaurant in downtown Toronto which Macadam haunts with compulsive predictability, that was the last I saw of them until *Connections I* and *II* [the first series] hit the air two and a half years later with an impact you could have measured with a seismograph.

To say that I was glad to be out of crime reporting myself would be a shocking understatement. While it is among the most fascinating and challenging areas of endeavour for an investigative reporter, it can also be by far the most frustrating and the least rewarding.

The main problems are Canada's rigid libel laws and the enormous expense involved in mounting an adequate defence in court. But there are others. Good sources are difficult to come by, and understandably so. Crime victims and informants inside the mob may well be risking an encounter with goons wielding baseball bats in talking to a reporter: they may even face death. So they seldom talk. And it is almost as difficult to get information out of the police. The organized crime bureaus of the major police forces are perhaps the most security-conscious branches at such organizations, and reliable sources within these departments take months of painstaking work to develop to the stage where they will be willing to help you out from time to time on a difficult story. To do his job effectively, a reporter needs dozens of such sources. And there is a Catch-22 here. Generally, one develops this kind of informed source by trading information; it is a "you-scratch-my-back-and-I'll-scratch-yours" kind of arrangement, and it works best when the reporter can offer worthwhile trade bait. This, of course, means that the reporter needs to develop his own body of intelligence before he can begin swapping for what is available from police sources.

Most information-swapping with reporters goes on at a personal level. This kind of hanky-panky is generally frowned upon by book-bound senior officers, and in any case a good police officer will deal only with reporters with whom he has developed a relationship of mutual trust and respect. He could, after all, be putting his career on the line by divulging police information to the press, and a reporter who uses the information irresponsibly could wreck an important investigation by tipping-off its subjects. Often, clandestine arrangements for meeting a good police source are just as elaborate as they are for a rendezvous with a mob informant or victim.

There can be few reporters involved in this kind of cloak-and-dagger business who have not often asked themselves if they wouldn't be better off asking for a transfer to real estate or obituaries – especially on those, albeit infrequent, occasions when his byline has appeared over a story likely to do some real damage to the underworld and he has to endure a brief twinge of fear every time he turns the key in his car's ignition for the next few weeks.

While it is true that the mob seldom attacks reporters (to do so would draw too much heat from the authorities), it is also true that there are exceptions to this rule. In June, 1976 forty-eight-year-old *Arizona Republic* reporter Don Bolles, father of six children, was killed when a bomb placed beneath his car exploded. He had been investigating high-level corruption and mob infiltration in the Arizona state legislature. In the spring of 1973 a hood named Tony Mucci walked into the newsroom at *Le Devoir* in Montreal and began blazing away with a .22 revolver at crime reporter Jean-Pierre Charbonneau, missing twice and hitting him once, in the left forearm. Dick Levitan, a reporter who runs an investigative team for the *Boston Herald*, returned home one night in 1978 to discover that someone had doused his apartment and furniture in bucketsful of animal blood. It must have been a sobering experience.

Added to all of this is the fact that reporting on crime – organized variety or otherwise – has traditionally been among the lowest-status jobs in journalism. The crime beat has been seen as a repository for dead-beats, rookies and alcoholic derelicts who have been around for so long it has become impossible to fire them. Anyone who shows any talent for investigation on the beat is quickly moved to a more respectable (usually political) assignment. Those who are left behind are often the subject of ugly rumours about being on the take from criminals or the police, or both.

This was some of the bad news I felt obliged to pass on to Dubro and Macadam that December afternoon.

I have no way of knowing what the two thought of my litany of woes (neither can remember) but from their air of polite interest, I suspect they felt I was laying it on a bit thick. In my own defence, I think I can accurately state that I had a sneaking suspicion even then that if anyone were ever to bring organized crime reporting to television, it would be those two: they were just . . . unorthodox enough to pull it off.

The Secret Office

"Organized crime? Very simple. It's just a bunch of people getting together to take all the money they can from all the suckers they can."

Former mob member Vincent Teresa

December, 1978. Four years have passed. *Connections I* and *II* have become part of Canadian television history, and now three promising sequels are nearing completion.

And here I am, outside the secret *Connections* headquarters on the fourth floor of the crumbling Film House building on Front Street in Toronto, a freshly-signed and witnessed contract in my briefcase for a book about how they did it. I am to meet with Dubro, first on my list of about fifteen members of the *Connections* crew whom I will have to interview.

There are three doors to the office, all unmarked, distinguished only by chrome Abloy lock fixtures – the pick-proof kind that take a special half-round key. I select a door and knock and seconds later it opens about eight inches. Jamie Boyd, the office manager and general factotum peers out at me and then opens the door wide.

"Hi, come on in. I've been expecting you."

I step inside and the door swings closed behind me, locking automatically.

Jamie is in his mid-twenties, but he looks quite a bit older because he is beginning to lose his hair. He wears his jeans tucked into a pair of leather riding boots; his shirt is full-sleeved and collarless. He would fit in better at the CBC drama department.

"Well, this is it," he says with a sigh, sweeping his hand out in a modest theatrical gesture.

"I'm sorry it's such a mess . . . I'm really going to have to tidy up a bit."

It is a formality – he doesn't give a damn about the mess any more than I do.

He leaves me to browse until Dubro arrives, and to amuse myself I slide open a drawer in the huge card index file and flip through the names. The fabled *Connections* files.

Investigating organized crime is initially almost entirely a matter of making the right connections, of establishing associations. Most of the people in whom you are interested are walking the streets, which means that even the police have been unable to pin anything on them. You know they are mixed up with the mob partly by their past records, but mainly by the company they keep, and you establish this through surveillance of various kinds and by meticulous cross-referencing of every name that comes up in the course of the investigation. This is why Dubro has been such an invaluable member of the *Connections* crew. He is a researcher and a connection-maker *par excellence*.

In the four years he has been researching organized crime in Canada for *Connections*, Dubro and a staff that has varied from one to as many as half a dozen assistants, has helped put together a collection of information on criminals and their methods that is astonishing. There is nothing like it anywhere in Canada, outside the criminal intelligence services of a few large police forces and federal enforcement agencies. It is the backbone of the whole *Connections* operation; the brain of the organism. It is the reason why the doors to the *Connections* office must always be kept locked; why no one who is not directly attached to the production team is ever allowed to set foot in the office; it is why everyone on the production staff who has access to the office has had to sign a contract containing punitively rigid secrecy and disclosure clauses. It is the most complete compendium of information on Canadians, well-known and obscure, and their criminal records and associations that has ever been assembled in private hands. This means it is also potentially the most explosive body of research in existence in Canada, outside the major law enforcement agencies. It is Dubro's pride and joy; his baby.

On a low table against a wall, opposite the paper shredder, is a collection of thirty-two index-card file drawers containing thirty-five thousand names, completely cross-referenced. Along another wall is a bank of eight, four-drawer legal-sized filing cabinets, which contain the tapes, photos and printed information referred to in the numerical code on the index cards. The information has been painstakingly collected from books, magazines, newspapers, surveillance reports, police wiretap transcripts and other police documents, court records and transcripts, corporate ownership records and interviews with hundreds of law enforcement officers, civil servants, businessmen, union officers, journalists, lawyers and criminals. The mass of information has grown so large that at one point the *Connections* crew discussed banking it all in a computer for convenience. But that would have led to security problems, and anyway, it was too expensive.

I pull out the card-index drawer marked Re-Rz and after a moment of thumbing through the cards, extract one bearing my own name and three reference numbers. And just then, Dubro breezes through the door and takes the situation in at a glance.

"You see? We've got every crook in the country listed here." He chuckles at his joke. "Actually, that will be the notes from our first meeting with you, back when we were just starting out."

Dubro's ensemble today is a muted blue tweed jacket, broadcloth shirt, conservatively striped tie, grey flannel trousers and black loafers. He looks like he's just stepped out of an ad in *Gentleman's Quarterly* as he hangs his Aquascutum on the coat tree.

"I'll be with you in just a few minutes. I have a couple of calls I have to make first."

"Fine, me too."

His calls are definitely more interesting than mine. First, he sets up a screening for later that afternoon: the *Connections* crew had purchased some film in Italy shot for an Italian documentary on the Mafia, and it has to be looked at to see if any of it might be useful to them. The trouble is, it's in Italian and the only translator they've checked for security is not available. Dubro rustles up an RCMP sergeant who is fluent in Italian and who is willing to translate.

Then he puts in a call to Calabria, Italy. He is calling a reporter for the London *Times* who is covering a Mafia trial there: the call goes through unexpectedly rapidly, and there is a scramble to get the tape recorder attached to the phone before she comes on the line.

Dubro learns from the reporter that the key to the trial is turning out to be the kidnapping of John Paul Getty III, one of the younger members of the famous oil family. The kidnapping is something the *Connections* sequels would be delving into. He also learns that Granada TV in Britain is sending a crew to cover the trial. That's good news: *Connections* would be able to buy film from them.

Then a call to the film editor who is cutting the Getty piece to give him the news. "Yes, that's right Granada . . . It's going to be making big news . . . I suppose we could get scooped a bit depending on what comes out . . ."

No one is very concerned about the possibility of having to scrap *Connections* material – they have more than they know what to do with. The biggest problem at this stage is cutting it back into some kind of manageable length. (The latest in a series of tentative schedules for the programs is pinned to a bulletin board in the office; it shows three programs, *Connections 3, 4* and *5*: the first ninety minutes long and the following two sixty minutes each. The airdate is set for early March, 1979, about two and a half months away.)

Dubro has also received a message, he tells me, from an informer named Lou.

"This is very unusual. In the past we have set up all the meetings somewhere on neutral ground, but this time he wants to see me in his office. Says he's got something very important to tell me."

"Isn't it a bit risky meeting him in his office?"

"Yes, I suppose it is, a bit. He's actually taking bigger risks than the mob characters we've talked to who have gotten out and are co-operating with the police. They get protection, but Lou is dealing with these guys every day."

"A stool pigeon?"

"That's right, I guess that's what you'd call him. And remember what Volpe said about stoolies on the last show?"

I remembered it well. The very idea of trying to interview Paul Volpe, the most influential figure in organized crime in Toronto and a fully-initiated member of the Mafia – a "made man" in the argot – had the kind of spunk, the kind of chutzpah that made *Connections I* and *II* the most-watched public affairs documentaries ever aired by the CBC.

Macadam had enviegled his way into Volpe's home on the pretext of filming a re-enactment of Volpe's discovery of a police bug planted near the patio in his chain-link fenced, flood-lit back-yard. Macadam claimed to be sympathetic to Volpe's protestations of police harassment and, incredibly, Volpe had agreed to the filming, a portion of which duly appeared on *Connections II*.

Following the shoot, Macadam had a private, friendly chat with Volpe over coffee in Volpe's kitchen. Macadam had been wired for sound with a button mike attached to a Nagra SN tape recorder concealed beneath his shirt, and the pocket-book sized machine recorded the following comment of Volpe's for posterity:

"They have stool pigeons all over the world . . . and the minute a stool pigeon gets killed . . . someone kills him . . . which to me is rightly so – you gotta kill them, you gotta get them out of the way . . . anybody that's an informer, he's only looking to hurt people."

I recall the murder of an informer a few years earlier: this particular stool pigeon paid for his transgression by being garotted to death . . . but only after his murderers had set him afire and then carefully carved thirty pounds of flesh from his body while he was still alive, in the kind of macabre ritual that is a hallmark of Mafia killings.

The point is that Lou is taking quite a risk.

Dubro and I decide to go out for some lunch, mainly to get away from the telephones so that we can talk about how this whole extraordinary project got started. He introduces me to a nearby greasy spoon where we both order the special of the day – toasted ham and cheese with tepid french fries.

We are just finishing our food when Dubro looks up and says, "There's Lou. He's coming over to our table."

"Uh, do you want me to clear out? Won't he be uncomfortable with a stranger here?"

But there is no time for a reply: Dubro is already standing, his serviette in one hand, the other extended in greeting.

I look up to see a swarthy gentleman with a black moustache. He is wearing a battered khaki car coat with an ersatz fur collar.

Dubro blithely introduces me.

"Hi," I say, "pleased to meet you."

Lou gives me an unexpectedly open smile as he shakes my hand.

"Jim, I'll see you in about half an hour. I've got a couple of people to talk to first."

He waves as he walks toward the door, and Dubro sits down to resume his lunch.

"Well," I manage, "he certainly seems cool."

Dubro looks at me, nonplussed, and then smiles a weary smile. "No, no, you've got it wrong. That's not Lou the informer. That Lou's name isn't Lou. We only call him that. This Lou was the police sergeant who'll be doing the translation for us on the Italian footage."

My first day on the book project, and already I'm being infected by the notorious *Connections* paranoia.

On our way back to the office, I ask Dubro why *Connections* is interested in the Getty kidnapping story. I can't see what it has to do with organized crime in Canada. Dubro begins to reply, but then interrupts himself:

"You see that old guy running the news kiosk over there on the corner?"

I glance across the street and see a blue and white *Toronto Star* vendor's stand, and an old man – probably sixty-five or seventy – huddling out of the wind, pulling his blue serge greatcoat tightly around him and stamping his feet to keep the circulation going.

"That's Shorty (not his real name). He's with the mob. They say he's got a small fortune, and he's got some of it out on the street."

"On the street?"

"He's a loan shark."

"You mean he does business right there on the street?" I ask, taking a closer look. This guy could be someone's grandfather.

"We're not exactly sure how he works it, but you'll often see cars of organized criminals pulling up there and he goes over and talks to them right there on the curb. He's apparently a sort of information depot as well."

I am thinking that Dubro walks by here every day on his way to the *Connections* office.

"Does he know who you are?"

"I don't think so . . . if he does, he's never let on. I get most of our out-of-town newspapers there."

As we wait for the traffic light, I have a sudden flashback to an old Cagney movie. Cagney looks strangely like Dubro. I can hear the dialogue . . .

"You gotta help me Shorty, you gotta tell me who did it. Otherwise the best dame that ever set foot in this town goes up the river for life!"

Shorty slips another paper to a passing customer, snatches the nickel out of the air, drops it in his apron.

"Awright kid, I guess I owe ya one. It was Pinky and his boys."

"Pinky!" . . .

Except that this real-life Shorty, if he's like other real-life loan sharks, doesn't have a heart of gold. Witness this excerpt from the *Connections I* transcript:

Narrator: July 27th, 1971. This is U.S. Senator McClellan's permanent subcommittee [on organized crime]. Vincent Teresa testifies about his loanshark operation.

Teresa: Piranha. We named the company after one of those fish from South America, you know, the one that eats you up as soon as you fall in the water.

Sen. McClellan: What?

Teresa: You know, the fish that . . . piranha fish . . . that when you fall in the water, they clean you right down to your bones in a matter of minutes.

McClellan: They eat . . . the man-eating fish.

Teresa: The man-eating fish. That's it.

McClellan: Do you think that was an appropriate name for your company?

Teresa: Well, we wanted to be known as a tough outfit. That's why we named it the Piranha Finance Company. One of the guys that ran it, Pete, he was cuckoo, you know he was a junkie, he used to take stuff, he was always floating around in the air. They had to shoot him down off the ceiling once in a while and he had this big tank with two piranha, Pete and Gladys . . . it's a fact. We used to tell the customers, if you don't pay, we'll stick your hand in.

McClellan: Do you think they got the message?

Teresa: They got the message. One day this kid, Tally Yacha [phonetic spelling] comes in the place, that owes us a lot of money and was behind in his payments and I liked him. He was a very likable guy, and kidding with him, I says . . . you know, you son of a . . . if you don't pay, I'm gonna stick your hand right in there and I did. I never thought anything'd happen to him and the damn fish bit his finger off . . . the top of it. You know I said that in front of the sub-committee and Jesus, it made nationwide headlines about fish eating people . . . that's a lot of foolishness. I've had piranhas since then and put my hand in and they never done a thing to me. It was just hungry I guess, or maybe he liked that greasy thumb he had.

Narrator: But for the victims, the reality is not so amusing . . . What you are about to hear is the actual conversation between a loanshark and his victim.

[The tape used here of a wiretapped telephone conversation was provided for *Connections* by the Montreal Police.]

Loanshark victim: All right, I appreciate it very much that you loan me the $100 but what I do not understand is this . . . why do you charge me 25 bucks a week extra every time. $125 is the charge, I could give that to you any time. But hell, $400, $500, $600 . . . how much do you want?

Loanshark: I told you I wanted $400. I'm selling it anyways.

Victim: You're going to sell that.

Loanshark: Yup, I don't want to fuckin' bother with this.

Victim: Well, alright, what the hell they going to do to me?

Loanshark: What they're going to do to you I don't know. Whatever they want.

Victim: Why can't you give me some work to do?

Loanshark: [shouting] I don't have no fuckin' work for you to do. I give you money. I want my fuckin' money, understand? . . . You listen now, okay?

Victim: Yeah.

Loanshark: When I give you that fuckin' money, you were supposed to come and pay it. Now you didn't pay. You owe $400. You understand? . . . Now don't tell me to give you work to pay back fuckin' money! I'm selling the account. Somebody else will go up there – you won't know them and you'll see if you like borrowing money and not paying.

Victim: Well, alright, now you sell the account to someone else, okay.

Loanshark: Now if your windows get blown out tonight, that's your fault.

Victim: If they're blown out . . . alright, it's my fault.

Loanshark: Okay, if your kids get hit with bullets, that's your fault.

Victim: Don't touch my kids! If you touch my kids, I'm telling you right now, I'm going after you!

Loanshark: Yeah?

Victim: You! You, you yourself!

Loanshark: I'm telling you . . .

Victim: That's right! What . . .

Loanshark: . . . that someone is going to grab you and there's going to be trouble.

This particular victim wasn't in as deeply as some . . . *Connections* interviewed one terrified man who had had to repay $10,000 on an initial $300 loan.

But back to Dubro . . . and my question about the Getty kidnapping.

"Why are we interested in the kidnapping? Because the guy who supposedly masterminded the whole thing, Dominic Barbino, is a first cousin of Paulo Violi, who was the boss in Montreal until he was murdered last year. And the police logged phone calls between the two of them during and after the kidnapping. There was no tap on the line, so all they have are the logs.''

''But it's another connection.''

Dubro smiles. ''Right. Another connection.''

3
The Collaborators

"I couldn't believe it myself, I felt, you know, this can't happen here. It's Canada, and everything should be peaceful. When I realized that these people were actually members of organized crime I decided I had to stand up and fight.

Union official Jean-Guy Denis detailing an attempt by Mafia to take over control of an Ottawa plasterers' and cement masons' union.

January 1979. Bill Macadam has just arrived back in Toronto after having spent Christmas and New Year with his family in England. I am waiting for an interview in the Norfolk Communications offices on the eleventh floor of a new high-rise office building on Toronto's University Avenue. A fine address. Norfolk, Macadam's film production company, has apparently come a long way since the days of cadging space from the CBC in windowless cubbyholes and enlarged broom closets.

Macadam emerges from his carpeted office to greet me with a boyish smile and hearty good wishes for the new year. I am tempted to ask him: "How's the Queen?" but think better of it. There is no telling how this kind of ribbing will go down with him. His family background can be a sensitive area, as writer Ron Base discovered in interviewing him for *Quest* magazine a couple of years ago:

"I broach the subject of money in an intimate little wine bar with dark wood, ceramic tiles and a cheerful waiter who in season carries spears at Stratford. And Macadam, until now the personification of aloof cool when I'm around, abruptly loses it. His mouth twists into several strange shapes before he says: 'Who told you my family had money? Who told you that?' Actually, just about anyone acquainted with Macadam at CBC apparently regards him as a man of some means. 'Money certainly doesn't seem to be a problem

for him,' says a colleague. But I'm not about to say that. . .'
'Well, I don't care what you've heard,' Macadam says. 'I mean,
this isn't something I want to get into, but my family isn't wealthy.
And I've worked hard for everything I have.'''

Certainly no-one who has spent any length of time around
Macadam can doubt that he works very hard indeed. The fact is,
he does almost nothing else. The lights in the Norfolk offices
can usually be seen burning brightly long after everyone else in
the building has gone home, had dinner and settled down in front
of the television set for another evening of brain damage.

Still, few young television producers that I know of can afford to
indulge a taste for etchings of Rembrandt, Whistler and Milne, or
hop over to London for a weekend when the fancy strikes, or dine
out nightly in sumptuous surroundings, or for that matter be as
overwhelmingly generous with thoughtful gifts and dinner invitations. And still fewer could afford to bankroll a private production
company like Norfolk, which has poured tens of thousands of
dollars into program development and research.

It has occurred to me on occasion that part of the secret of
Macadam's success in the difficult business of freelance television
production has been that he can afford to make mistakes, and he can
afford to insist on doing things his way, because when push comes
to shove he has the security of knowing he can afford to drop out of
a project and take a bath doing it.

One of Macadam's most famous ancestors is John Louden
Macadam (1756-1836), inventor of the macadamizing system of
road paving, a method so cheap and easy that it revolutionized
highway transportation in Britain in the nineteenth century. He very
nearly went broke developing his idea, but Parliament eventually
granted him a yearly pension for his efforts.

Macadam's father, who died in 1975 at age eighty, has been
described as ''part of the hegemony that whispered advice into the
British Establishment's ear during World War II,'' and he in fact
wrote Neville Chamberlain's tragic speech declaring war on the
Nazis in 1939. His obituary in the London *Times* remembered him
thusly:

''Sir Ivison Macadam, KCVO, CBE, FRSE; founder and trus-
tee, National Union of Students . . .

''At Chatham House [The Royal Institute of International Affairs, where he served as Secretary and Director-General] he is
remembered for his Scottish drive and application in pure admin

matters. He organized persons, events, and work with equal stern objectivity, and he got a lot done accordingly, though sometimes making opponents by his singlemindedness . . . He worked early, late and continuously, and he never shunned unpleasantness which fell to him to handle . . ."

Macadam's mother, Lady Caroline (to whom Macadam writes with touching regularity in his clotted ball-point scrawl), is great-granddaughter to Henry Winslow Corbett (1827-1903), an American entrepreneur in the classic mould. With the help of a wealthy backer, at age 19 Corbett leased a small ship, stuffed it with dry goods and sailed it around Cape Horn from the Atlantic seaboard to the booming Pacific northwest. He made a killing selling the merchandise on board and went into the railroad business. He settled in Oregon in 1851, and became Portland's leading businessman, founding Oregon's First National Bank and *The Oregonian* newspaper. Later, as the first United States senator from Oregon, he was an early supporter of the presidential aspirations of Abraham Lincoln.

In the pantheon of Macadam heroes, this great-great-grandfather ranks high, right up there with T. E. Lawrence (of Arabia), in whose book *Seven Pillars of Wisdom* Macadam has found strong moral inspiration; the late, great broadcaster Edward R. Murrow, who is his journalistic inspiration; Henry Luce (founder of the *Time* empire) and Winston Churchill.

At the age of one, Macadam was shipped off to his grandparents' home in Oregon just before World War II, his father having been in a better position than most to know what horrors lay in wait for England.

With the end of the war Macadam, along with thousands of other young British refugees, returned home. Unlike most of the others, he was soon enrolled at Eton, one of the pillars of the crumbling institution known as "the old boy network." He was not a very good student, and will sheepishly admit to having been in the lowest form longer than any student in Eton's history.

At nineteen, his Eton education under his belt, Macadam was encouraged to seek his fortune in the Pacific northwest he had come to love as a child during the war. To emigrate to the United States, however, seemed too big a leap: he chose instead British Columbia, where he could work for a cousin who owned orchards in the Okanagan Valley. Within eight months he had moved on to a logging job on Vancouver Island. Fresh out of Eton, his head full of

Latin and his manners honed by years of hob-nobbing with par-
liamentarians and chiefs of state at home, and their scions at school,
he of course had nothing in common with the men with whom he
now found himself living and working. The trials that befell him out
there in the bush are not difficult to imagine: Macadam will say only
that the first of those years "were the loneliest of my life."

"It was one of the major mistakes of my life, to stay there for so
long. I often wanted to leave, but I just couldn't until I knew that I
could make it. In the end, I knew that I was better at doing what we
were doing than they were, and so did they. I was there for three or
four years . . . when I arrived I was a terrified kid, but by the time I
left I could walk into a fight with broken beer bottles and everything
and tell them to stop fighting, and they would."

The mere remembrance of all of this has brought a flush to his
face. He pauses, and then adds, "Once you've gone through
something like that, you know there's nothing you can't do. Nothing."

Macadam repeats the "nothing" with a queer intensity; there is
a powerful knot of emotion behind it.

A strike of the potent International Woodworkers of America
union finally got Macadam out of the sawmills. With the logging
industry shut down, Macadam and a few union friends decided to
build an airstrip near their Campbell River headquarters: the nec-
cessary heavy machinery was all there, made idle by the strike, and
the company agreed to let them use it. That job completed, the
group pooled their savings to purchase an ancient fabric-covered
Aeronca two-seater plane and hired a former RCAF instructor to
teach them how to fly it.

A new world was opened up for Macadam, one which fitted
perfectly with his romantic vision and newly-found self-
confidence. In 1964 Macadam and one of his flying friends got
together with a sympathetic bank manager to form a tiny air charter
business, which they named Trans-Mountain Airlines. After five
years of operating mainly in and out of remote inlets up and down
the coast of Vancouver Island and the British Columbia mainland,
the airline had accumulated a stable of more than a dozen light
aircraft.

During that period, Macadam was also busy becoming a force to
be reckoned with in the federal Conservative party. In 1960 he had
been coaxed into taking over the presidency of a moribund Vancouver Island riding association, and within a couple of years he

had become vice-president of the national party. He ran for Parliament in 1965 as a sacrificial Tory lamb in the NDP-dominated riding of Comox-Alberni and was soundly thrashed, despite an attention-grabbing campaign.

Politics had become a full-time preoccupation – in 1968 he served as Robert Stanfield's campaign manager – and he gradually eased himself out of the airline business. But it wasn't long before the frustrations of opposition politics became evident, and by 1971 he had successfully extracted himself from his party responsibilities and was once again casting about for something to do – something that would satisfy what one begins to suspect is a powerful sense of personal destiny.

He chose television journalism. And, of course, he jumped in with both feet. His first major interview, taped for a CBC Ottawa local public affairs program, was with former Conservative Prime Minister John Diefenbaker. During their chat, the Chief waxed uncharacteristically candid, admitting that there had been times as Prime Minister when he didn't really have much of a handle on what was going on in the lower echelons of government. He soon had second thoughts about what he'd said and ordered Macadam not to use the offending sections.

"You've made me look like a goose," he accused Macadam.

When Macadam proved unsympathetic, Diefenbaker railed at higher-ups in the CBC, threatening dire consequences if the interview was aired uncut.

There were a few frantic, soul-searching meetings with CBC management. But the interview was aired complete, and nothing came of Diefenbaker's threats. Another lesson learned.

A little later we find Macadam, dry of throat and clammy of palm, walking into a bar in Hull, just across the Quebec border from Ottawa, and sitting down at an empty table. He is there because he has been told it is the headquarters of an outlaw motorcycle gang called Satan's Choice, and he wants to do a film about the burgeoning rivalry between gangs in Ottawa and Hull. A waiter walks over to him and suggests he move to another table. It is not a particularly polite suggestion.

"Why? This table will do just fine."

"That table is reserved."

Macadam has chosen one of the tables set aside for members of Satan's Choice.

His voice involuntarily rising, he toughs it out with the waiter.

"That's okay. I want to meet some of the people anyway. It'll be okay. Just bring me a beer."

The waiter glares at him for a moment, and then shrugs it off.

"Awright, what'll it be?"

Macadam's knowledge of beer brands has suddenly left him.

"Uh . . . I'll have a Molson's 50."

"A what?"

If Macadam's motorcycle machismo bluff had ever had any credibility with the waiter, this gaffe has blown it. There is no such beer.

"A Molson's. Just bring me a Molson's," he replies lamely.

Later, in recounting the incident to a friend, Macadam says: "What I should have done was grab the waiter by the lapels and say, 'I said a Molson's 50. You get a glass, you take a Labatt's 50 and a Molson's X and you pour them in together. Got it?''

Before long, however, Macadam has indeed met and talked with members of Satan's Choice and soon he has permission from that gang and two others to interview and film them for a television documentary. The item was eventually aired on CBC Ottawa in two twenty-minute segments. A colleague later remembers them as having been "technically atrocious, but journalistically quite good. And the big thing is that nobody else thought it was even possible to do, and that counts for a lot. All in all, for a first effort, it was pretty good stuff."

For Macadam, it had been an opportunity to bring his personal credo into his efforts as a filmmaker. He later told an interviewer:

"The motorcycle thing was done as a challenge, accomplishing what seemed to be too difficult . . . [My] approach is to try to do things everyone thinks are impossible."

Macadam felt he was ready for the big time, and went looking for assignments from the CBC network public affairs department, whose flagship at that time was a big budget affair called *Weekend*.

Come up with a few good ideas, and we'll consider letting you do them, he was told: the standard response to inquiries from unknowns. Since developing good ideas involves research, Macadam eventually phoned the best researcher he knew, Jim Dubro, and asked if he'd be willing to help.

Macadam, filled with WASPish proscriptions about introspection (it softens the brain) will only occasionally, and only when pressed on the subject, admit that perhaps he might harbour one or two mild eccentricities. But Dubro, he will tell you with affectionate relish, now there is a *true* eccentric.

"Do you know, when he first started working on *Connections*, he was a part-timer in a department store tobacco shop to earn extra money!" The very thought of so outrageous an undertaking breaks him up.

"That's what's so great about him," he continues to marvel. "He is completely unselfconscious. I'll bet if he needed the money right now he'd go right back to working in a tobacco shop selling cigars and wouldn't think twice about it!" More laughter.

In Macadam's world such an occupation is clearly inconceivable for someone with Dubro's impeccable credentials.

Born in Boston in 1946, Dubro graduated *magna cum laude* and *Phi Beta Kappa* from Boston University before moving to Columbia University for a Master's degree in English literature (thesis: Dr. Johnson's *Life of Savage*), then to Harvard, and finally to the University of Toronto and a teaching fellowship at Victoria College. At that time, his best-known work was perhaps an article published in *Eighteenth Century Life*, based on his discovery of the manuscript of an obscure opus by the poet John Lord Hervey. The poem was called: "The First Ode of the Fourth Book of Horace Imitated in a Letter from Mr. Edgecombe to Mother Lodge."

But it was not Dubro's academic record which had impressed Macadam as much as his work as a fund raiser during a stint as research assistant to the Dean of Harvard and before that, at Vassar College in the United States. Fund-raising, you might think, is a relatively harmless undertaking, having little in common with the racier aspects of research into organized crime. This may be so at institutions where it is not taken very seriously, but it is not so at Harvard and Vassar, where it is taken very seriously indeed.

Dubro's main job at Harvard was to set up cross-indexed reference files on all known foundations. From the material in those files he prepared profiles of foundations not yet giving money to Harvard, and suggested ways in which their funds might be tapped by the university. But from time to time he was also involved in more specific fund-raising research.

"I remember one time the dean called our office and told us the daughter of a big Wall Street broker who had given five million dollars for a library, was coming by to have a look at the site. He wanted to know what the broker's life expectancy was and whether he had any sons. We checked the files and there was an insurance report in there that said he was expected to live only about four to six years. And we also found he had no sons. That's the kind of thing good research will tell you.

"She was only about twenty-one . . . normally some associate dean would have shown her around for a few minutes, but after we checked we had the Dean and the Vice-president out there showing her every hole in the ground. If the guy had had a son, there would have been no point in wasting the time on her.

"Terribly sleazy. All very unethical, I thought," he remarks cheerfully. Then he blushes and shifts his position in his chair.

On second thought he adds, "What's a few million to these guys. Probably nothing, and it's very important to the schools."

When he received the phone call from Macadam back in March 1973, Dubro was unemployed and rapidly going broke, studying for his oral examinations for his PhD. He agreed to try to develop some story ideas, he recalls, "partly because there was the chance of some income there, but mainly because the idea fascinated me."

Within a few days, he met with Macadam, a neat list of about twenty ideas in his briefcase. Among them was the proposal to investigate CIA activities in Canada, about which he had noted simply: "They're operating everywhere else . . . why not in Canada?"

The resulting program, *The Fifth Estate: The Espionage Establishment* had originally been planned as a ten- to twenty-minute item for insertion into the regular *Weekend* TV magazine-style format. But as Macadam and Dubro continued digging into the subject and developing new leads, it became clear that there was at least enough material for an hour-long special report. It was aired on the full CBC network in January, 1974.

It caused a House of Commons sensation by exposing the activities of a super-secret intelligence-gathering outfit fronting as a branch of the National Research Council. And in the process of putting it together, the two had also come close to causing an international incident when Dubro had diligently, if inexpertly, staked out the Virginia home of the RCMP's chief liaison officer with the CIA, in hopes of filming him leaving for work.

Dubro, accompanied by a cameraman, mounted his stake-out in a rented car parked across the street from the liaison officer's house, concealing himself for hours on end behind a smudgy copy of the *New York Times*. Of course he was spotted, and his vigil was eventually interrupted by the Virginia police, who arrived to ask what the hell he thought he was doing. Dubro explained that he and his cameraman were CBC journalists and argued that since they were on public property they had every right to remain there. But the police insisted that the two make themselves scarce, and in the end there was nothing to do but to comply with the order or be arrested.

By the time Dubro had driven back to the CBC's Washington bureau offices, the Virginia police had reported the incident to the RCMP, who, it developed, had been the source of the initial complaint. The RCMP had informed the Canadian Ambassador in Washington, who had contacted the CBC Washington bureau to state in no uncertain terms that CBC crews had no right to be operating in the United States without first being cleared through the embassy. He threatened to withdraw future embassy co-operation, and to have the whole matter raised in the House of Commons – a threat which can usually be relied upon to strike terror into the hearts of CBC bureaucrats.

The CBC's Washington bureau manager, Jack Rutherford, greeted Dubro with a wild stare – he had the embassy shouting in his ear in one phone, and CBC Ottawa demanding to know, on another line, what in God's name was happening. He was so upset he was shaking. (Rutherford later told a friend, "It was the worst day of my life.")

Dubro decided he'd better call Macadam in Toronto to ask for instructions. Macadam, in instantaneous high dudgeon over what he saw as the rankest kind of political interference with freedom of the press, told Dubro to sit tight. He then telephoned the Washington ambassador, threatening to hold a press conference if the ambassador did not offer a prompt apology to the CBC and promise to call off his dogs so that his crew could get on with their job. He gave the ambassador a half-hour deadline.

The luckless ambassador, outflanked and outgunned, chose dis-cretion and within fifteen minutes had complied with Macadam's belligerent demands.

"But that wasn't the end of it," Dubro was to tell me later. "Before long I got a call from the RCMP liaison officer himself. He said he'd heard I wanted to see him. 'No problem. Anytime. You want to film me? That'd be just fine. Whenever you like.'"

So Dubro and his cameraman drove to his office in the annex

to the Canadian embassy, this time to face another, unexpected problem.

"This time he was *too* co-operative. He kept looking at the camera, and we wanted it to look like surveillance film – we wanted him dodging out of his office and jumping into his car. We had to do three takes out on the parking lot to get it so that it looked right."

Here Dubro paused, an embarrassed smile playing on his lips:

"I've always felt a bit funny about that one."

If episodes like this – and there were others – proved nothing else, they demonstrated that this pair had a rare singlemindedness and determination. It is the kind of incident that executive producers and network vice-presidents like to file away in the back of their minds for retrieval on that day when they have a difficult story to assign. Macadam no longer found it necessary to go to the CBC scrounging assignments for his fledgling production company. The CBC came to him.

4
A Close Encounter

"Lookit here. See the hole here? That's the hole where it was in. And here's where the wire led . . ."

Paul Volpe describing to Bill Macadam how police bugged his poolside patio.

In the spring of 1974 Peter Herrndorf, Harvard whizkid and *enfant terrible* of the CBC administration, was appointed head of CBC television current affairs. In recent years, the department had lost much of the zest, sparkle and *esprit de corps* that had characterized it during the late sixties, and its programming reflected this. The critics were becoming more and more vicious: much of the acclaim received by *The Fifth Estate: The Espionage Establishment* had been couched in phrases like: "Now this is the kind of thing the CBC should be doing more often," or, "At last, something really interesting from CBC current affairs."

Herrndorf, determined to shake up the moribund department with an infusion of new blood and new ideas, went looking for talent even before his appointment had been made official. In April, he met with Macadam and asked him to submit a list of ideas for television documentaries.

The list Macadam produced was headed by a proposal for a look at the problems of maintaining Canadian sovereignty over the Arctic. He had come across information on American intrusions into Canadian territorial waters in the Arctic Ocean, and was eager to document the incidents and make them public. A second proposal was for an examination of the monopolistic role played by banks in the Canadian economy. And farther down the list was a suggestion that it might be worthwhile to have a look at organized crime in the country.

Macadam had hoped to get one of the projects underway within a few weeks, but it was to take nearly six months for Herrndorf to reorganize his department and sort out its budget: it was December before he asked Macadam to prepare a detailed preliminary research report on the subject he had finally selected from the list of proposals – organized crime in Canada.

Initially disappointed that Herrndorf had not chosen the Arctic proposal, Dubro and Macadam nonetheless plunged into the new project with the enthusiasm of the unsuspecting. On December 9, 1974 Dubro noted in his diary: "Today started Mafia project. Spent $8.45 on material . . . including this diary." A modest enough start to a project that eventually consumed well over half a million dollars in direct and indirect costs, and took two and half years to complete.

The working title given the project was "Commerce", a name deliberately chosen for its odour of turgid annual reports and dry balance sheets: it was a sure conversation-stopper at cocktail parties. This was part of the tight security imposed on the project from its inception, security that was so effective that until a few weeks before the two programs went to air in June 1977, only a handful of senior CBC personnel knew they were in production.

Within a few days of signing the research contract, Macadam heard that his father was dying: he left immediately for England, and it was February before funeral arrangements and the press of other family business permitted him to return.

Meanwhile, Dubro had comfortably ensconced himself in the main branch of the Toronto public library, cheerfully wading through the hundreds of books, reports, studies, magazine articles and newspaper clippings on organized crime and the Mafia, making notes on file cards. The approach was no different than if he had been researching some obscure Renaissance writer: locate the literature on the subject and read it, or at least skim through it, paying special attention to the footnotes and the bibliographies. Once you have listed and cross-referenced the footnote references and the bibliographies, you begin to have a pretty clear idea of who the authorities are and what evidence they have to support what they are saying. Then you go to those sources and do the same thing, locating *their* sources and references and cross-indexing them. Before long you find yourself dealing with the same basic raw data that has been used by the authorities you have been reading, and you are in a position to interpret their conclusions and to draw some of your own.

Dubro was also happy to take advantage of whatever opportunities his social life offered to learn more about the subject. At a City Hall Christmas party he buttonholed Alderman (later Mayor) John Sewell, who had made veiled accusations of organized crime involvement in the area's land development industry. At another party, he discovered Marshall McLuhan among the guests.

Dubro gleefully recalls, "I said to him, 'Alright Marshall, what do you think of the Mafia?' And he immediately came out with this whole theory about oral and anal culture . . . the police represent the anal, in that they won't believe anything that isn't written down. The Mafia is an oral culture and that's what has allowed them to survive: they can function by telephone or orally – they don't have to have things written down, and a big paper-publishing bureaucracy like the police.

"I thought it was all bullshit . . . I remember saying to myself, 'My God, he's so glib . . .' But in retrospect I can see that he was quite accurate. The police spend a lot of time following people around and writing reports and sending memos here and there, but they often miss the broader picture, or some crucial event."

This initial phase of the research took Dubro two months to complete. The research report he prepared for Macadam was three pages long, and it contained a list of about 200 names of criminals, law enforcement officials, journalists and authorities on crime whom Dubro felt would be worth talking to in person, to get more information and to locate potential interview subjects for the program.

The research had not, however, been as straightforward as the two had expected. At least one fundamental question could not be resolved simply by examining the literature on the subject.

At that time – and it still seems strange in retrospect – there was a powerful movement afoot in academic and political circles, and even among some journalists and police officials, to deny that organized crime existed, at least in any highly sophisticated form. Chiefs of police across the country had gone on record denying that there was any such thing within their jurisdictions even though, in many cases, their departments held information gleaned from wiretaps and other sources that proved beyond any doubt that organized crime was thriving.

Quebec was an exception. Evidence of the existence of organized crime had become so blatantly obvious there following a series of spectacular gangland murders that the provincial government had reluctantly given in to demands for a full-scale crime probe.

The Mafia had become a particular *bête noir*. Ontario's Attorney General, Allen Lawrence, speaking in Toronto before the Federation of Italian-Canadian Associations and Clubs had recently stated: "I want to assure you that there is no such monolithic monopolistic criminal group here in Metro that, on the Godfather pattern, controls an area of criminal activity."

The very word "Mafia", along with its synonym, La Cosa Nostra, had been politically unutterable for the past couple of years, ever since the Italian-American Civil Rights League had held its first big rally in New York's Columbus Circle. Canadians of Italian descent were quick to adopt some of the American organization's techniques. Politicians and public officials, including chiefs of police, found themselves the targets of powerful lobbies backed by considerable political clout (there were several hundred thousand Italian-Canadian voters in Toronto alone). The gist of the message was that any reference to the Mafia or La Cosa Nostra represented a racial slur against all Canadians of Italian descent, and that anyone who made such a slur must be prepared to pay the political consequences. Newspapers and other periodicals that dared use the offending words were deluged with subscription cancellations and angry letters accusing them of irresponsible sensation-seeking. It did not take very long for the words to all but vanish from the nation's public vocabulary.

In the United States, the Italian-American Civil Rights League was successful in embarrassing the U.S Department of Justice into dropping the terms from its official vocabulary. The makers of *The Godfather*, a film that is explicitly about life in an American Mafia family, were persuaded by League pressure to delete all references to the Mafia from their script. The word is never used in the film.

The irony of all this was that the Italian-American Civil Rights League had been founded in 1971 by Joseph Columbo, the leader of one of New York City's five Mafia families. He had originally conceived it as a way to reduce the pressure federal authorities were exerting on the mob. Unfortunately for Columbo, the more traditional among his fellow family bosses in New York did not agree with his high-profile tactics, and at the second annual Unity Day rally of the Italian-American Civil Rights League, he was shot point-blank in the head and neck. He died several years later, having never regained consciousness. The marksman was himself murdered in the slickest professional style within seconds of pumping the bullets into Columbo: the second gunman vanished in the Unity Day crowd and was never captured.

But this episode did not, as one might have expected, bring a speedy end to the movement to remove the word "Mafia" from the language. Several more years were needed for the more timid politicians and law enforcement officials in Canada and the United States to again risk admitting the obvious – that the Mafia was indeed a power to be reckoned with in the big cities of both nations.

While it is true that one must be Italian–Sicilian or Calabrian – to become a member of the Mafia, it is also, of course, true that one need not be a member of the Mafia to become involved in organized crime. "Mafia" and "organized crime" are not synonymous (though they are sometimes lumped together in the broader term, "the mob"). As one might expect, people of many different nationalities are involved in organized crime.

It is therefore all the more difficult to understand why during this period it was not merely the existence of the Mafia as an organized force in North American life that was being questioned, but the existence of organized crime itself. There could be no question of racial slur being involved in a reference to "organized crime."

On the other hand, for a ruling politician or a law enforcement official to admit to the existence of highly organized and extremely lucrative criminal conspiracy within his jurisdiction was to admit that he had not been successful in carrying out his duties with regard to the security of the community. Denial, even in the face of evidence, was apparently less embarrassing. And they could always look to academia for support of their denials. Respected American sociologists like Daniel Bell and criminologist Gordon Hawkins were among the leading academic naysayers of the period. In an article coyly entitled "Organized Crime and God", Hawkins had argued:

"In regard to our own society, Ruth Benedict has pointed out that 'the fundamental opposition of good and evil is a trait of occidental folklore that is expressed equally in Grimm's fairy tales and in the *Arabian Nights*. It determines some of the most deeply seated world views of western religions and western civilizations. The opposition of God and the devil, of Christ and Antichrist, of heaven and hell, is part of the fundamental intellectual equipment of those who participate in these civilizations.' It is probable that a large part of the appeal of such TV series as 'The Untouchables', 'The Corrupters', and 'The F.B.I.', to mention only three, rests on the fact that they dramatize the struggle against organized crime in terms of this fundamental myth. In this, too, it seems likely lies some of the appeal of televised and reported congressional investigations, newspaper accounts of *crusades* against organized crime and a vast literature dealing with law enforcement efforts against it.''

Organized crime, thus, was merely a figment of the collective unconscious, conjured up through some deep-seated psychological or cultural need for clarity and organization. It was simply a quaint cultural myth, its literature mostly folklore.

Dubro, inclined by training and temperament to accept the opinions of the academics, wrote into his initial research report a section arguing that the program would have to deal with the whole question of whether or not organized crime was really organized, in the sense of having a corporate structure complete with a board of directors, advisors or *consiglieri*, enforcers, soldiers, and elaborate international connections. Dubro was convinced that this kind of organizational sophistication was beyond the capabilities of the thugs he had been reading about.

Macadam on the other hand, his judgement unencumbered by months of research, unsullied by learned speculation into aspects of Western consciousness of good and evil, temperamentally inclined to accept the word of a reporter over that of an academic or self-styled authority, was just as certain that Dubro was wrong. The working titles he was toying with for the program at that stage made Dubro cringe with embarrassment. One was, *The Secret Government*; the other was *The Sixth Estate*.

''Where's your evidence?'' Dubro would demand. ''What proof do you have? Show me the documents.''

''We'll get the evidence,'' Macadam would reply. ''We'll just have to keep digging.'' For Dubro, however, it seemed to be a clear case of not letting the facts stand in the way of a good story. The argument was to carry on more or less continuously for several months.

''At that stage,'' Dubro recalls, ''I was still behaving pretty much like an academic. I saw the study of crime as criminology and that was a branch of sociology. Therefore the sociologists were the ones who would know something about organized crime. The press was not to be trusted, because they exaggerated – that was what the sociologists argued – and of course those policemen who were willing to talk about it were not to be trusted; they were simply in the category of generals asking for more tanks. It was in (their) interest to make things look as bleak as possible.

"Later on I did get a chance to talk to Daniel Bell, and it was a waste of time. He didn't know anything. But by that time I'd already figured that out for myself."

Working now as a team, the two began methodically to run through the list of potential sources Dubro's research had identified. They set up a schedule that kept them busy for twelve or fourteen hours each day, interviewing reporters, academics and policemen. Their list of names continued to grow, as interview subjects referred them to others who might know something, who might have something to say. Macadam had early decided it was necessary to talk to everyone, to track down every reference, and in the end more than a thousand interviews were conducted for *Connections I* and *II*.

For Dubro, whose lot it was to locate most of these people and talk them into being interviewed, it was a daunting prospect. But he knew as well as Macadam that it was necessary. In researching *The Fifth Estate* he had routinely checked through the catalogue of spy novels, and had discovered one author who seemed to have written with a good deal of insight. This author, a former CIA officer, had been an assistant to the agency's director before resigning. And he was willing to talk. He turned out to be a gold mine of inside information, by far the best espionage source they were to develop. The lesson was obvious: turn over every stone – you never know what you'll find underneath.

Tracking down leads, the two travelled to Montreal where they spoke to the head of the Quebec Crime Probe, and to reporter Jean-Pierre Charbonneau. Charbonneau, they discovered, was an extremely valuable and co-operative source, and Macadam gave him a small contract to develop information on the Montreal mob.

Toronto police referred them to sources in Calgary and Vancouver, and Macadam flew west to talk to them.

Every name mentioned by their sources, each document they were shown, every report they were able to obtain, was carefully indexed and placed in the growing filing system they had set up in their tiny windowless quarters in a downtown Toronto CBC building. By March, 1975, they found they needed a full-time file clerk.

But although the files were growing to alarming proportions, Macadam and Dubro were becoming seriously concerned about the quality of the information they were getting: it was all too sketchy, too ephemeral. There was little that was solid enough to build a credible documentary. With some tantalizing exceptions, most of their sources were telling them one of two things: yes, there was a problem, but it was small and it was being taken care of by law enforcement agencies; or, there had been a problem back in the early 1960s but it no longer existed. For Dubro, the fact that a number of the criminals he had read about in the reports of government crime commissions had died or been murdered or had fled the country tended to support the latter point of view.

Again, Macadam's response was to dig harder. He decided it was time to start talking to the criminals themselves. Paul Volpe, reputed to be the most powerful organized crime boss in Toronto, a Mafia member and one of the best-connected criminals in the country, was an obvious first target.

How do you interview a Mafia boss? Macadam first visited Volpe's lawyer, David Humphreys, who told him, "organized criminals are like unicorns; everyone says they exist, but nobody's ever seen one."

But he was willing to try to arrange an interview with his client, to set the record straight. He would phone Volpe first, and then Macadam could call him to find out whether an interview would be okay.

When Macadam got through to Volpe, it was clear he had been expecting the call. Humphreys had kept his promise. He identified himself and told Volpe he was doing research for a CBC program on organized crime.

"Yeah . . . so?"

"Well, uh, I've been told . . . uh, there have been a lot of allegations that you are a pretty big man in organized crime."

"What organized crime? I'm just a businessman."

"Well, uh, if you're just a businessman, how would it be if we had lunch together and we could go over some of these allegations people have been making?"

There was a pause. And then Volpe responded, apparently amused by Macadam's straightforward approach.

"Sure, okay, where do you wanna do it?"

They agreed to meet outside Humphrey's office and then find some place to have lunch.

Macadam phoned Dubro at home – it was a holiday, Easter weekend, 1975.

"I've got a meeting with Volpe!"

"Good God," was all Dubro could manage.

Dubro spent the rest of his ruined holiday pulling together all the information they had on Volpe: his alleged connections with known underworld figures, the allegations that had been made during United States Senate investigations into organized crime, the rumours they had heard about him from police in Canada, the charges made in newspaper reports. He stapled a photograph to the top page.

Armed with this research, Macadam set out the next day. It was a sunny spring morning, and he was early; despite the butterflies in his stomach he was enjoying himself; it was a pleasure to see all the shirt-sleeved people out strolling in the sun, liberated at last from the encumbrances of heavy winter clothing.

He had almost arrived at the meeting place when one stroller in particular caught his eye. He was in his fifties, dark complexioned, medium built, with a lantern jaw and a prominent nose that appeared to have been broken sometime in the past. But what made him stand out was his clothing: a white fedora, white raincoat belted tightly, and a white tie on a cream-coloured shirt. Macadam could scarcely believe what he was seeing. The man looked exactly like central casting's idea of a Mafia boss . . . like something out of a B movie.

Macadam crossed the street and approached him.

"Mr. Volpe?"

Volpe was startled: "Yeah. Hi. How did you know?"

"I just thought I'd take a chance."

They had trouble finding a restaurant in the area that was not closed for the holiday – eventually Volpe reluctantly agreed to Macadam's suggestion that they eat at the Courtyard Cafe. At that time the Courtyard was Toronto's principal celebrity hangout, a place where you might find yourself a table away from Donald Sutherland, or Patrick Watson or Jane Fonda.

It was entirely too public a setting for Volpe's liking.

The lunch lasted an hour and a half and was more productive than Macadam had dared hope. He played the carefully conceived role he was to use with great success throughout the project – that of the slightly stupid but sincere and likable CBC researcher, naively asking explosive questions but clearly too thick-headed to understand the significance of the answers. The kind of friendly dummy you like to humour, to keep around for laughs. A pain in the neck sometimes, but amusing to be with.

"Let's just go through the list I have here and I'll ask you about each one, and you can tell me the real story . . . but if you don't tell me the truth I'm just not interested in talking to you."

Volpe agrees with a toothy smile.

"You know Natale Luppino, right?"

Luppino, Macadam knew, was a lieutenant in the Luppino Mafia family operating in Toronto and Hamilton.

Volpe was seated with his back to the wall, the entrance in view, his dark eyes darting constantly from table to table.

"For God's sake, keep your voice down . . . Sure I know him. I stood up for his son."

"What does that mean, 'stood up'?"

"I was the godfather to his son."

Macadam scribbled furiously in his notebook. That connected the two Mafia families; in the tradition of La Cosa Nostra it indicated an alliance as surely as a medieval marriage between a Spanish princess and an English king.

"How about Vito de Filippo, do you know him?"

Volpe stalled, pretended to search his memory . . . Vito . . . Vito . . . de Filippo . . .

"Now, come on," Macadam interrupted. "It says right here . . ."

"Yeah, yeah, right. Will you keep your voice down? Vito de Filippo. He used to be a partner of mine in the casino in Haiti . . ."

Once again, Macadam was scribbling notes, trying to conceal his excitement: Dubro's research had identified Filippo as a key figure in the New York Mafia family of Joe Bonnano, and later with Bonnano's successor, Carmine Galente. Both Bonnano and Galente had strong ties to the Montreal underworld.

By the time they had finished talking, Macadam had several pages of notes. Volpe had ordered a Campari, but had taken only a few sips from his glass.

Macadam paid the bill with a flourish of his well-worn American Express card, and made a suggestion.

Since Volpe insisted he was simply a small businessman and that he was virtually unknown, why not take a walk through Little Italy and see whether anyone seemed to recognize him?

Volpe, still amused and feeling expansive, agreed.

Macadam rode with Volpe in Volpe's Cadillac to the heart of Toronto's Italian district. They got out of the car and strolled east down St. Clair Avenue West. Macadam was not sure what he had expected to happen: maybe he expected Volpe's appearance to stop traffic, to cause shopkeepers to bar their doors and shutter their windows. Maybe he was just enjoying the experience of being chummy with a Mafia boss, and wanted to prolong it. In any case, nothing was happening.

"You see," Volpe said with a grin. "Nobody knows me here."

"Alright," Macadam responded, "what I want to do is to go into this little store here and say: 'This is Mr. Volpe and he has been named in a U.S. senate investigation as a key organized criminal here in Toronto, and I would like to know if you know who he is.'"

Volpe chuckled. Of all the dumb . . . "No, I won't do that."

"Why not?" Macadam insisted.

"Because it would be embarrassing to me."

They continued their walk, and at one point Volpe stopped in front of a bakery and stared in the window for several seconds before continuing on down the street. He made no comment, but Macadam made a mental note. He learned later that the bakery is owned by Mike Racco, boss of another Toronto Mafia family.

Finally, Macadam asked Volpe, "What do you suppose people are thinking?"

"I'll tell you what they're thinking," Volpe replied, "they're thinking you're a policeman." He laughed, delighted by the thought.

Macadam was to have several more meetings with Volpe, maintaining friendly, first-name relations with the Mafia chief right up until *Connections* finally went to air. He was even able to obtain permission to film Volpe at his home on a secluded lot overlooking Toronto's Bayview Avenue and the Don River valley.

Macadam remembers: "When I phoned him to arrange the meeting he suggested I come to his place and we could order out for Chinese food. I picked up a bottle of wine and drove over there, and parked beside his red Cadillac in the driveway. When I got out of my car there was a tremendous uproar from several dogs inside the house, and it took quite a while before Volpe answered the door. He ordered one of the snarling dogs to the basement and showed me in. As you come into the house, there are cupboards on the left and a stand-up bar, some couches and an old slot machine on the right. Straight ahead the roof cantilevers and there is a largish open living room with windows overlooking the swimming pool. To the left of this area there is a kitchen and breakfast room . . . At the rear of the living room is Volpe's den. It has high windows looking out over the ravine to Bayview Avenue. It's quite large, but it didn't seem to contain a working desk or any books – just some couches and chairs – it was an unusually harsh, sparse room. Outside the breakfast room there are some very elaborate dog kennels . . . the whole back yard is fenced and lit with floodlights and immaculately tended . . . On the whole, though, with the dogs and the fences and the lights, you had a feeling of a place under siege.''

When *Connections* was broadcast, police sources advised Macadam to leave town for a few days, to give Volpe time to cool off.

''You've really made a fool out of him and there's no telling what he'll do in the heat of the moment,'' he was warned.

(Macadam stayed in the city. ''You have to remember,'' he explained later, ''that the police's first reaction to my idea of going to see Volpe was 'He'll kill you.' I asked how they knew that – had anyone tried it? They had to admit that they didn't think so, and then they started to think that it wasn't such a bad idea. People do not usually look at these things logically . . .'')

The success with Volpe was encouraging, but it was clear that they needed much more solid information than they had been getting from most of their sources. The sooner they could get to Washington and New York, the better. The American authorities possessed a great deal of information on organized crime in Canada, because of the Canadian connections of the American mob in New York, Buffalo, Miami and Seattle. And all the journalists they had talked to had told them that the Americans were far more open with reporters than Canadian authorities, and far more likely to give them the kind of information they needed without an elaborate song and dance. Moreover, Macadam and Dubro had learned by this time that the best way to get information from police sources was to give them information in return: they were desperately in need of good swapping bait. They hoped the Americans would provide it.

Nor were they to be disappointed. That first American foray was a watershed in their investigation.

5

The Hidden Network

"I phoned Jim (Dubro) in Toronto and told him, 'There's a common thread in all of this and it's Violi. We've got to concentrate on Violi.' "

Bill Macadam

Macadam had already been in Washington for a full day when Dubro arrived to join him on June 18, 1975. When the two got together in Dubro's room at the Hay Adams Hotel, Macadam was plainly excited. He had spent much of the previous day talking with officials in the United States Drug Enforcement Agency (DEA), where he had been shown the agency's "war room" complete with its huge wall charts showing world-wide drug distribution networks. High on several of the organizational charts had been the names of Canadian criminals – the same criminals whom their Canadian sources had assured them were no longer active. The DEA officials were insistent that they were indeed active, and in some cases were able to produce for Macadam documentary evidence to reinforce their case.

That meeting was to set a pattern: during fourteen days in Washington and ten days in New York, the two conducted four or five interviews each day with experts and law enforcement officials in various government agencies. In the evenings, back at their hotel, they would go over the day's haul like kids sorting through hallowe'en booty. Much of what they were being given during their interviews was information that had originally been obtained by the Americans through liaison with Canadian police forces – in particular with the RCMP's criminal intelligence branch.

Within a very few days it became painfully obvious that their Canadian sources had been witholding information from them –

even deliberately misleading them – on a wholesale basis. Why? They couldn't know for sure, but part of the reason clearly involved a lack of trust. Police sources in particular were apparently afraid that any information they gave Dubro and Macadam might be used irresponsibly, in a way that might hamper continuing investigations. In some cases it also seemed likely that police sources feared the information they possessed might be used to discredit their own activities – to support arguments that they were not doing their job, that they were allowing organized crime to flourish.

And there appeared to be another factor, one which most investigative journalists eventually have the misfortune to experience. For many confidential sources, dealing with journalists is a kind of power game, in which the sources themselves hold all the marbles and are therefore in a position to be able to manipulate the reporter. They dole out their information sparingly, because once the reporter knows as much as they do, the game ends and their power evaporates. Watergate's mysterious Deep Throat is perhaps the classic example of this syndrome, and he drove *Washington Post* reporter Bob Woodward almost to distraction with his refusal to tell the whole story.

Macadam and Dubro's initial delight at uncovering this trove of information in Washington and New York slowly turned to anger as they began to realize the extent to which their Canadian sources had withheld or misrepresented similar intelligence in dealing with them. Before returning to Canada, the two spent an evening plotting a new strategy for dealing with their contacts there. It was a plan they hoped would provide answers for both the problem of trust and the power-play syndrome.

They would go back to every source who had proved to be of any value, but this time they would operate singly rather than as a team. In a one-on-one interview, informants would have the security of knowing they could later deny having met, or having passed a specific piece of information, and their denial would be plausible because there would be no third party witnesses. The two would also work hard to develop personal relationships with their most valuable sources, meeting for coffee or drinks or dinner whenever it could be arranged, soft-pedalling the requests for information until a solid mutual trust had been established. Claims to journalistic professionalism in dealing with sources had not been enough to allay their fears: Dubro and Macadam would also have to demonstrate their trustworthiness as individuals.

Dealing with the power-play syndrome presented a more straightforward problem. The tactic here would be judicious use of the information they had collected from their American sources to hint that perhaps they knew a few things that their sources didn't know. They were at last in a position to get into the information swapping game. To make it work for them, they knew, they would have to be careful to make their hand appear as strong as possible.

"We were very coy about it," Dubro says, "always careful to imply that we knew a lot more than we actually did. But it worked marvellously well. The minute we'd drop a name like Baldassari Accardo (a virtually unknown Torontonian whom DEA officials in Washington had identified for Macadam as a key figure in the Canadian drug trade), our sources would sit up and take notice. If you knew about Cotroni and Violi, well, so what? Everybody knew about them. But not many people know about Baldassari Accardo, so you'd work on that."

The game would develop, slowly, according to guidelines that were unspoken, but clearly understood by both sides. It was, "I'll show you mine if you'll show me yours" – a simple enough rule, and one universally understood from childhood.

As the research progressed, interviews with criminals conducted by members of the *Connections* team provided an even more valuable source of swap material: few of the police authorities dealing with organized crime had even so much as seen their quarry in the flesh, having gleaned what information they had almost exclusively from surveillance reports and wiretaps. If there was an ethical problem involved in divulging details of such an interview to the police, it was not a difficult one to resolve in most cases. Normally, the story told by the criminal would be a tissue of lies, by that time perfectly transparent to the interviewer. The really valuable information would often come in response to seemingly innocent questions about friends, relatives, and associates – like Volpe's admission to Macadam that he is godfather to the son of Mafia boss Natale Luppino. Knowing that they had been blatantly lied to throughout their interviews, Macadam and the others had few compunctions about breaking their half of the understood agreement between a journalist and his interview subject: that is, that information is supplied for the exclusive use of the journalist.

Where a source, even though a criminal, dealt honestly with a *Connections* interviewer, this agreement would be respected and the information gleaned would be out of bounds to police contacts, no matter how tantalizingly valuable it might have been as swap material. In some areas, the *Connections* crew wound up knowing considerably more than the police, and in many cases this information was not used in the programs for legal or technical reasons or because it would clearly compromise the source. It remains buried in the files, under lock and key. (In fact, less than a third of the information available to them was used in producing the five programs.)

The Washington leg of the trip had had a special significance for Dubro: it was there that he and Macadam met and interviewed Robert Blakey, a leading criminologist from Cornell University, an academic whose credentials were faultless, even by Dubro's knowledgeable standards. Blakey had spent several months listening to police wiretap recordings of conversations between leading organized crime figures in the U.S. as part of a special assignment he had been given by President Lyndon Johnson's 1965 crime commission. Dubro brought to the interview his skepticism about the degree of organization within the mob, and left without it.

"There was just no denying what Blakey had to say. He had actually heard these guys talking about the organization, the bosses, about moving a soldier from here to there, about who was in charge in what places and so on."

And any small doubts that may have lingered after the meeting with Blakey were dispelled forever shortly after the Washington trip when Dubro interviewed DEA investigator Paul Teresi, in Buffalo. Teresi had worked as an undercover agent in several North American cities, including Toronto. His files, which he allowed Dubro to study, corroborated Blakey in every respect, and made it clear that the mob was well entrenched in Canada, and highly organized. The evidence was irrefutable. The arguments with Macadam ended.

Conversations with American officials had also made clear something Dubro and Macadam had suspected for months: that the RCMP held by far the most complete and authoritative files on organized crime of any police force in Canada. Time and again, the Americans would refer in glowing terms to the criminal intelligence work of the Mounties.

The problem facing Macadam and Dubro was that the RCMP is also the most security-minded force in the country, and the least willing to co-operate with the news media. There are very, very few reporters in the country who can boast a solid source inside the

RCMP. Few have even bothered to try to develop one, so formidable is the force's reputation for invulnerability.

This, then, would be a third part of their new strategy on returning to Canada: to make a concerted effort to break down the RCMP.

The campaign was worked out in elaborate detail during the final evenings in New York, and put into action immediately on their return home. Stage one would be a direct appeal to the RCMP Commissioner in Ottawa by Macadam, who hoped that if appeals to the public's right to know would not do the trick, discreet references to political contacts might.

Stage two would be to establish good relations among junior and middle-ranking officers on the force. Again, this was to be Macadam's project: it had been decided that to involve Dubro would risk muddying the waters by increasing the level of mistrust. Among those officers was one obvious target, a senior Toronto-based investigator. Macadam and Dubro had talked to him early in their research, and had been impressed with his relaxed attitude toward dealing with the news media.

The appeal to the Commissioner proved to be worse than fruitless: although he did not know it at the time, Macadam was to learn later that it had provoked a directive issued to senior officers instructing them to discuss nothing with *Connections* personnel that was not already on the public record. Macadam was told merely that the best the force could do was to arrange a series of general briefings by senior officers dealing, once again, exclusively with public information.

The avenue of officially sanctioned co-operation closed. Macadam began to haunt the fortress-like RCMP headquarters on Jarvis Street in Toronto, talking with anyone who would give him the time of day. He focussed much of his attention on the friendly investigator, visiting him as often as seemed judicious. He cadged invitations to the officers' mess for drinks, and to the cafeteria for coffee, where he would regale his hosts with stories of hunting and fishing in British Columbia or on the estates of family friends in Britain. On one occasion he arrived for an interview with his source lugging hip waders, shotgun and shell jacket. This attracted a certain amount of attention in the security-conscious headquarters building:

"Sorry about all this," Macadam would say when looked at askance. "I've just flown back from a goose shoot in northern

Manitoba and I didn't have time to drop it off at home on the way in from the airport.''

He explained to a skeptical Dubro: ''Those guys are all hunting and fishing nuts. This way they know I'm not just another long-haired CBC type, that I'm a regular guy who goes hunting and fishing too.''

Discovering that among the many amenities in the headquarters building were bachelor rooms for officers visiting from out of town, Macadam explained to the friendly source that he had not yet been able to move from Ottawa to Toronto and was consequently forced to stay in hotels: it would be much more convenient, he suggested, if he could simply move into one of the vacant rooms at RCMP headquarters . . . The answer was ''No.''

Slowly, however, his persistence began to pay off, and by the end of the summer it was not unusual to see Macadam huddled over a corner table at Noodles with one of a number of law enforcement friends, discussing crime over pheasant or *tutto mare* and Alfredo noodles.

In later interviews with criminal sources, *Connections* personnel wired themselves for sound with Nagra SN body-pack tape recorders and hidden microphones, so that nothing would be missed, no matter how freely flowed the wine. But it was an early and emphatic rule that this was never to be done with police sources.

By the late summer of 1975, the months of patient effort Dubro and Macadam had invested in developing sources began to pay dividends. It was almost as though a dam had burst. Everyone began talking to them, feeding them more information than they could easily digest. The key source at RCMP headquarters was offering what seemed to be unreserved co-operation, introducing Macadam to others of his own force and in other police departments. He made it plain to subordinates that they were to answer questions as accurately as they could – whether or not the questions concerned matters of public record. Contacts in the Ontario Provincial Police and the Metro Toronto police force opened up. The Quebec Crime Probe was providing volumes of data each week. Macadam's contacts in Calgary and Vancouver finally began giving him information he had been seeking for months. The filing cabinets bulged.

Patterns began to emerge; connections began to click into place.

"I was in my hotel room in Calgary one night in August going over notes from interviews during the day," Macadam recalls, "and suddenly it all seemed to come together. I phoned Jim in Toronto and told him, 'There's a common thread in all of this and it's Violi [Montreal crime boss Paolo Violi, murdered in 1978]. We've got to concentrate on Violi.'

"There were too many coincidences. In Vancouver I found out that the head of the Italian mob there, Joe Gentile, was godfather to one of Violi's children, and that Giaccomo Luppino, who is a Mafia boss in Hamilton and also Violi's father-in-law, had recently come to the city. Violi was cropping up everywhere . . . in Ottawa, too. Connections between Violi and the Commissos in Toronto came out at the Quebec Crime Probe . . .

"Jim, I think, was pretty dubious at that point . . . and rightly so, because it was just a hunch I had. As usual, he wanted to know what evidence I had – where the proof was. I told him I thought that if we concentrated on this approach for a week, we would be able to come up with all the evidence we needed. If I wasn't borne out by that time, we could always continue with the city-by-city approach, looking at each operation individually, as a satellite of some other American operation, as we had been up to that time. But we never did go back to that, because the hunch paid off.

"It seems incredible now, but at that time no one had been looking at all this information as pointing to an integrated conspiracy that stretched across the country. The police were mainly interested in what went on in their own jurisdictions and nobody was looking at the broader picture.

"It had enormous significance; it meant that organized crime was much more powerful than anyone believed. It was quite an exciting discovery."

The Third Man

6

"Well, in 1946 after the boys came home from the war . . . a group of people called the Volpes — the group of brothers had a car wash and from there diamonds were being sold, bootlegging was consistent . . . People started gathering there . . ."

Mob associate describing the beginnings of organized crime in Toronto.

Dubro and Macadam had little time to enjoy the euphoria of their new successes: they were both near exhaustion after months of gruelling research and frequent tension. They were also aware that their CBC research contract expired in September 1975, and they could not tell whether the inscrutable Peter Herrndorf was genuinely committed to proceeding with the production to the filming stage. Herrndorf was so well protected by his staff that it often took days of effort to arrange a five-minute telephone conversation with him.

In October, 1975, the two prepared a fifty-four page report on their research for Herrndorf's second-in-command, Paul Wright. It was marked, "Strictly confidential: for Paul Wright's eyes only," and it began:

"Since the initial research for this program there have been a number of developments which must be considered of great importance . . .

"We believe that we are dealing with a new national problem. The police forces are not yet able to deal effectively with crime on a national and international scale. Hence we have been working in some cases ahead of law enforcement and in others we have become an information source.

"Our research has led us to believe that organized crime is far more serious a threat today than it is generally understood to be. It has already gone a long way in infiltrating almost every segment of our society in Canada, including businesses and high government office. We consider it as a cancer in advanced stage of development and a cause for very serious national alarm . . .''

The report went on to describe in detail the structure of organized crime in Toronto, Hamilton, Windsor, Ottawa, Montreal and Vancouver, to name scores of key criminals and their associates and business enterprises, and to outline several cases of police, judicial and political corruption.

Two weeks later, they submitted a program outline – a synopsis of how they felt the research could best be organized for television presentation. Appended to it was a list of eighteen cities in Canada, the United States and Britain described as ''places advisable to visit prior to filming,'' and eighty-four potential interview subjects, most of them criminals.

But the negotiations for a production contract dragged on and on. By that time, Macadam estimated he had spent well over $5,000 of his own company's money to supplement the $15,500 Herrndorf had assigned to the research project – even though he had drawn no personal salary, living instead on proceeds from the recent sale of his airline. Still uncertain whether the production would be given a ''go'' by Herrndorf, and with Norfolk's bank overdraft mounting alarmingly, he balked at investing more. Moreover, he insisted that any production contract make some allowance for his losses to date. Dubro found himself having to survive weeks on end when there was no money to pay his meagre $200 a week salary. Several times he threatened to quit, and once or twice he though he *had* quit, but Macadam kept him on the job through the simple expedient of refusing to acknowledge either written or verbal resignations. On one occasion, Dubro reinforced his resignation by leaving town, accepting an invitation to address a meeting of the American Society for Eighteenth Century Studies, at Indiana State University. The meeting was held in co-operation with the Kinsey Institution for Sex Research, and Dubro's topic was, ''The Third Sex: Lord Hervey and his Coterie.'' But this resignation proved no more successful (though perhaps more diverting) than the rest, and Dubro found himself stopping off in Chicago on his way home to interview contacts in the local police force.

The financial frustrations grew so intense that early in December Macadam rented a small truck and, in the dead of night, removed from the *Connections* office in a Bay Street CBC building the files he and Dubro had accumulated over the past year and took them to his apartment a few blocks away for protection. As far as he was concerned, the project was dead. Herrndorf could go to hell.

I have managed to achieve a sense of some of Macadam's frustration for myself: for more than two months I tried to arrange an interview with Herrndorf, to get his version of what went on during those months of negotiations. Herrndorf was, during that period, CBC vice-president in charge of planning. His secretary always has the same response for me: "Sorry, Mr. Herrndorf is out of town."

"Can you tell me where he can be reached?"

"No, sorry. I don't know where he is."

"Oh. Is there anyone in CBC Ottawa who can tell me where I might locate him?"

"No, I'm sorry, no one knows where he is."

"He's a vice-president and nobody knows where he is?"

"Yes. Sorry. Can I take a message?"

I have no doubt that he was a few feet away from her, behind the door to his office.

Once, he did return my call. He said that he might be here in Toronto over the weekend but that if he was he would be extremely busy. He would see if he could squeeze me in. I gave him three phone numbers where I could be reached, but I didn't hear from him.

Eventually, with the deadline for this manuscript perilously close, I met Herrndorf quite by accident at a party given by a mutual friend and over the course of the evening was able to extract the promise of an interview, which took place the following day. He turned out to be friendly, straightforward and generous to a fault in his interpretation of events.

He explained that during this period he was being besieged by CBC accountants who were scandalized by Macadam's seemingly profligate spending habits. Not knowing in detail the nature of the project identified only as *"Connections"*, they could see no possible justification for dinner bills amounting to several hundred dollars, among other things. They were convinced somebody was robbing the CBC blind.

"It's an open question as to who got screwed," Herrndorf acknowledges. "Certainly, I don't feel that we got screwed. The project went five hundred percent over budget, but I was quite happy to live with that given the results we got. But it meant that we [in the CBC] had to do an enormous amount of finessing . . . an incredible amount . . . and the hero of that is a financial guy named Don Richardson who managed to squirrel it away here, there and everywhere over a period of two to three years, allowing us to keep going.''

Despite the financial headaches it was creating, Herrndorf remained solidly committed to carrying on with the project, though he was naturally anxious to minimize its costs. Those connected with the project who, unlike Macadam, did not have to get involved in financial dealings with him, have a good deal of respect for the courage this commitment took. *Connections* was operating in uncharted waters, at huge expense, and if it didn't work it was Herrndorf who would be left carrying the can.

Moreover, Herrndorf had early in the project made a crucial decision without which *Connections* would never have seen the light of day. It had to do with libel suits. Given the fact that it was important to name names, there was no doubt that suits would be filed; the only question was how many.

Two criteria can be used in judging whether or not a given piece of information or name should be used on a show like *Connections*:

The first is purely journalistic, and must answer questions like: ''Are the journalists convinced in their own minds that what they are saying is true?''; ''Can they prove it to their own satisfaction?''; and, ''Is it important that it be said publicly?''

The second criterion is purely legalistic. Can the accusation be proved in court? The ultimate decision in every case would be Herrndorf's, and he chose deliberately to operate on the basis of journalistic criteria, seeking the advice of lawyers only on how to minimize the CBC's risks. Journalists, and not lawyers, were thus making all the journalistic decisions.

It is worth taking a small detour into the laws of libel to understand some of the risks involved. In general, a journalist can be said to be on safe ground so long as he sticks to writing about known criminals – those who have been convicted or who have been identified as crooks in some legislative or judicial inquiry. In that way he is not actually accusing anybody of anything . . . he is merely reporting what legally constituted bodies have said. But if a reporter is seriously investigating the conspiracy that is organized crime, there is little point in his writing exclusively about individuals who have already been publicly identified as criminals. It is the people who have not yet been identified and exposed that interest him most – or should: the "legit" businessmen who invest dirty money for the mob, the real estate swindlers, the "respectable" loansharks, the politicians who lend their support, the public officials who have been bought off. And this is where the problem crops up. To commit libel, a story or TV program need do nothing more than lead members of the general public to think less of the person involved than they did before they saw the story. And in Canadian libel law, unlike American, there are no special exemptions that apply where the subject of a story is a public figure: everyone, including politicians, has exactly the same protection. (Reporters Carl Bernstein and Bob Woodward could not have conducted their Watergate crusade in a Canadian legal environment, mainly for this reason.) Merely to report, for example, that a federal cabinet minister has been seen on several occasions socializing with known criminals, could land a reporter in court faced with an expensive libel action.

Everyone knows that the ultimate defence in a libel case is proof that the story told the truth. But investigative reporters soon learn that knowing you have told the truth can sometimes be cold comfort. For it is not merely the bare facts of a story that are at issue in a libel action, *but the conclusions that an average reader might reasonably be expected to draw from those facts.*

In the case of the cabinet minister who consorts with known criminals, the reporter who tells the story is letting himself in for trouble. All the evidence may be available that is needed to prove beyond doubt that the minister has indeed been hanging out with rough trade. But the clear implication of the story will almost certainly have been that the minister is up to something shady. Otherwise, why would the reporter have bothered to write the story (after all, he is not a gossip columnist), and why would his newspaper or television station have bothered to publish it or put it on the air? So, when he has his day in court, the reporter is likely to be required to prove two things: that the minister has indeed been consorting with criminals, and that in doing so the minister was up to something shady or illegal.

Strictly speaking, for a reporter to *imply* that someone is a crook, he must be prepared to prove in court that he *is* a crook. The difficulties this presents are enormous and obvious. It can usually be presumed that the police know what's going on – in fact, in many cases the reporter's information will have come at least in part from police sources. If the police, with all of their resources, haven't been able to establish that a conspiracy exists or that the law has been broken, how can the reporter be expected to provide the necessary proof?

It is true that the court has the option of assessing only token damages where it feels that the reporter was justified in writing the story, as it might well do in the case of the tainted cabinet minister. But that, again, can be cold comfort: the cost of the journalist's legal defence will have been enormous and the journalist or the journalist's employer will in all likelihood be stuck with those costs.

The long and the short of it is that the libel lawyer's first question to a reporter or a producer who has a problematic story is more likely to be, "Do you think he'll sue?" than, "Is it true?" Lawyers will argue that they have been hired by publishers or broadcasters to protect the company concerned: being prepared to provide legal vindication of a reporter's charges is only one aspect of that protection. They must also consider whether the legal costs involved in going to court are likely to cripple the company. The result is that most libel lawyers are extremely cautious and conservative. Most organized crime reporters thus live in a perpetual state of frustration, permitted to publish or broadcast only a tiny portion of what they know to be true and important. Herrndorf's decision was to make the *Connections* team exceptions to that rule.

In his lengthy contract negotiations with Macadam, Herrndorf also had another concern and that was whether Macadam would be able to pull such an enormously complex show together and package it singlehandedly for television. On this score, at least, he and Macadam were in agreement: it would be helpful, if not absolutely necessary, to appoint an experienced television director before filming began. And the best director either could think of for the project was Martyn Burke.

Burke, though still in his early thirties, had already achieved a solid reputation as one of the country's best young filmmakers. And he had proved more than once that he had the kind of guts and industry that would be necessary to take on the mob.

His flamboyant career had first attracted attention in 1966 when his by-line began appearing on a series of stories run in the Toronto *Telegram* under the headings: "Martyn Burke's Vietnam Diary", and "Martyn Burke's China Diary". Schoolmates who had, a year earlier, dozed with him through final year classes in economics and business administration at McMaster University in Hamilton, were agog. Burke had been taking the courses, after all, as part of his grooming to take over his father's business in construction equipment. He had spent his summers working in the company shops, and on finishing college had been rewarded with a white-collar job in the front office. A nice setup, some might think. But not Burke.

For Burke, the idea of carrying on in his father's footsteps, living in Etobicoke, a suburban Toronto split-level heaven for executives and their wives, was absolute anathema. Not only did he despise Etobicoke, but he was unable to get along with his father. His father, for his part, couldn't understand a son who was more interested in movies and writers like Albert Camus than in the family business he'd struggled to build. Eventually, they stopped speaking to one another. Burke still carries with him a bit of baggage that grew out of their conflict: a slight stutter that one notes with surprise in a person so apparently self-assured. (When his father was dying in hospital a few years ago, a CBC colleague of Burke's urged him to visit him before it was too late. Burke later told an interviewer, "I went to the hospital the next night, but he was dead . . . It is one of the great regrets of my life that I never saw him one last time.")

His career in the family business ended just a few weeks after it had begun, when his father forestalled his plan to resign by firing him. After that there were a few months spent booking acts for a CBC-TV folksinging series called *Let's Sing Out*. But for Burke it was urgently necessary to be where things were *happening*, to be immersed in a rip-tide of events. In 1966, that could only mean Vietnam: in the spring of that year, while thousands of American youths desperately schemed to stay out of the war, Burke plotted to get into it – not as a soldier, but as a correspondent. At twenty-two, with no more journalistic experience than a handful of articles for a Toronto *Telegram* youth supplement (one of which told of an American friend living in Canada who had been drafted into the war), Burke approached the *Toronto Star* and the Toronto *Globe and Mail* with a proposition: if they would accredit him as a correspondent, he would pay his own way to Vietnam and file stories for them. Not news stories, but features and colour pieces. Both papers showed him the door. Nothing daunted, he approached the *Telegram*, where editor J. D. MacFarlane decided to take a chance. And it was no small risk: once he had been accredited, whatever havoc Burke caused in Vietnam would be the *Tely's* responsibility.

Burke sold his car, withdrew his savings from the bank, and bought a safari jacket and a plane ticket to Hong Kong. With the "cultural revolution" in full swing just across the border in China, Burke could not resist having a look, and he managed to talk his way through the frontier post, posing as a college student. He mailed a series of articles on China back to the *Telegram*: what they lacked in depth they made up for in exclusivity – a virtue of no mean significance to editors in the competitive Toronto newspaper scene of those days.

From China, it was on to Laos and a boat across the besieged Mekong River delta to Saigon. While most established American correspondents were enjoying the luxury of exclusive compounds replete with servants and the finest of food and drink, Burke's meagre resources dictated a bug-ridden fleabag of a hotel which he shared with penurious freelance writers like himself, down and out American entertainers who could find work nowhere else and the embarrassed Canadian members of the International Joint Commission, a bad joke about peacekeeping. It was the stuff of novels, that hotel in Saigon, and Burke decided to write one. (He finally found time to complete the manuscript in the spring of 1979, and shipped it off to Doubleday in New York. Its title is *Laughing War*.)

His Vietnam columns for the *Telegram* were, to be kind, not of Pulitzer Prize calibre. In one, headlined "A battle seen from under a dead man's helmet," Burke begins:

"(Da Nang) – 'You're going into Hastings?' yelled the marine sergeant above the roar of the helicopters at Dong Ha air base. 'You better grab a helmet. Get one from that pile over there – but find one that ain't got blood all over it.'

"So I rummaged through a pile of equipment that had formerly been worn by combat marines who will never have any need of helmets – or anything else – again . . ."

But to criticize the writings of a twenty-two-year-old freelance war correspondent is no doubt to cavil: in any case, for Burke the stories were merely an excuse to experience the war; a justification for taking risks. The important thing was that his press credentials allowed him to test himself in a Viet Cong ambush and on a jet fighter mission along the Cambodian border and in the exotic sordidness of Saigon by night.

Years later Burke said to me: "Once you been through what I went through in Vietnam – the hustling, the starving, the fighting, the lying – nothing intimidates you much. You find out you can do anything.'' A little bell went off in my head and I could hear Macadam saying through his own brand of speech impediment essentially the same thing about his particular cathartic experience in the forests of British Columbia.

After Vietnam, Burke spent the next nine years indulging his lust for travel and adventure and producing, writing and directing some of the most interesting television of the period.

There were documentaries about the fighting in Northern Ireland; an earthquake in Peru; the merchandising of riot control equipment in the United States; voodoo rites in Haiti; a satirical look at social change in Britain; an apocalyptic film about California in the wake of the Manson murders (*California Movie*); a sad and sordid look at life in a touring carnival (*Carnivals*); an angry examination of McCarthy-era blacklisting in Hollywood (*The Hollywood Ten*). He also co-authored a screenplay for CBC drama about neo-Naziism in Toronto (*Black Phoenix*).

When no one else could get to talk to Uganda's Idi Amin Dada, there was Burke posing as ''a close personal friend of Pierre Trudeau,'' being given the Cook's tour of Kampala in the dictator's personal Maserati, chatting with the Man himself while cameras rolled.

Next it was a quickie, a low-budget feature thriller called *The Clown Murders,* based on the bizarre Toronto kidnapping of Mary Nelles. Reviews were, if not ecstatic, at least encouraging.

When Herrndorf caught up with him to ask him to take on *Connections*, he had just completed directing European sequences for a feature film he had written about a coup d'etat in a fictitious Mediterranean country (later to be released as *Power Play*) with Peter O'Toole, Donald Pleasance, Barry Morse and David Hemmings. The big time. But things had gone sour with the producers – they wanted script changes and he refused to make them. The producers pulled out and it was 1978 before Burke found new financing to complete the film.

Along the way he separated from his wife of six years, and endured the turmoil of a doomed romance with a beautiful German girl he had met while filming in Europe.

If his colleagues in the film and television business had a criticism of Burke's work, it was that his approach was sometimes too flashy . . . too sensational for CBC traditionalists.

Macadam harboured no such reservations about Burke and his

work – he simply admired his gutsiness. And it was with delight that he welcomed him to the *Connections* crew as co-producer late in December 1975.

Burke's first task was to familiarize himself with the research, and he spent two weeks toiling through the files and asking questions. Then, working with Dubro and Macadam, he put together a new program outline, one which they hoped would convince Herrndorf that the research could successfully be translated into film. The program would begin with a "teaser" in which the major figures in organized crime in the nation would be identified. From there, it would move on to a look at the activities of organized crime: drugs, the laundering of "dirty" money through real estate and "legitimate" business; labour racketeering; loansharking; the subversion and corruption of officials and institutions. Finally, there would be a look at the history and geography of organized crime in Canada – how it had grown and who was in charge in which cities.

A meeting was set for December 22, 1975, the last working day before Christmas, in a CBC current affairs boardroom. As the four worked through the outline and thrashed out final contract details, a boisterous office party raved on directly above them. The agreement stipulated that filming was to begin in February, 1976 and run through to May. There would be a four-month layoff from May to August to minimize expenses, and then there would be a final four weeks of update shooting in late August and early September. The program was to be an hour long, with the airdate in the early winter of 1976. The budget was set at slightly less than $80,000, a figure largely without meaning since, in keeping with CBC accounting practice, it excluded all so-called "internal" costs such as overhead, equipment, and salaries to CBC personnel attached to the production.

The last details resolved, the meeting broke up at 7 p.m. "And then," Burke recalls, "we all went upstairs to the Christmas party and promptly got drunk."

The Shooting Begins

7

Burke: "What kind of activities were you involved in?"
McSween: "All kinds of things... murder and anything like that..."

Martyn Burke interviewing Montrealer Pierre McSween.

January, 1976 was devoted to organizing the complex logistics of the project. A long shopping list was drawn up detailing what "visuals" would be needed: still photographs, film of people and places, interviews with sources, informers, criminals and victims. The list was twenty-eight pages long. Because the filming would take them to cities all over North America, a travel itinerary had to be worked out and scheduled in detail.

A crew had to be selected, and that was Burke's responsibility. On camera, they would need someone who was more than technically competent: he had to be willing to assume the risks occasionally involved in surveillance filming or filming confrontations between Macadam or Burke and assorted thugs, and he had to be able to show initiative in situations where unorthodox techniques or unusual equipment would be needed to get the required footage. Burke selected Francis Granger, a Yugoslav who had worked mainly in France before moving to Canada, and with whom Burke had worked on one or two projects for CBC current affairs. Granger had a reputation for coming through in the clutch: in 1969 he had been working with a French ORTF crew shooting a documentary on the first year of the regime of the Greek Colonels, and he brought out the first film of the inside of a Greek concentration camp for political prisoners. This had involved getting himself arrested and escorted inside the camp, where he was able to film surreptitiously for several minutes before being discovered. When the authorities demanded that he turn over his film, he gave them only what was in the unexposed side of the camera's duplex magazine, keeping the exposed film safe until he was released a few hours later.

The sound man was to be a CBC staffer named John Crawford. Like Granger, he brought to his work an interest and dedication far beyong the normal call of duty.

Of course, few of the scores of criminals they intended to film had any desire to have their pictures taken: filming would have to be surreptitious. What was needed was a nondescript "window van" with one-way smoked glass, inside which the cameraman could set up his equipment and film without being observed.

CBC regulations stipulated that the truck had to be obtained through the Corporation's transportation department. Burke asked the department for a used van, "something that was pretty well beat-up on the outside," one that wouldn't attract attention by being new and shiny. Twice, the department offered trucks that looked like they had just rolled off the assembly line. Both times, Burke sent them back. A third offering looked just as perversely spiffy: this time Burke accepted it. That night, when the underground garage at the CBC's Bay Street offices had emptied, he drove it into several concrete pillars. When he had finished, it had just the kind of lived-in look he had wanted all along.

A signmaker was commissioned to paint the names and phone numbers of two or three fictitious small businesses on magnetic plates which could be attached to the sides of the van. Cardboard cutouts were made to block out light from the windows behind the cameraman's position: once the backlighting had been eliminated it became almost impossible to see inside the van through the smoked glass and the cameraman could do his job in relative safety. Walkie-talkies were ordered – they would be needed to allow the cameraman to keep in touch with his driver, who would normally have to leave the truck to avoid attracting attention during a stake-out. One final piece of essential equipment for the van was be-latedly added immediately after the first surveillance shoot: a container into which the cameraman could urinate.

Filming got underway at last on February 11, 1976, with two days of shooting in Toronto. The first quarry were Montreal Mafia bosses Vic Cotroni and Paolo Violi and Hamilton boss John Papalia, all of whom were caught walking into a Toronto court-house for the preliminary hearing in an extortion trial. Then the crew was off for a two-week swing through Detroit, Buffalo and

Montreal. In the weeks that followed they would branch out across North America, filming in Vancouver, San Francisco, Miami, New York, Hamilton and Guelph, Ontario.

It took only a few days for the dream of wrapping up the program on schedule to be punctured. The first trip to Montreal had been organized by Macadam, working through researchers Jean-Pierre Charbonneau and Michel Auger. Macadam had given the two a shopping list, which they were to organize in such a way as to maximize the crew's efficiency: interviews with police contacts carefully scheduled; surveillance filming timed so as not to interfere with interviews; "scenic" shots of criminal hangouts filmed somewhere in between, and so on. But when Burke, Macadam and the camera crew arrived, they found that the plans did not work at all smoothly. Police sources who had been gold mines of information in private interviews clammed up on camera, skirting sensitive topics and talking in the vaguest of generalities. Criminals did not appear for the hidden surveillance camera when they were supposed to, and it was sometimes difficult to identify them when they did. Or the light would be bad . . . or someone would be standing in front of the camera.

Meanwhile the meter would be ticking away at the rate of thousands of dollars a day. The mounting frustration and tension came to a head over an interview with a Montreal police narcotics expert who, typically, became remarkably uncommunicative once the camera started rolling. Macadam, well aware that the expert knew a lot more than he was divulging, kept probing, using every interview technique he knew to try to obtain something of value. Burke paced back and forth behind the cameraman, growing increasingly impatient as two, three, four and finally five rolls of expensive film went through the camera. Five rolls! Burke had never used more than four rolls on an interview in his life . . . not even with Idi Amin. And the policeman had said nothing worth using. Back at their hotel, Burke exploded at Macadam for what he saw as a poor job of organizing and for wasting crew time and valuable film on a useless interview. Macadam shouted back that Burke did not understand the complexities involved. It was the first of a continuing series of battles between the two, in which there never seemed to be any resolution. Both men were used to having their own way, and neither was ever willing to give an inch. At times, they came close to blows: it was Macadam the immovable object against Burke the irresistible force.

More than a conflict of super-strong personalities was involved; more than the haughty public school product versus the street-wise scrabbler. There was a fundamental difference in approach to the whole project. Macadam cast wide nets, whether in researching an area of crime or in conducting an interview. He would cover every angle, going after detail with infinite patience, checking out every lead, taking as much time as necessary to learn everything there was to know. It was a costly, time-consuming approach, but it could pay unexpected dividends. Worn down through sheer attrition, interview subjects would sometimes say things on camera they had had no intention of disclosing; researchers driven to distraction by Macadam's incessant demands for more and more detail often turned up a piece of information no one had suspected existed.

Burke, on the other hand, placed more trust in his intuition – on the sudden flash of inspiration, on the quick, killing thrust in an interview. While Macadam would cover a subject like a blanket, smothering it until the one essential fact crawled out gasping for air, Burke would go after the story within the topic like a ferret after a rabbit, ignoring "irrelevancies." The result was that Macadam often believed that Burke was careless and superficial, while Burke would accuse Macadam of not knowing a story when he saw one.

Looking back, it is obvious that the two approaches dovetailed beautifully, the weakness of each often being minimized by the strengths of the other. But this was by no means clear at the time. When Burke says today: "There were times when I was more worried about reprisals from Macadam than I was about the mob," he is only half joking. Little things took on mountainous proportions: Burke had his own spacious CBC office, while Macadam was forced to share cramped, windowless quarters with secretaries and researchers; while Macadam was always the anonymous unseen interviewer, Burke would occasionally show up on camera along with the interview subject – and Macadam interpreted this as a deliberate ploy on Burke's part to inflate his own role in the program.

Who was in charge? Macadam believed he was. After all, the program had been his idea and he and Dubro had done all the initial research and he had negotiated the production contract. Burke was a johnny-come-lately, a hired gun, a technician. Burke however, believed he was in charge. The CBC was paying the bills, and Herrndorf himself had been responsible for his appointment as co-producer. Besides, he had vastly more experience than Macadam.

In one typical encounter, Burke stormed into the *Connections* office one afternoon and in front of all present accused Macadam of bungling a shooting schedule and wasting time and money.

"Once more," he shouted, stabbing a finger at Macadam, "once more and you're out!"

He slammed the door and stamped back into his own office, slamming that door too.

Moments later, his door was kicked open and there was Macadam, beet-red, shaking, blood in his eye:

"If you ever do that again, Buster, I'll punch you right in the nose!"

Burke still savours the moment. "'Buster' he called me! Can you believe it?"

I asked cameraman Granger who had appeared to the crew to hold ultimate authority.

"Nobody," he replied. "That was half the trouble."

There were also disagreements over priorities and techniques between Macadam and Dubro, although they could generally be resolved amicably. One perennial source of argument was the filing system and how it should be organized for quick access. Another was the preferred technique for concealing a body-pack tape recorder. Macadam, normally a casual dresser, favoured taping the machine to his body and hiding the microphone beneath a sweater. Dubro preferred to slip the recorder into the breast pocket of his jacket, clipping the microphone behind his tie. Macadam insisted that Dubro would appear suspiciously formal if the thug he was secretly taping decided to remove his jacket and Dubro left his on. But Dubro, one suspects, was simply not prepared to suffer the indignities involved in following Macadam's technique.

Researcher Clarissa MacNair recalls her initiation into the Macadam method:

"There were about four of us in that tiny office one afternoon and Bill suddenly slammed down the telephone and said to me, 'Quick, get some toilet paper. I've got an interview in fifteen minutes.'"

"Well, I went to the ladies' and got some paper and when I got back there was Bill without his shirt on, all pink and naked from the belt up. He held his arms up in the air and had me wrap several layers of toilet paper around his waist. Then he held the tape recorder against the small of his back and I had to tape that to his body, over the toilet paper.''

Macadam, meanwhile, twisted round and round, arms aloft, like a torero being cinched into his cummerbund.

''The idea was that the toilet paper allowed you to take the tape off later on without pulling out all those tiny hairs on your body,'' MacNair explains. ''He'd tried it without the paper and getting the tape off was agony.''

(As for Burke: ''I certainly didn't go through all that bullfighter shit. I used to just stick it in my belt.'')

Even a seemingly straightforward problem like finding adequate office space from which to co-ordinate the production and carry on research proved to be a headache of no mean proportions. CBC facilities and offices are scattered all over Toronto's core in everything from renovated automobile showrooms, to a decrepit skid row theatre, to a former girl's school, to a handful of more modern office towers where space has been subdivided into rabbit warrens awash in teetering stacks of paper, books, film cans, video casettes, promotion posters and Centrex telephones. *Connections* occupied five different offices during the research and filming of the first series, all windowless. The first office was big enough for a single desk, which Macadam and Dubro shared. The second was large enough to accommodate two desks, which were shared by Macadam, Dubro, a secretary and a filing clerk/researcher. A few weeks' relief from the overcrowding was obtained when the office moved into a large space used for storing surplus furniture, but that was taken over by the *90 Minutes Live* staff when that program began, and *Connections* was moved into yet another tiny, airless space about fifteen feet square, containing two desks. By this time there were six people on the staff, not counting Burke. It was an intolerable situation, and Macadam finally broke his rule about never allowing anyone not directly connected with the production into its offices. He invited Herrndorf in for a visit, and shortly thereafter Herrndorf arranged to have a nearby staff lounge converted into office space for the production. This time there were four desks, but still no windows. Macadam's approach to Herrndorf had been straightforward: either *Connections* was given the lounge, or his staff would occupy the nearby boardroom.

The need for more office space was in a way symptomatic of a problem with the production itself, one that was growing to critical proportions as the first filming deadline of May, 1976 approached: Burke, Macadam and Dubro were being overwhelmed by information. New names kept cropping up, and an investigation of each new name would turn up several more. And all of this new data tended to cloud the original thesis of the program – that Paolo Violi of Montreal was Canada's pre-eminent criminal figure, and that the program could usefully be focussed on that one criminal. There were too many leads to be tracked down, and it was increasingly unclear which ones deserved priority.

Moreover, the criminals to which they had attached a priority for surveillance filming were proving extremely difficult to capture. Surveillance shoots to which half a day had been assigned in the original production schedule were often stretching into three-, four- and five-day projects. Most of the subjects were simply not predictable in their movements. The delays meant ballooning costs . . . the budget was on its way out the window.

Early in April, Burke and Macadam wrote a memo to Herrndorf explaining that translating the program outline to film, "is a much more complex and expensive process than could have been envisaged" when the contracts were signed.

"Generally," the memo said, "we are pleased with the material we now have. Yet, in terms of what we feel must be achieved by this program, we are convinced that more filming is needed. The program has emerged much like a jig-saw puzzle, with all kinds of tiny pieces being fitted together to make a whole. It is important to note that, in saying we need more filming, we are not trying to construct a larger or more artistic puzzle. We are merely struggling to find the minimum number of pieces needed to put together the existing puzzle we all set out to solve a couple of months ago . . .

"It comes as no surprise that we find this program one of the most difficult and exhausting enterprises that could be undertaken by this department. What we are doing is putting together on a national scale what literally dozens of police forces, royal commissions and crime probes have tried to do on a more local or specific scale . . .

"We feel that we have worked as hard and planned as efficiently as was possible. Yet, the past several weeks have abounded with inefficiencies and wasted time. We know of no way to avoid this. At times, we have spent hours or days on surveillance filming when caution might have told us to go for the safety of the interviews we could have arranged in its place. Yet, we feel that in other instances, we have spent too much time doing interviews when we should have been out searching for those visuals that require so much waiting. It is an endless debate with no real answer.''

The memo wound up with a plea for an extra $24,000 to complete the filming, arguing that without the additional expenditure, much of the film already shot would be rendered useless.

Herrndorf granted the increase, but not without first demanding an accounting from the two producers.

Those ''accounting'' meetings were held in an atmosphere of intense hostility, Herrndorf sitting behind his desk twisting the ends of his huge moustache while Macadam and Burke sat opposite him. By this stage, Herrndorf and Macadam were scarcely capable of carrying on a civil conversation, so Burke often found himself stuck with the job of having to explain the delays.

''I used to gauge Herrndorf's mood,'' Burke says, ''by how fast he was twiddling his moustache. If it was a twenty RPM twiddle, I knew he was absolutely furious, and we were in big trouble. And I would sit there absolutely livid because I was in the position of having to explain why we weren't finished, after having just spent days trying to get one hood, whom we couldn't get, and he was giving me shit for not having the thing completed . . . and I wanted to yell at him and he wanted to yell at me . . . and I would sit there quite red-faced and he would sit there twiddling his moustache . . . And we had a lot of twenty RPM meetings, all over the question of, 'Why aren't you idiots done?'''

Face to Face with the Mob

"Domenic goes by the 'twenties style. Which is . . . you just drive by, roll the window down and just shoot somebody. That's his style. And there's people that like that style."

**Toronto mob member on Domenic Racco, a
leader in the Siderno Mafia family in Toronto**

Why weren't they done? Of course, there was the problem of tracking down new leads, with no real sense of precedent to help in choosing the correct path through the maze of information. But even more serious were the difficulties involved in obtaining the film they needed.

Connections was dealing with four categories of information. First, there was information in the public domain, such as newspaper and magazine articles, the transcripts of inquests, trials, public inquiries and so on. Second, there was the information that was not generally known, but that a well-informed interviewer could coax an interview subject into revealing openly. Third, was information gained from sources who wanted or needed to remain anonymous, but who would co-operate on an off-the-record basis. They might be criminals, reformed criminals, undercover agents or other police sources.

Exploiting these first three kinds of resources was a more or less predictable process, and predictability is of utmost importance in television, where an error in scheduling during a production can run up thousands of dollars in crew and equipment costs.

What was new and unpredictable, and therefore costly, was dealing with the fourth category of information: that only obtainable first-hand from the criminals themselves. Included in this category was much of the visual content – the pictures that were needed if *Connections* was to be good television. Television is after all a visual medium, and if you don't have the pictures, you don't have a program. Yet, the *Connections* team could not simply telephone the person they wanted and set up an appointment to talk to him on camera about his criminal activities. Where interviews were possible at all, it was only under carefully contrived false pretences (as in the case with Paul Volpe) or through a planned confrontation in which Macadam or Burke would approach his quarry on the street and start asking questions. In the latter case, hidden cameras and concealed microphones would follow the action.

Where an interview was clearly impossible under any circumstances, as it was with many of the more dangerous criminals, it was necessary to carefully research the subject's daily movements and then try to be at the right place at the right time with a surveillance camera.

The vignettes which follow illustrate the difficulties met by the *Connections* team on an almost daily basis.

David McGoran and Raymond "Squeeker" Greco both have long criminal records, and have been described by police as "enforcers" for Toronto Mafia boss Paul Volpe. Among their pastimes is collecting money from loanshark victims. Their methods are not always pleasant.

To try to film the two for a *Connections* item on loansharking, Macadam decided to use the direct approach. The filing system told him they could usually be found in McGoran's Danforth Avenue real estate office, which does double duty as a mob meeting place. So one afternoon in May, 1976, Macadam and cameraman Granger walked in off the street. Granger had his camera rolling, but he held it as casually as his nerves would permit, at hip level. Macadam's body-pack was switched on and recording.

McGoran was leaning bulkily over a desk when they entered, talking to a receptionist. As Granger deftly tilted his camera in McGoran's direction, Macadam asked to speak privately with him.

"What is it that you want?" McGoran demanded, his voice registering clearly on Macadam's body-pack.

"I'm from the Canadian Broadcasting Corporation and I just wanted to ask you . . . to get some advice from you . . ."

McGoran points at the camera. "What's this for?"

"Pardon me? Oh. It's a camera. Uh, is there anywhere I can speak to you privately?"

Macadam was ushered through a centre office in which several heavies were lounging: among them he spotted "Squeeker" Greco.

As McGoran and Macadam entered a rear office to talk, Squeeker got up to see what was going on. He poked his head through a doorway into the front office, and Granger tilted his camera up at him. Gotcha.

Meanwhile, Macadam, more than a little nervous about being separated from his cameraman, is brazening it out with McGoran:

"We have been told . . . you know this whole thing about loansharking and everything . . . that you've been involved sort of in enforcement and so on . . . I wanted to come right to you and find out if there was any truth in it . . . ."

"I've been hearing about this shit for twenty years. I try and sell fuckin' houses, that's all I do."

"Is there anybody in your view that's trying to get at you, spreading this . . ."

"The police department. They're all retards." He pauses to answer his telephone. Then he continues: "I don't want to appear like an obnoxious person . . ."

"Pardon me?"

"I don't want to appear like an asshole, but none of this is for publication of any kind."

"No, I'm not print . . . I'm . . ."

"The last time I talked to a guy like this I picked up a fuckin' magazine and I was written up as all kinds of terrible fuckin' people in different ways . . . they went around interviewing all my customers . . . they never found anybody who was dissatisfied anywhere and yet they still made a shitty thing out of it, you know . . ."

"Yeah."

"You can't win. All they're lookin' for is to sell newspapers. I can't gain by it. How do you defend yourself against innuendo? You might as well . . ."

"Yeah. I know." Macadam is trying hard to appear sympathetic, to make himself an ally. It is a technique he uses frequently in these interviews. He suggests to McGoran that maybe somebody is out to get him by spreading false rumours, and that he might just know who it is. McGoran is intrigued.

"I don't know where you get this kind of lead, even," he says.

"How do I find out who's out to get me if you don't tell me who's telling you this?"

"Well, you know, maybe I can get to the bottom of it . . . Let me tell you the story I've heard, and you can tell me whether it's absolute nonsense or not. What I have heard is that you have people that go around and collect debts for loansharks . . ."

"That's the Mafia's shit."

"What?"

"That's Mafia shit you're talkin' about. What would be the point in doing anything like that?"

"Well, I suppose one would get a percentage?" Macadam suggests.

"Great. What am I gonna do . . . collect eight hundred bucks off some guy . . . breaks his legs or something? Make eighty bucks? Would I commission the job out to somebody to do it, and I get twenty and he gets twenty? I mean it's all such fuckin' hog-wash . . ."

"Then it's not true that . . ."

"In respect to me, it's not true."

"Has anyone that's ever worked for you been involved in this? Is that why . . ."

"I hire all guys that need chances," replies McGoran, gesturing to the next room where Squeeker and the others are waiting. "I hired two guys just out of jail and nobody'll give them a job . . . They're selling houses for me. One guy's already got the mortgage department more organized than I ever had it in twenty years."

"And because of this, these idiots follow me around, the I squad [police intelligence] . . ."

Suddenly, McGoran stands up behind his desk.

"Are you wired up? You got a tape thing on you?"

Macadam's stomach contracts to about the size of a pea.

"No, but what . . ." He is trying to carry on with the conversation. But McGoran has walked over to where he is sitting on the edge of a sofa.

"You puttin' this on tape?"

"No. But what . . ."

"Listen you [unintelligible] . . ."

McGoran slips his hand down the outside of Macadam's sweater and finds the concealed microphone. There is a scuffling noise on the tape.

"Now just a minute here . . ." Macadam protests.

McGoran's voice is very cold: "Get out of here, and take your friend with you."

Macadam leaves as quickly as dignity will allow. In the front office he says to the cameraman, "He doesn't want to talk to us . . . he doesn't want to do an interview right now."

The concealed tape machine keeps rolling as Granger and Macadam return to their car. Macadam is too rattled to remember to turn it off.

"You want any exterior shots?" Granger asks.

"He started to ask if I was wired up," Macadam says, but Granger doesn't understand.

"You want any exterior shots?"

"He said, 'You're wired' and he jumped on me . . ."

"Who? The big one?"

"Yeah. I went in the back by myself, so that blew that . . . but they're all there. I think if we turn the car around we can get them. And there's that place next door too, those are all enforcers too."

The tape continues to roll. Macadam is behind the wheel of the car, trying to negotiate the traffic to put Granger in a good position to shoot the exterior of the building.

"What next door?" Granger asks. "The barber shop?"

"Yeah."

"Yeah, okay. Now you go make . . . go up left and across the street and we can maybe stop . . ."

"Left?"

"Left," Granger says. He sounds as flustered as Macadam.

"Keep to the left!"

Macadam wants to know, "Did you get Greco? He was there. Did you see him?"

"You see you are in the right lane now and you should be in the left lane."

"Okay, I know, just calm down, I'll get it. But did you get Greco?"

"Yeah. The young one . . . That place should be raided by the cops!"

There is traffic noise on the tape, and then Macadam speaks again.

"He said, 'Are you wired?'"

"He said 'Are you wired?'" Granger repeats, incredulously.

"Yeah, he said 'Are you wired' and he jumped over and jumped me . . ."

"He was touching you to find you've been wired or not?"

"Yeah."

"He found out?"

"Yeah."

"He found out you were wired?"

"Yeah. I said, 'Oh shit . . . you know, come on' . . . I can't remember what I said . . .''

Of the film thus obtained of McGoran and Greco, about eleven seconds was used in the ninety minutes of *Connections I*, to cover part of the narration explaining the role of the enforcer in loansharking.

Claude Dubois leads a Montreal organized crime family that is unique in that it actually *is* a family: it consists principally of Claude and seven of his eight brothers. Over the past decade, the Dubois brothers have earned a reputation as the most vicious, bloodthirsty collection of hoodlums anywhere in the country. They make a living through extortion, loansharking, prostitution, and other related activities, operating mainly out of the St. Henri section of the city. In recent years, their power has grown to overshadow the Mafia's in some areas. To obtain film of Claude Dubois, in particular, was an early and obvious priority for the *Connections* crew. Attempting to interview him was judged to be too risky, given the Dubois' reputation for violence. Two brothers, Roland and Norman had been filmed while being served with subpoenas outside their St. Denis nightclub hangouts, and there was even a little film of Claude, but all of it had been shot using a special night lens developed by the United States military for use in Vietnam. Its pictures were acceptable if nothing else was available – they served to document – but the colour was poor and the figures were not as distinct as with a standard lens. On his third trip to Montreal, Burke decided to try for Claude Dubois once again, this time in daylight.

It was April 21, 1976 and Jean-Guy Dubois was on trial for murder. Researcher Michel Auger had told Burke that during the trial there were normally at least two of the Dubois brothers seated in the spectators' gallery, from where they glared menacingly at Crown witnesses. On this day, Auger had learned, Claude himself would be there. Burke hoped to catch him leaving the courthouse and follow him in the hope that a better filming opportunity might present itself.

The crew was divided between two rented cars: Burke drove one and the other was occupied by cameraman Granger, soundman Eric Hoppe and researcher Auger; the camera car was parked outside the main entrance to the courthouse, while Burke circled the block to keep an eye on a rear exit. They kept in touch with walkie-talkies.

It was nearly rush hour by the time Claude Dubois emerged – from the front entrance – with his long-haired brother Adrien and the lawyer of Jean-Guy, their accused brother.

Burke got the message on his walkie-talkie: "They're getting into a car!" He swung his own vehicle into a parking lot behind the courthouse and sprinted around the building to catch the camera car just as it pulled away on the Dubois' tail. He leaped into the back seat beside Auger; Hoppe drove, cursing the downtown traffic.

The Dubois drove their green Chrysler Imperial to a square near Place Ville Marie, where they parked, and walked with the lawyer across the plaza to his office. Granger's camera ground away, exposing precious footage of the three. He now had Dubois twice: once outside the courthouse, and now here. But Burke wanted more, if only for insurance.

Hoppe parked the car in a spot which gave Granger a clear shot of the building's entrance. But it was a rush-hour tow-away zone, and within minutes, a Montreal police cruiser had pulled up beside them, demanding that they move.

"We pretended we couldn't understand French," Burke recalls, "and at the same time we pointed to the camera and told them we were doing undercover work. It confused the hell out of them . . . I think they thought we were RCMP or something. Anyway they went away and left us alone."

And just in time, for Claude and Adrien Dubois were emerging from the lawyer's building. They climbed back into their Chrysler and pulled away, Burke and the others close behind. This time, the *Connections* team followed them to a bar north of St. Catherines Street, the Fontaine de Johannie, where Adrien got out. Claude continued on alone, driving north.

A car containing four animated men is something you notice in traffic, particularly if one of the men in the front seat has a film camera with a long zoom lens balanced on his shoulder. Dubois noticed that he was being followed. But there was little he could do because the rush-hour traffic made evasive tactics impossible. Burke and the others could see him nervously checking his rear-view mirror every few seconds. Finally, he pulled into a gas station, and the surveillance car was forced to drive past. Soundman Hoppe swung down the first side street he could find and sped around the block, just in time to pick up Dubois' tail as he left the gas station, glancing over his shoulder at them.

The traffic thickened as the two cars approached the Metropolitan Boulevard, one of Montreal's main expressways, and Hoppe tried to manoeuvre to give Granger a good clear shot of Dubois behind the wheel of his car. On the access ramp to the Metropolitan, traffic finally stopped completely – Burke and the crew found themselves in the embarrassing position of being trapped in the space directly behind the car they had been following. Dubois' eyes kept flicking up to his rear view mirror. There was sweat on his forehead.

Granger turned to Burke: "You got your body-pack? You're crazy if you don't try for an interview with that guy."

Within seconds, Burke had slipped the Nagra into his belt, clipped on the tiny microphone and jumped out of the car. He did not want to give himself time to think about what he was doing. Next thing he knew, he was pounding on Dubois' window. Dubois jumped like he'd been shot.

"Mr. Dubois . . . Mr. Dubois. I'm from CBC television. I was wondering if we could have an interview . . ."

"Why are you following me?"

"Well, because we were hoping to interview you, and we were trying to find you . . ."

"You got a camera. Why?"

"Right, because we'd like to film you. We'd like to interview you about your family and about what's going on, and I was just wondering if we could talk to you on camera."

"Well . . . but you could speak to me before trying to . . ."

"Well, I'll tell you, I'm awfully sorry about that except that we tried to . . ."

Dubois, apparently relieved that it was only a CBC crew that had been following him, pointed to the shoulder of the access ramp, interrupting Burke:

"Let's park there for now."

The two cars pulled over. As Dubois emerged from his Chrysler, cameraman Granger climbed out of his car and carefully placed his camera on the hood, pointing in Dubois' and Burke's direction. He switched it on, and then stood back with his arms crossed.

"Are you the one that phoned me once?" Dubois asked Burke.

"No, it was somebody in our unit though . . . I mean there was a guy who phoned you one time, and we've been trying to get hold of you . . ."

"Somebody phoned me from Toronto."

"Right. It was this guy Macadam."

"Don't take nothing now. We'll speak first and then we'll manage something."

"Okay."

"I got nothing against [an interview], you know, as long as it's positive."

"I'm sorry for following you . . . we were trying to stop you at one point and we thought that would be ridiculous . . ."

"First of all, I'm ready, like I told the other guy that phoned me once . . . I'm ready to speak with anybody, to film anything, but we're passing, on the seventeenth, in front of the [organized crime probe] . . . so I think before talking with you or taking a film that I finish with that, and after that we'll do something."

Dubois launched into a brief harangue about police harassment of the Dubois family.

"Between me and you, if they [the police] have something against me, they would put me right away inside, believe me. You know, believe it. They would put me right away inside."

"Okay. I'm sorry for following you, but . . ."

"One of my brothers right now that's got a murder charge . . ."

"I know."

"He's in court since yesterday, the trial is on you know. I would like to try to finish [that]. And I'm telling you before he will come out of it. That one thing we know, he's not guilty of that sort of thing. So you come out of it with a positive on that, and after that we'll get out from the [crime probe] and after that we'll talk with anybody."

(Jean-Guy Dubois was convicted of murder and sentenced to life imprisonment early in 1977. His first trial in 1975 was declared a mistrial, and three months later a juror was charged with accepting a $2,000 bribe to "hold out" for a not guilty verdict. The juror got two years in jail.)

The impromptu interview was to carry on for about twenty minutes, with Dubois seemingly eager to talk, ranging over a host of topics from the cost of his house to his views on rival Montreal gangs. Burke was scarcely able to get a word in edgewise.

At one point Burke tried to wind up the interview on his own:

"Okay, well, look Claude, thank you very much, and I'm sorry we bugged you this way, and I didn't mean to scare the . . ."

"I wasn't scared."

"Well, I was," Burke chuckled.

But Dubois insisted: "I wasn't scared."

Burke, anxious to finish up, brushed the comment aside.

"Well, anyway . . ."

"Scared of what?" Dubois would not let go.

"Well," Burke replied wearily, "I mean you've got guys trailing you . . ."

"I'm not afraid to die," Dubois volunteered. "And there are some people that are afraid to die, you know . . . there are people who are afraid to die. Me, I'm not afraid to die. If I die, I die. So. That's all . . ."

Burke's interest is aroused. This was good stuff.

"Haven't you got enemies though that . . ."

"If a guy is forty or sixty, he's still going to die."

"Haven't you got enemies though that would . . ."

"Well, we must. Who has got no enemies? You got enemies?"

"Yeah. A few."

"Well, you got enemies . . . you got to die, that's true . . . you must have given a punch in your life to somebody, so that's an enemy. And when you are ten brothers, you must have enemies. Even if myself I didn't do nothing . . . one of my brothers punch somebody, the guy, he's going to hate me just the same, because I'm a Dubois."

Burke began to move away once again.

"Well, good luck at the crime probe . . . thank you, Claude."

"Well, after that I think we'll talk more, and I'll give you more. If you want to know who's really collecting the nightclubs [extorting protection money], I'll tell you who's collecting the night clubs."

Burke stopped: "You can't tell me now, so I can go and find out somewhere, can you?"

". . . Right now if you want to know who's really the king in Montreal, in collecting, everything, it's the cops themselves."

Burke's face must have betrayed incredulity.

"Well it's a true thing. I'll give you all the nightclubs, all the names of the cops, who are their partners, and how much they collect there, which one belongs to there . . . I'll give it all. I got everything."

"Well that's very interesting, because I had heard . . . the newspaper stories were that you guys had pushed out the Cotroni organization [the Cotroni/Violi Mafia family]. That was what they said. And there was a truce that had been arranged between you and the Cotronis and that it's you who are now really powerful here and the Cotronis are not any more . . . that's what the newspaper stories . . ."

"The only difference between me – us, I mean – and the Cotronis, is the Cotronis, when they saw it hot with the cops they ran away. When it's hot, we stay there. We're gonna face the fucking thing, you know. But no, they didn't want to face it, they run away. Us, we'll face the thing. That's the only thing . . . that's why we're still here."

Burke probed a little farther: "Violi's in jail though. He faced it in a way." [Paolo Violi refused to testify before the Quebec Crime Probe and was given two one-year sentences for contempt.]

"That's another thing. They put Violi as a big king . . . to me, Violi's a punk. He tried to go and collect a guy for $100 a week with a punch in the nose. You don't call that a king. For me, he's a punk, no? They didn't want to face it, they run away."

"Okay, well . . . we'll give you a call after you're through and we'll come down again, and if we can get together . . . Okay, thank you Claude."

Burke waves goodbye as he climbs back into his car. As Dubois eases his Chrysler into the traffic, Burke checks his body pack:

"I hope to Christ I was . . . well, I twisted it on, but I hope the switch was working okay . . . and I hope my finger worked on the switch okay . . . let me check . . . oh, it's on! Oh, Jesus, Christ!"

The Dubois interview was featured in *Connections II*, as part of *The French-Canadian Connection*. Interwoven with it was an interview with another French-Canadian gangster, Pierre McSween, the only survivor of a gang that once shared power with the Dubois, before being wiped out in a vicious gang war. McSween had testified before the Quebec Crime Probe, telling what he knew about the operations of the Dubois gang. Immediately afterward, he prepared to leave Montreal for a police-protected hideout in rural Ontario, having dyed his hair and changed his appearance in other ways. He was contacted for *Connections* by a friendly Montreal police captain, and agreed to an interview before going underground. It was perhaps the most sensational interview of the first series of programs, containing as it did an admission from McSween that he had participated in murders for which he had never been charged.

Burke: So then your gang had a squad with some people who were killers . . .

McSween: Yeah.

Burke: Some people who would handle extortion . . .

McSween: Well, you beat people at the nightclub like, uh, some they don't want to pay protection, but most of the time you break everything in the nightclub, you know. That guy, it's worse for him because, you beat him it's nothing – he doesn't lose no money you know – but when you break everything it's worse, you know?

Burke: How were you involved in murders?

McSween: It's something that you do for your brothers . . . but I wouldn't kill anybody for money. I mean, most of the time the things happen because you gotta revenge yourself, or you're going to get it, you know . . . But even somebody give me five thousand dollar, I wouldn't kill anybody for that. No, it's not that . . .

Burke: You would only kill for revenge for your brother?

McSween: Oh, yes.

Burke repeated the question later in the interview:

Burke: What about murder?

McSween: Oh, I seen a few murders. I was there for about five, six . . .

Burke: You yourself were there for about five or six murders?

McSween: Yeah.

Burke and cameraman Granger are sitting in the surveillance van in a north Toronto parking lot, waiting for Mafia member Rocco "Remo" Commisso to appear at his Eglinton Avenue West banquet hall, Casa Commisso. Commisso belongs to the "Siderno" group in Toronto, a Mafia alliance so-called because its founders come from the Siderno area of southern Italy and maintain strong ties with the Mafia there. Despite several murders and bombings, the public was as yet unaware of the existence of this branch of the Mafia in Toronto. The *Connections* crew planned to change all that. To do so, they needed pictures of Rocco Commisso. Commisso, of course, was unlikely to co-operate: he liked his anonymity and wanted to preserve it. It was going to be a touchy confrontation.

To relieve tension while they waited, and to test Burke's body-pack recorder, Burke and Granger conducted a mock interview with Granger playing the part of a fictitious Mafia boss, in an unintelligible Donald Duck squawk:

"Mr. X, is it true that you're a key member of organized crime in Toronto?"

Squawk, squawk.

"Does that mean that you are in fact involved in extortion, rape, murder, arson?"

More squawks.

"I see. Uh, there have been reports that you have very strong ties with the U.S. and are in fact tied up with the Magaddino family over in Buffalo."

Squawk, squawk, squawk.

"I see. Mr. X, is it true that the construction industry in Toronto has been almost entirely taken over by you and your family by incredible instances of arson and brutality and that you have had people's legs broken?"

More squawks.

"Okay, well I guess that pretty well sums it up Mr. X."

Burke and Granger are still chortling over their nervous little burlesque when real life intrudes: Commisso is approaching the banquet hall. Burke, hoping to delay him outside long enough for Granger to get a good shot of him, runs across the street. He calls out:

"Excuse me . . . Remo? Are you Remo? I'm looking for Mr. Commisso. That's you, isn't it?"

Commisso pauses, giving Burke a chance to catch up.

"What you want?" His voice is icily threatening.

"Mr. Rocco Commisso?"

"Come inside." It is not a request, it is an order. But Burke has to keep him in camera range.

"No . . . I'd just as soon talk to you out here rather than . . ."

"Inside!" Commisso demands. (Later, Burke was to recall, "His eyes just turned to stone. I've never seen anything like it. He just emanated violence.")

"I'm from the Canadian Broadcasting Corporation . . ."

"Yeah?"

". . . and I'm told that you're Mr. Rocco Commisso. Is that your name?"

"I am Rocco Commisso. What you want to know?"

"Oh." Burke stalls. At this moment he doesn't want to know anything. He just wants to delay Commisso long enough for Granger to get his footage, and then get out with his skin intact. "Uh, we were doing something . . . uh, and we were told to talk to someone named Remo Commisso. Is that you?" Burke is pretending to be confused by Commisso's nickname, Remo.

"Come inside. I don't wanna have to talk out here. Come inside."

Commisso enters the banquet hall, and Burke has no choice but to follow him. Inside, he notices several men who had apparently been waiting for Commisso's arrival. They do not look friendly.

"I'd rather not talk in here," Burke is saying, ". . . if we could just . . ."

"Well, I've got nothing to hide. You talk to him," Commisso says. He points to one of the men moving toward Burke out of the gloom.

Burke inanely repeats his question: "Well okay, our producers were trying to find a man by the name of Remo Commisso and I was wondering whether that was you. Is it you?"

Commisso's anger flares: "Who give you the right to go around and look for name of Commisso?" he shouts at Burke. "Producer, no producer . . . I don't give a *fuck* for your producer or your anything!"

"Oh." Burke is edging toward the door. His mouth is dry.

"Okay?" Commisso shouts.

"Okay," Burke replies, and he is out the door, back on the street.

Now what? He can't return to the truck, because they will be watching him from the banquet hall and that would blow its usefulness as a surveillance vehicle. On the other hand, maybe the men inside saw him get out of the truck to chase after Commisso. What if they decide to check the truck and find Granger and his camera inside? They could as easily break his arm as look at him . . .

Back at the *Connections* office, Dubro and Macadam were waiting for Burke to check in, to let them know how the shoot had gone. It was a safety routine they followed on risky shoots. When the telephone rang, Dubro picked it up and Macadam lifted an extension.

Burke was breathless from running to the phone booth. "Can you get up here right away," he said. "We're in trouble."

"He sounded terrible," Macadam recalls. "I didn't realize he was out of breath from running . . . I thought he'd been beaten up or something. I asked him, 'Do you want the police?' and he said 'Yes.' "

Dubro began dialing the number of a Metro police contact and before he could finish Macadam was out the door on the way to the parking lot and his car.

"I don't think I've even driven so fast in all my life," he says. "I went through all the red lights, driving at about ninety miles an hour from Bay Street up there to where Martyn was. I figured that if the police noticed me, fine . . . they would follow me up there and perhaps we would be able to utilize them. I couldn't find the phone booth Martyn was supposed to be in and I was zooming up and down Eglinton until finally I spotted a police car – Jim had been dealing with the Metro police and they had the area pretty well surrounded. I stopped the police to ask them what was happening, and at the same time I saw the surveillance van coming down the street with Martyn and Francis. Luckily the police hadn't moved in or anything, because they were okay."

Burke explained later that he, too, had flagged one of the police cruisers and hurriedly outlined his predicament to two baffled constables. He asked them to see that the marked police cars kept out of sight, while he retrieved the truck. He had worked out a route, down an alleyway, that would take him back to the parking lot without being visible from the Casa Commisso. Minutes later, he and Granger were safely on their way back to the *Connections* office. The police were called off. It was the first and the last time *Connections* asked for police protection.

Giacomo Luppino is probably the closest thing there is to a Hollywood-style Mafia "Godfather" in Canada. Whatever individual differences they may have, Mafia groups from all over the country pay Luppino respect. When there is a dispute, it is often Luppino who is asked to mediate. Now in his late seventies, he lives quietly in a modest bungalow in suburban Hamilton.

It was three o'clock on an April afternoon in 1976 when Burke parked the battered white *Connections* surveillance van in front of the Luppino home on Ottawa Street. On the side of the truck was a magnetic plate bearing the name of a gardening company and a telephone number. Granger was in the back, adjusting his camera tripod. It was the first of half a dozen attempts to film Luppino, before he was finally caught raking leaves from his front lawn a month later.

Burke, clad appropriately in his oldest, scruffiest clothes, slid out of the driver's seat and walked around to the back of the truck, where he opened the door a few inches and pulled out a rake and a hoe. He perched the tools on his shoulder as he walked off down the street, leaving the truck apparently empty.

When he returned an hour later and opened the rear door of the van to replace the tools, he was greeted by a gust of exhaust fumes. Granger was on the floor, almost unconscious. Burke leaped into the driver's seat and quickly moved the van out of sight of the Luppino house; then he helped Granger into the fresh air.

It was several minutes before the cameraman had recovered sufficiently to explain what had happened. About half an hour after Burke had left, a car had backed up to the van so that its exhaust pipe was only a few inches from the van's grille. The driver raced its engine for several minutes and Granger, having no way to get out of the truck without being seen (the back door was locked from the outside), had gradually been overcome by carbon monoxide fumes. Whether the incident was simply an accident, or an attempt to smoke Granger out, or even an attempt to kill him, there was no way of knowing. But it convinced Burke and Macadam that they had to have a reliable communications system between the truck and the outside world at all times. A set of police-quality walkie-talkies was purchased, and from then on, at least three crew members were involved in all surveillance shoots.

If the *Connections* team was embarrassed at calling in the police at the Casa Commisso, it was not simply because it had been a false alarm. There was also the reporters' reluctance to rely too heavily on police resources in putting the program together. Journalists, after all, maintain their integrity only so long as they operate outside the establishment, of which the police are a part. When they begin working too closely with the establishment, they lose the outsiders' perspective that permits them to maintain some semblance of objectivity in their reporting. They then cease to be journalists at all – they become public relations officers and, as such, are of little use to anyone, least of all the public they should be serving.

In operating in foreign countries, however, there was little need for concern about being compromised: there, they were outsiders by definition, and could be nothing else. In the United States, and later in Italy, *Connections* occasionally relied heavily on police co-operation to get the film they needed.

In New York City, a prime *Connections* target was Carmine Galente, the most powerful Mafia chief in America, and perhaps the most ruthless. (Galente was murdered in a spectacular gangland rub-out in New York, on June 12, 1979.) Prison psychologists had diagnosed him as a pathological killer. As boss of the New York mob, Galente maintained considerable influence in Montreal, just as Buffalo Mafia figures exercise some authority in southern Ontario. In crime, as in other things, Canada is to a greater or lesser degree a branch plant operation. It was Galente who, working as an emissary of the New York mob in the 1950's, helped Vic Cotroni to become the supreme Mafia boss in Montreal. Cotroni had long since retired to the quiet life and an honoured role as family counsellor and advisor, but the links to New York were maintained under his successor, Paolo Violi, until Violi's murder in 1978. Although at this writing it has yet to be decided who will succeed Violi, there is no doubt that the new boss, too, will keep up the New York connection.

Dubro's research had established that Galente split his time between his daughter's home in Greenwich Village, and the apartment of a mistress on East 38th Street. (The mistress represents a Montreal connection of another kind: she is the wife of a Mafia member from that city, a fugitive wanted by the police for his alleged role in a diamond swindle.) However, stake-outs at both locations during an early trip to New York by Burke, Dubro and Macadam had produced no results, and its was difficult to justify the expense of further surveillance there, without some assurance of better rewards.

Dubro had been invited to Columbia University to give a talk to the university's Eighteenth Century Association later in April 1977 (he titled it "Walpole, Hervey and their Associates") and Macadam suggested that he spend two or three days while he was in New York trying to get a better fix on Galente's movements. Fellow journalists, Dubro soon discovered, would be of little help: the

American television networks had been trying to film Galente ever since his release from jail several weeks earlier, and had come up with nothing. (One of them was later to offer a handsome fee for a copy of *Connections'* film.)

Dubro had heard that the Brooklyn Organized Crime Strike Force of the United States Justice Department had taken an active interest in Galente in connection with a drug investigation. A contact there gave him the name of a small bar near the Brooklyn Bridge where Galente was frequently to be seen meeting with associates. Dubro visited the bar that afternoon, and found himself the only customer. One of three husky men who were eyeing him suspiciously from behind the bar finally spoke to him:

"Waddya want?"

"Uh," Dubro replied, "I guess I have the wrong bar."

Later, he was to explain, "It would have been an awkward place to film there anyway. I mean, it was right under the Brooklyn Bridge . . ."

Dubro then contacted a source on the New York Police Department's intelligence squad. He told Dubro that Galente had to visit his parole officer once a week, and he gave him the name of the officer. From him, Dubro learned the time of Galente's visits to the parole office. Here, finally, was a sure-fire filming opportunity: the parole office was in a court building in Foley Square where it would be a simple matter to establish a hidden camera position.

Burke flew in the next day with cameraman Granger. To be on the safe side, Dubro had arranged with the New York police intelligence squad to have police surveillance squads waiting outside both the daughter's home and the mistress's apartment. He, Burke and the cameraman would wait outside the courthouse.

Dubro's communication system with the police consisted of a pocketful of dimes and a convenient phone booth: every twenty minutes he telephoned a police officer who was in radio contact with the surveillance cars. He was emerging from the phone booth after one of those calls (nothing to report) when he noticed a short, balding man with a professorial air mounting the courthouse steps. Galente! Dubro ran up to the man and stopped him on the steps.

"Mr. Galente?"

"Who?"

"Mr. Galente. You *are* Mr. Galente, aren't you?"

"Never heard of him," the man said, and continued on his way.

The sequence was duly recorded by the cameraman, but nobody was sure whether they had the right man.

Another phone call gave them the answer. Galente had in fact just left his daughter's apartment and driven off in his car. Dubro warned Burke and the cameraman to get ready. They waited, and waited. No Galente.

Dubro dipped into his pocket and placed another call to his police contact.

"He's not going anywhere near the courthouse," he was told. "They're on his tail and he's headed for the Long Island Expressway."

Dubro was still on the phone when someone rapped on the booth door. It was the parole officer.

"He's not coming," he told Dubro. "He's going to a confirmation ceremony at a church somewhere out on Long Island."

He didn't know which church.

Dubro, Burke and Granger jumped into their rented car and sped off, stopping every few miles for Dubro to telephone the police for an update on Galente's position. Eventually, he learned that the police had followed him to St. Christopher's Church in Baldwin, Long Island. He was instructed to park his car a few blocks away from the church, where the police surveillance squad would meet him and advise on filming strategy.

An hour later and without further difficulty, Granger was able to film Galente leaving the church. They were the first pictures anyone had obtained of Galente since his release from prison. About thirty seconds of that film was used in *Connections I*, to cover narration designed to set up the New York-Montreal connection between Galente and Paolo Violi.

As with most of the film used in the series, the unavoidable cost per second in terms of time, money and emotional and physical wear-and-tear was prodigious.

9
The Code of Silence

Judge: "You have no idea what the Mafia is?"
Witness: "No."
Judge: "But you were designated by the (Italian) anti-Mafia
law!"
Witness: "I don't know what anti-Mafia means."

Witness testifying before the Quebec Crime Probe

For law enforcement authorities the world over, the biggest stumbling block in combatting the Mafia has traditionally been *omerta* – the Mafia code of silence. A member or associate who discloses the smallest detail of the workings of the Mafia faces almost certain retribution in the form of a violent death. Witnesses in cases involving Mafia members routinely chose long prison sentences for refusing to testify rather than co-operate with government prosecutors.

In 1958 the United States government began developing a scheme that has gone a long way in breaking the iron grip of *omerta*. It is called the Witness Protection Program, and under it federal law enforcement officials can offer lifetime protection to criminals who agree to testify against other criminals, together with elaborately documented new identities, relocation assistance and help in finding a legitimate job. It is a controversial scheme, involving in the minds of its critics something akin to a pact with the devil. Law enforcement officials call it the best tool they've got in fighting organized crime.

An unanticipated spin-off of the Witness Protection Program has been the evolution in the U.S. of a small and unique industry – the Mafia consulting business. Several of the more than 2,400 criminals now protected by the program use their expertise on the inside workings of the mob to earn money. Some publish books, some are consultants to crime-prone businesses such as race tracks or casinos; some even work as undercover agents for various police forces.

One such success story was Vincent Teresa, who in 1970 traded his job as number three man in the New England Mafia for a new identity under the program. His testimony at organized crime trials since then has resulted in the conviction of nearly fifty criminals, and information he has provided to law enforcement agencies has led to the arrest and conviction of scores of others. During that time he has had to change identities not just once, but several times, to keep ahead of the mob's assassins. As the highest-ranking Mafia member ever to defect, he is a walking advertisement for the effectiveness of the Witness Protection Program and his murder could cause it serious damage.

Dubro read Teresa's book, *My Life in the Mafia*, during the early research stages of *Connections* and identified him at that time as having prime potential as an interview subject for the program. The problem was to find him, and then to get him to agree to talk on camera.

In *My Life in the Mafia*, Dubro found acknowledgements to three men: FBI agent Jack Kehoe, United States Attorney Ted Harrington and Teresa's ghost writer, veteran *Newsday* reporter Tom Renner.

He contacted all three men by telephone, and then made personal visits to their offices in Boston and New York, asking them to contact Teresa and persuade him to telephone the *Connections* office in Toronto. He followed up with frequent telephone calls to all three men, during which he would remind them of his interest in talking to Teresa.

Four months after the initial attempts, Teresa finally phoned: Dubro was not in the office, so the ex-Mafia boss spoke to Macadam.

After a few minutes of chatting about organized crime in Canada, Teresa, never a man to mince words, came to the point.

"Lemme ask you this. What do youse guys have in mind for me?"

Their conversation, and one the next day in which Dubro was involved, provides an insight into the technique adopted by *Connections* for dealing with the several criminal informers eventually involved in the programs. The challenge was to get them to co-operate without paying them anything beyond legitimate expenses, in deference to the long-standing journalistic dictum against bribing sources to talk. Dubro and Macadam, and later Burke, all used the same technique: vagueness liberally sprinkled with flattery.

"Well," Macadam replies, "I was thinking, if there was an area . . . I mean, I know there are areas we'd like to talk to you about, and then if you might feel interested in coming on the air . . . we're in a tight budget situation, but of course we would expect to pay some honorarium."

"What kinda money you talkin' about?"

Macadam carefully ignores the question:

"Well, uh, uh, we'd either fly down or fly you up or whatever, you know, to do an interview with you. We'd have to discuss what would be a satisfactory way of protecting you . . . probably have your voice altered . . . I don't know what precautions might be necessary . . ."

"Yeah, well I can probably get some of my own protection."

"Right. But we're, uh, uh, normally . . . let's put it this way. Normally we don't pay anything but I realize that in a situation like this we would want to pay an honorarium . . . something. It wouldn't be much, frankly, because we're in a very tight budget situation and we just don't have the money."

Teresa laughs: "Why do I always hear that from producers? I just done a thing for ABC, I don't know whether you caught it . . . it was on a coupla weeks ago . . ."

"Gosh, no I didn't."

" . . . organized crime in this country and so forth and so on. I had about sixteen minutes with them and, uh, like I said, all producers are always cryin' they got no money."

"Well, it's ridiculous, I agree with you. I mean, it's a fact of life. They never give us enough money to do the thing properly you know. They give us X number of dollars and it's just never enough to do the thing at all, unlike the feature film business, or whatever, where they seem to have money to burn. We're always scrambling for every last dollar, and it's not a good situation."

But Teresa persists: "Well if you give me some idea how much money's involved I can . . ."

"Well the thing would be, I'll tell you it would be a better situation, I could give you a better answer once you've talked to [Dubro], if it's possible for you to ring us again collect – I hope *this* was a collect call . . ."

"No."

"Oh gosh."

"I don't call collect. Then my telephone number would be on your bill. And I'm not sayin' I don't trust you, but you might have a bad secretary."

They set up a call for the following afternoon, when Dubro would be available. Teresa has by now tired of pursuing the question of money.

"To tell you the truth," he says, "I'm thinkin' very seriously of goin' to Canada to live."

"Really?" says Macadam, apparently fascinated.

"Yeah, but I don't know what I would do up there."

"Well, it's a country of great opportunity, I can tell you."

"Well, I just wish I had one opportunity, I'd be up there tomorrow I can tell ya." Teresa laughs. "Because this country is bad for me, you know. People are startin' to find out where I am."

"Yes, I can imagine that would be a problem."

". . . and it's gettin' a little touchy. And, uh, it's kind of tough to go to another country without knowin' anybody."

Macadam can legitimately sympathize here: "Yes, yes, I know."

"I'd like to go to Australia, but, like I say, without knowing anybody, it's kind of difficult."

"It's a big move alright. The only thing is a move from the U.S. to Canada is not like going . . . it's not an enormous jump. One can always move back if one doesn't like it, whereas in Australia you're an awfully long way away." (Macadam, of course, knows that a man with Teresa's record would have no hope of clearing Canadian immigration.)

"Right. Well, okay," Teresa says, "I'll call you back tomorrow at this number."

The next day Dubro answered the phone.

"Jack Kehoe asked me to give you a call," Teresa begins.

"Right. I was talking with him . . . gosh, it must be weeks ago now. I guess Bill told you roughly what we were doing . . ."

"Yes, a documentary kind of thing."

"We're doing a documentary on organized crime in Canada, including some of the relationships with the United States."

"Right."

"And I read your book, which I think is very, *very* good."

"Thank you," Teresa says proudly.

"It's one of the best that I've ever . . ."

"I'm going to be signing a contract this coming Tuesday to write another book, as a matter of fact."

"Really! Well that should be *very* interesting. I really think the first one . . ."

"Yeah . . ."

". . . is one of the most entertaining I've read."

"Yeah. Right." Teresa is lapping it up.

"And I've had to read a lot . . . I've read just about everything on the subject . . ."

"Uh huh."

". . . of organized crime and there's just very little that's as good, including the *Valachi Papers* [the original Mafia exposé–a classic], and uh . . ."

"Yeah, well, I lived it, so . . . that's the way it was."

"It certainly is . . ."

Dubro now solidifies his gains by dropping a name:

"I saw Phil Manuel when I was down in Washington." [Manuel is an investigator for the United States Senate's Permanent Subcommittee on Investigations.]

"Oh yeah? He's a good friend of mine."

"He recommended you quite highly."

"Uh huh."

"In fact, he said you were *the* expert on gambling junkets."

"He's right there," says Teresa, "I originated 'em."

This takes them off into a long question and answer session about Canadian criminals who were involved in casinos in Haiti during the regime of Papa Doc Duvalier.

Then Dubro drops another name.

"I was talking to Ted Harrington down in Boston as well . . ."

"Geez, I spoke to him yesterday."

"Oh, did you? How is he?"

"He's fine. He's tryin' to do something for me on something else."

"He's a great guy . . . a good lawyer," Dubro volunteers.

"Oh, he certainly is," Teresa agrees.

"He ran for attorney general [of Massachussetts] you know . . . too bad he didn't make it . . ."

"Yeah, I know. One of my brother-in-laws was helpin' him out . . . but what're you gonna do?"

"He told me you knew Raymond Patriarca and Meyer Lansky."

[Patriarca was a New England Mafia boss and Lansky, a former contract killer and later a key mob financial figure, was often involved in Canadian laundering operations.]

"I know 'em both well."

Then he offered Dubro some advice about attempting to interview them:

"You gotta understand somethin'. They can't possibly tell you the truth. You understand? Whatever you ask them they're gonna go against. If you ask Lansky if he knows Raymond Patriarca he's gonna say 'I've never heard of him.' If you ask Raymond if he knows Lansky, he's gonna say the same thing. If you ask either one of 'em if they know me, they're both gonna say 'no.' You see? They have to say that. They're into this conspiracy and they can't let their hand down."

"Yes, I understand that," Dubro said. "But the interesting thing about television is that you can see the *way* they deny it."

"I was just on television a couple of weeks ago," Teresa says proudly.

"Yes, I know, and I *missed* it."

"There was a few other people on there like Mickey Cohen . . . he talked for ten minutes and didn't say nothin', because he's punch-drunk now . . . people don't realize that. I told the producer that . . ."

"Well, yes. I don't think we're going to use him at all."

" . . . when he told me Mickey Cohen is gonna be on. I told him 'You're not gonna be able to make sense out of anything the man says because he's a vegetable now. He's been pounded around so many times he don't know what he's talking about no more."
[Cohen is a veteran of mob wars dating back to Prohibition.]

Finally, Dubro says, "Well look, I think there are so many areas to talk about . . . is it possible for me to come down and see you, or . . ."

"Yeah, well the thing was that the other fella I talked to said that we, uh, he said that you people wanted to pay me but that you didn't know how much, and that you would have a better idea than him."

"Uh, in terms of the financial aspect, Bill has to approve it, but it really . . . what I'd like to do is to be able to come down and talk to you about what you might be able to do . . . Uh, I was going to ask you about Montreal . . ." and the conversation drifted off into names and connections in that city.

"Well, look," Dubro says, once again," I think the best thing would be if I could come down to visit you sometime in the next couple of weeks . . .''

"Well I'll be in New York City next week to sign that book contract for a couple of days and then from there I have to be out on the west coast to do some business with the race tracks . . . I do some consultin' work for them.''

"Right.''

"And for Las Vegas, too, by the way. And I have some business to do for them. Then after that I'll be startin' this new book and I'll be tucked away someplace and you won't be able to reach me for a week or so . . .'' This was beginning to sound like an interview on the *Tonight* show.

Then, abruptly, Teresa changes the subject and the sudden belligerence in his voice startles Dubro:

"Say listen, I understand from Jack Kehoe that you know where I am. Is that right?''

"Uh, well yes I do,'' Dubro confesses.

"You mind tellin' me where you found that out?''

"No, I'm afraid I can't,'' Dubro says with a nervous little laugh. "I can't reveal sources.''

"I'm not askin' you to. All I wanna know, was it legitimate or a 'wiseguy?''' ['Wiseguy' is mob jargon for a Mafia member.]

"Oh no, nothing like that. It was strictly legitimate.''

"Okay, that's all I want to know. That don't bother me none.'' Teresa sounds more relaxed once again.

"I, uh, just tracked it down . . . that's, uh, my job . . .''

"That's okay.''

"But I think it would be pretty hard for most people to find out.''

"Well, I don't know whether it's hard or easy. I know they'd better not come near me because I'm ready for 'em.''

Eventually, they agreed to meet in Poughkeepsie, New York. The filming took place nearly six months later, in a New York city high-rise office that was vacant for the weekend. *Connections* had in the end agreed to pay Teresa's first-class air fare from a West Coast city to New York, but that was all.

Teresa, a short, stout man in his late forties, arrived at the office with three armed and burly United States marshals, who seemed to take their job very seriously indeed.

"They looked like a bowling ball and three pins,'' Burke recalled.

As the cameraman set up his tripod and adjusted the lights, two marshals flanked Teresa while the third stationed himself near the locked door to the office. All three seemed very tense.

Suddenly, a key was inserted in the door lock. An instant later the door swung open, to reveal a chunky cleaning woman stooping down to pick up her pail while she propped the door open with her mop. When she straightened up, she found herself staring down the muzzle of the marshal's .38 Police Special. With a brief shriek, she dropped her pail and backed into the hallway: it took several minutes for the marshal to calm her down and explain that he was a policeman.

The interview lasted for nearly two hours, with Teresa giving a dazzling display of underworld wit and wisdom, and thoroughly enjoying himself in the process. To conceal the new look he had given himself to avoid recognition, he had personally selected a disguise that reflected his dramatic flair – a black fedora and a large black bandana covering his nose and the lower part of his face.

His reply to Burke's very first question provided the opening lines to *Connections I*. Burke asked Teresa to define organized crime.

"Organized crime . . . very simple. It's just a bunch of people getting together to take all the money they can from all the suckers they can . . . Basically, it's like a large corporation, with department heads all over the country . . . all over the world for that matter . . . and naturally you have to show loyalty to somebody . . . to a certain man, and when you don't that man gets a little angry with you and spanks you – in a hard way."

Later, Burke asks him about the enforcers, the men who do the "spanking":

"Who are the killers? What are they like?"

"Oh, wait now . . . you'll have to excuse me, but I don't want to start naming no names when it comes to any murder or anything, 'cause the next thing you know I'll be in front of a Grand Jury for indictment. I can't do that. But I'll tell you what they are: a stone killer's a guy that the mob will call up and say, 'Look, we want you to go kill this Frenchman that's directing this show,' and they don't ask no questions or nothin'. Just, 'What's his name and where can I find him?'

"And they'll stake you out for a few days, and one way or another – if they have to lay on a bed of rattlesnakes – they'll get ya. Now don't make it sound like a western cowboy outfit . . . they'll get ya, whether they gotta hit you in the face with a baseball bat like an old friend of mine, Paul Lanny [phonetic spelling] used to do, or whack you over the head with a club, or a knife, or a gun, or whatever. But they'll get ya and they'll take their sweet time, but when it's done it'll be done professionally. There won't be anyone chasing them down streets or anything like that. It'll come off just as smooth as silk.''

"Is there anybody out trying to get you?" Burke asks.

"I would imagine quite a few. But listen, when the time comes, they'll get me eventually. If they don't, something else will. Maybe I'll die of cancer . . . It ain't the worst thing in the world to get shot, you know.''

"I don't know," Burke confesses. "I've never been shot.''

"Well, you know, I mean, would you rather have cancer in your chest, or a bullet?''

"That's a good question. I'd rather have neither right now.''

Teresa's bravado contrasted strangely with the trepidation he had expressed to Macadam about moving to another country.

Only a few minutes of the interview could be used in the programs, but all of it was fascinating. Teresa knew his subject well, and spoke in almost epigramatic style:

On the roots of the mob's power: ''The backbone of all organized crime . . . is gambling. That is the backbone, that is where it all started. With nickel and dime numbers and horses and ball games, football games, basketball games, sports betting. This is where it all started, because that's where they got the biggest edge [where the odds most favour the ''dealer'']. From there organized crime moved up to loansharking, from that into dope, and from dope into bonds and then into legitimate business . . .''

On life in the Mafia: ''How did I spend my time? Like a sucker. Gambling, running around, doing everything that I'm preaching about now that suckers do. I done the same thing, only I done it with a little bit of an edge . . . didn't make no difference, the percentage beat me anyway . . . gambling, you run around with women, you know, you gotta get yourself in trouble. I'm not sayin' I was the biggest runaround in the world, but I made a few mistakes. And everybody does, you know . . . that's the funny thing . . . the guys in the outfit [Mafia] they could have the most beautiful wives in the world, the most beautiful children in the world, the most beautiful homes. But when they're out on the street, they gotta have a tomato. They gotta have it. I guess it's a very simple reason . . . they gotta take their anxieties out, they gotta be able to curse in front of a woman, they've gotta be able to do something bad, what they want, you know, that they don't do in their own home . . . I don't think I ever ran into a mob guy that was married that didn't have a girlfriend at one time or another.

". . . they (Mafia bosses) will hug and kiss each other, and as soon as they walk away, they'll tell their man, 'Watch him.' There's no trust . . . They'll say 'yes' and 'yes' and 'yes' and when they turn around, they'll say, 'I'm not even payin' no attention to that guy.' . . . You can't influence them. They make up their own minds what they're going to do and it's gotta be their own thinking. So as friendly as you think they are to a man, it's just up front, it's not their inner thought.

". . . I think it's more power [than money]. They got all the money in the world. They couldn't spend the money they got, especially the way they live. I'm not being disrespectful . . . but most of them live like creeps. You know, they got a nice home and that's it. They never leave their back yard, they never enjoy themselves, they never go travelling or anything. I mean their enjoyment is to go down to the city and get a loaf of bread – hot Italian bread on a Sunday . . . that's their enjoyment. They got more money than God . . .

". . . I know one, Don Peppino [Joe Bonanno], that was driving an old . . . it was like a 1952 Chrysler, with a wheel this big in it. I asked him one day, I said, 'Joe, with all your money, why don't you buy a new car?' He said, 'You crazy? The Internal Revenue would be right down on my back if I buy a new car.' He said, 'You buy a new car, you're a big shot . . . I don't want no new car and that's fact.' They were afraid . . . these old geezers were afraid to take the money they had hidden out.

"Meyer Lansky showed them how to take it out. He took it, he brought it to banks, he made connections with other banks in other places out of the country and he turned dirty money into clean money for ten percent. For that matter, Jimmy Hoffa used to do the same thing.

"I'll tell you the truth . . . I don't believe in this malarkey that everybody that's in the mob is in it because they were poverty stricken because that's a lot of . . . that's just a lot of bull. It's as simple as that. I wasn't poverty stricken, and I could name ten guys that wasn't poverty stricken. I got into the mob because I wanted to be in it. I enjoyed being in it. I was a born thief, I enjoyed being out stealing. I really did. I could've went to work like anybody else. I coulda went to school, college or anything else. I'm not a stupid man. I might have got a college diploma and been something, but I preferred to steal. To me it was easier . . . nobody has to be in the mob, you understand. They're in it because they want to be and that's my firm belief.''

Months after the interview, Dubro learned that Teresa had moved once again, this time setting himself up in business as an importer of tropical birds somewhere on the United States west coast. Not long after that, Teresa was investigated for extortion and fraud in connection with his new business. He was never charged, but was reportedly dropped from the Witness Protection Program.

Another former Mafia member who figured in the *Connections* investigation was Pasquale "Paddy" Calabrese. Dubro began trying to track him down early in the summer of 1975, thinking he might be a useful source of information on links between the Buffalo mob – of which Calabrese had been a member – and organized crime in southern Ontario. Instead, Calabrese led *Connections* to the Member of Parliament for the Vancouver riding of Burnaby-Richmond-Delta, John Reynolds.

Like Teresa, Calabrese had been part of the Witness Protection Program in the States – in fact, he was its charter member. After being arrested for a spectacular hold-up at Buffalo's city hall in 1966 (some say the only time it's been done from the outside), he had resisted the blandishments of several varieties of law enforcement officials who tried to persuade him to feed them information about fellow Mafia members. But the fact that he was receiving visits from those officials was enough to convince the mob that he had turned stool pigeon. In revenge, they planned to have his wife photographed in a compromising situation with his best friend: the idea was to deliver the photos to Calabrese in jail, then sit back and watch him go "stir crazy." When Calabrese heard about the scheme, he decided to co-operate with the law in return for protection: He had little choice, since the mob already believed he had been talking and would doubtless seek retribution.

His testimony was instrumental in convicting Buffalo Mafia don Frederico Randaccio and his lieutenant, Pasquale Natarelli, of conspiracy in 1967. Each received a twenty-year sentence.

Since then, Calabrese has changed his identity at least six times. When Dubro caught up with him through a reporter at the *Buffalo Evening News* and a retired policeman who had originally helped "turn him around," Calabrese had completed five years working as a private security consultant to night clubs in Reno, Nevada. In that position he had frequent contact with members of the mob: federal police who had been following his career persuaded him to develop those contacts with criminals and become what would be called in the world of espionage a double agent. Calabrese was to use his intimate knowledge of the mob to infiltrate operations in various cities and feed information to the police.

In one spectacular case, Calabrese worked with an FBI agent in Alaska to break up a gambling and prostitution ring on the Alaska pipeline. His role brought him to the attention of the Co-ordinated Law Enforcement Unit in British Columbia. CLEU was established to co-ordinate activities of the RCMP and the Vancouver City police in dealing with the west coast's epidemic of major crime, much of it related to the heroin trade. It also employs civilian researchers. (Similar co-ordinating bodies for combatting organized crime exist in other provinces, for instance the Criminal Intelligence Service of Ontario, which co-ordinates the efforts of the RCMP, Ontario Provincial Police and several city police forces, along with civilians working for the Attorney General's department.)

Calabrese was hired by CLEU in 1975 to infiltrate the Vancouver Mafia and inform on its connections with other parts of the country. Within a few months he had turned up evidence which led to the breaking up of a huge counterfeit money and heroin deal among Mafia families in Toronto, Vancouver and Spokane, Washington.

Calabrese also provided CLEU with a great deal of detailed information on the operations of the Vancouver mob under its boss, Joe Gentile.

After preliminary meetings with Dubro and Macadam, Calabrese agreed to be interviewed for *Connections*. But by now it had become clear that the big story he had to tell was one of the Vancouver mob's attempt at political corruption at the federal level.

Calabrese had been told by Gentile and other Vancouver mob members that MP John Reynolds, a Conservative opposition backbencher, could prove helpful in providing information on goings on in government circles. (The series, however, made no claim that Reynolds had ever provided any direct service to organized crime.)

Calabrese in his Vancouver role as a mob member had met with Reynolds on several occasions, both with other mob members and alone. Their conversations had been secretly taped by a recorder concealed on Calabrese's body and the tapes were now in storage in a Vancouver police department safe. The police would not allow *Connections* to review the tapes, but B.C. law enforcement officials were willing to assign a researcher to listen to them and compare them with Calabrese's recollections of the conversations, as he described them during his interview with Macadam. The researcher confirmed the accuracy of what Calabrese had said.

Macadam later interviewed Reynolds, who had since announced his decision to resign his Commons seat, complaining that he was not being paid enough money as an MP to properly support his large family. He denied any wrongdoing. (Reynolds next appeared in the public eye as the host of a Vancouver hot-line radio program.)

The two versions of the story – Reynolds' and Calabrese's – were eventually combined to produce an item called *The Political Connection* for the second program.

As for Calabrese, his career in television was just beginning. He was to play a major role in the *Connections* sequels of 1979.

10
The Breakthrough

"He put himself above everybody else that I knew at that time in jail. For example he would always ask somebody else to clean out his cell or get him a place in the cafeteria..."

Montreal mob associate on jailmate Paolo Violi

Filming for *Connections I* and *II* finally ended May 17, 1976. Burke and Macadam did not have everything they wanted, but they had everything their tattered budget would permit, except for a few days' scheduled update shooting in late August and early September.

Now began the tedious process of editing into a coherent program the nearly fifty hours of film they had gathered. There was obviously much more material than could possibly be crammed into an hour, and Herrndorf agreed that the program could be extended to two hours. Work proceeded slowly during the summer, with Macadam, Burke and Dubro each taking several weeks' leave. Burke headed for his summer cottage to work on his Vietnam novel, *Laughing War*. Macadam flew to England for some relaxation on the family estate in Norfolk and some company business in London. Dubro was also in London, entombed in the British Museum for a month's concentrated work on his neglected PhD. thesis on Lord Hervey. But by early August they were all back on the job, pushing to meet a December completion deadline.

The editing was not going well. Without a strong central thesis, the volume of material seemed overwhelming. The original plan to divide the show into a first section describing several specific kinds of criminal activities and a second section which would amount to a kind of "who's who" in Canadian organized crime, simply collapsed under the sheer weight and complexity of the material they had amassed. Moreover, the difference in approach to the material between Macadam and Burke became ever more pronounced as more and more was pared away to get at the meat of the story. Macadam wanted the show to be as comprehensive and exhaustive as possible: Burke, who directed most of the editing, insisted on the excitement of a more dramatic, episodic style.

As winter deepened, it became evident that the program would not be ready on time. Herrndorf was becoming seriously concerned. By early 1977, four separate versions – rough cuts – of the program had been edited and discarded. Each was a disastrously confusing collection of facts with little continuity or direction. Herrndorf would leave each successive screening more worried than he had been the last time. The CBC's legal department was also concerned, for the legal risks involved in airing the program were unprecedented. Their demands for evidence to support the hundreds of separate and sometimes oblique or confusing allegations made in the film against individuals and corporations became increasingly insistent, and Dubro spent week after week talking to contacts confirming and re-confirming each of the hundreds of individual facts contained in the scripts.

In February, 1977, the screening of the fourth rough cut proved to be no better than the first three. Herrndorf left the screening room in a deep depression, convinced that he was going to have to scrap the entire project and somehow swallow the losses. There was only one other alternative: put the project in the hands of an executive producer with the authority to make whatever decisions might be necessary to put together a usable program, and pray that the producer would pull it out of the fire. It meant taking ultimate control over the program's packaging out of the hands of Burke and Macadam. The new executive producer would need considerable tact to deal effectively with both the warring producers, and would also, of course, need sufficient production expertise to find a way to make sense of the material. Faced with the disastrous option of cancelling, Herrndorf decided it was worth a try.

The following afternoon he met with Burke and was pleased to discover that Burke was happy and relieved to hear his proposition. They discussed potential candidates for the job, deciding quickly on Richard Nielsen. A phone call to Macadam confirmed that he, too, approved the plan and the selection. It seemed the only way out.

Nielsen is a filmmaker of vast experience, a former CBC current affairs producer who left the corporation to establish what became the country's largest independent film production company, Nielsen-Ferns International. He brought with him the singular advantage of being liked and admired by both Burke and Macadam – an asset made remarkable by the fact that by this time the two could agree on virtually nothing else.

It was not the first time Nielsen had been called upon to try to salvage a production and he approached his assignment with a wariness born of experience. Normally, he knew, when he was called in like this the production really *was* in trouble, and all that could be done was to make the best of a bad job, minimize losses, and prepare explanations about how he had been called in too late to be able to do much. This time, it was to be a different story.

Neilsen immediately arranged a screening of the most recent version of the program – this one three hours long.

"What I saw was the most exciting television film I'd ever seen," he remembers. "After a few years in the business of producing current affairs programming, everything begins to look the same – you're sure you've seen it all before somewhere. But what I saw at that screening all seemed fresh. And I was very impressed with the boldness and guts it showed in terms of the personalities involved . . . Macadam and Dubro in collecting the information, Herrndorf in being willing to put it on the air and shooting it."

Being able to feel a genuine enthusiasm for the material with which he would be working was important to Neilsen, because one of his biggest tasks would be to rebuild the shattered morale of the *Connections* crew. It was like being named coach for a team in a slump – he had to find a way to get them to believe once again in their own abilities.

Neilsen decided almost immediately to have the material re-cut into a series of self-contained vignettes or chapters – what is known in the business as a magazine format. He did this for two reasons: first, because it solved the production's most serious artistic problem, its lack of continuity or coherent structure.

"Everybody's first assumption about the program had always been that it would be a standard documentary – a narrative with a beginning, a middle and an end. Those kinds of assumptions can be very hard to get rid of. But I found that at that first screening what had fascinated me were a whole series of specific stories that had only a general thematic link," he explains.

The second reason was to give Burke and Macadam something each could do on his own – something that could be done relatively quickly and which each could see was good television. The production's editors were changed at the same time. Those who had been on the job since early the previous summer had reached an advanced stage of frustration and fatigue and Nielsen wanted editors who could look at the material with a fresh eye, as he had done, and be enthusiastic about its merits.

Within two weeks the first of the magazine items were completed, and everyone was enthusiastic about the results. The production was back on the rails.

Nielsen still had the task of advising on and approving final packaging, and there were still almost daily disputes between Macadam and Burke to be adjudicated, "a job," Nielsen says, "for which my only qualification was being a parent.

"They were not so much co-producers as unmatched siamese twins. The production just wouldn't permit them to operate separately. Both had to be involved in every aspect for it to work."

Screenings of each new item would renew the conflict between the two. Arguments usually had the same old source: the gap between Macadam's linear intellectual style and Burke's intuitive, emotional approach.

"Bill would ask a harmless question like why was a particular piece of information put in a particular place in an item, and Martyn would fly off the handle," said Nielsen. "He would be annoyed because he'd have no logical reason, and he would have to invent one . . . They never understood that the nature of their disagreements meant they could never be resolved . . . Paradoxically, though, it was a very creative relationship."

Nielsen also found that the tight security on the production could also sometimes cause problems:

"Normally, when somebody gives me a memo, I skim it to find out whether or not it's worth reading, and then if it is, I go back over it in detail. On *Connections*, somebody would hand me a memo and I'd skim it, but before I had a chance to go back over it, it would have been snatched from my hands and stuffed into the shredder."

The meetings with the CBC's lawyers became even more frequent and difficult as the programs began to take on their final shape. Burke and Macadam were glad to have Nielsen on their side.

"Bill and Martyn and I were about as awkward a group for the lawyers to deal with as one could conceive," Nielsen recalls with a chuckle. ''Martyn was very emotional and had a tendency to yell and shout; Bill was willing to argue the smallest point at endless length, until attrition would set in; and I of course had been around the CBC for years and I have a very good memory for corporation precedents, so I was able to question each decision from that point of view.

''And since there were three of us, we were able to work in shifts . . . for instance I frequently didn't listen to Bill for hours on end, but they had to.''

There were ultimately to be fourteen separate, self-contained ''magazine'' items divided into two ninety-minute programs. They are summarized in Appendix 2.

11
On the Air

"CBC to spill the beans on organized crime network."

Headline in the *Toronto Star*, May, 1977.

Normally, the story of *Connections I* and *II* would end here, in the spring of 1977. The programs have been edited and, with one or two minor exceptions, are ready for air. Soundman Bruce Nyznik has composed and mixed an elegant and brilliantly effective sound-track which pulls the items together and provides solid continuity. The sound track, in fact, is as much a *tour de force* as anything else about the program, though few viewers will even be aware of it.

A bit of update shooting and editing of script and film, a few last-minute legal checks and confirmations of scheduling times and then the programs are to be put on the network for everyone to see. However, as should be clear by now, nothing about *Connections* was normal, and so the story continues.

The original winter, 1976 deadline had long ago gone by the boards due to production delays. The revised April, 1977 deadline had been blown as well, by the editing delays before Nielsen arrived. But now that everything had come together successfully, a third air date was set, for late May. Everyone was now confident that the new deadline could be met and, in fact, the shows were ready in time. Unfortunately, the Ontario Conservatives chose to call a provincial election for that month, which meant that air time normally available for specials like *Connections* would have to be devoted to election coverage. *Connections* was once again without a time slot.

At this point something strange and inexplicable happened.

Macadam and Burke began to have doubts about whether the shows would ever be aired. They sprang partly from a rumour that on the agenda of the next CBC department heads' meeting was a proposal to cancel the shows. The proposal, the rumour went, had been placed on the agenda by Herrndorf himself – it was a way for him to dump the shows without having to take complete responsibility for the cancellation. Although Burke was (and is) an unabashed admirer of Herrndorf's abilities, he also understood the bureaucratic inertia and the cut-throat corporate politics that were ranged against the programs. Macadam was simply ready to believe the worst.

And so Burke and Macadam did not wait for confirmation of this rather vague bit of intelligence and, given Herrndorf's inaccessibility, there was little point in even trying.

Instead, they developed a two-part contingency plan. The second part of the plan, for which Burke claims responsibility, was to be implemented if the worst came to the worst. It involved simply stealing the work print – the master copy of the programs – and hiding it at the apartment of a friend of Burke's.

Burke explains, "We had worked bloody hard to get that footage, and in some cases even risked our necks. We were damned if we were going to sit around and see it get mouldy in some CBC archive somewhere, or get chopped up to be used as fill or leader in some other shows.

"In their context and in their own small way, some of those interviews we had done were historic . . . We were not going to let that film get destroyed . . . we regarded ourselves as the keepers of the vault."

The first part of the plan was designed to make the second part unnecessary, and it was carried out immediately. Burke telephoned Sid Adilman, a *Toronto Star* columnist and one of the most influential critics in the country, and told him about *Connections*. He gave him the general outline of the programs, and a few of the juicier production anecdotes, like the time cameraman Francis Granger had been gassed in the back of the surveillance truck. But most important, he gave fulsome credit to Peter Herrndorf for conceiving the shows and having the courage to carry them through. This was the master stroke, the psychological *coup* that would make it impossible for Herrndorf not to air the programs.

The story duly appeared on the front page of the *Star's* entertainment section under a four-column headline: "CBC-TV to spill the beans on organized crime network."

"A comprehensive CBC-TV documentary about organized crime in Canada and the United States, researched under tight security and filmed in tense situations, is due on Channel 5 next month.

"'It's going to prove beyond any doubt that there's a national organized crime network in Canada, embracing narcotics, loansharking laundering of money, corruption of officials and other activities', a source close to the project said yesterday . . ."

Adilman had, as expected, phoned Herrndorf for confirmation:

"Some CBC sources claim the program's budget has reached $300,000 but Herrndorf declined to give a figure. [It was actually closer to $500,000.]

"'It's a pretty expensive project,' he said. 'Until there's a final print and we sort out all the legal problems, we don't know exactly when it will be on the air. But we're close to a final print, and we're hoping to show it sometime in May, or at the latest in early June . . .'"

Accompanying the story was a column and a half-wide, five-inch high photograph of a smiling Herrndorf. The cutlines beneath the picture read: "CBC-TV's Peter Herrndorf: He initiated the investigation of organized crime."

Perfect!

Macadam had in the meantime been talking to Peter C. Newman, publisher of *Maclean's* magazine. The result was an excited mention of the shows in the magazine's "Preview" section.

Burke insists that, "those articles, especially the one in the *Star*, were the thing that absolutely saved the programs. Herrndorf had his picture in the paper with a story saying 'Herrndorf is fighting organized crime.' And he was in a terrible bind after that because he had put the cancellation on the area heads' agenda so that it would appear to be their fault for killing it. But after the articles it was clear that the responsibility for what happened with the show was all his. The reporters went to Herrndorf and interviewed him about this incredible, heroic show he was responsible for and he could not say he was cancelling it at that point. So we had a slight lease on life."

Macadam agrees: "I don't know if I ever was actually *convinced* that Herrndorf was going to cancel the show. But going to the press made it impossible for him to do it. It was insurance for us . . . once those stories appeared there was no longer any doubt that the shows would be run.''

But had there ever been any real reason to doubt that they would be run? It seems incredible that now that the programs had finally been successfully packaged, Herrndorf would consider cancelling them and writing off an investment of upwards of half a million dollars. And, in fact, he had no intention of doing so.

''The last time I seriously considered cancelling,'' he says, ''was the night of the screening of the last disastrous rough cut, before Dick Nielsen was brought on. Once Dick had things sorted out, there was never any question of cancelling.''

Nielsen confirms this: ''I don't think Herrndorf ever wavered for a minute in his resolve to put the programs on the air. I have no doubt of that . . . and I suspect I know how the whole cancellation fantasy got started.

''All of us would look at those items from time to time and wonder whether any of it could ever really be put on the air. It was all unique, all 'libellous' – although we felt we could defend everything on the basis of its being true – and even the hidden camera techniques we used had in the past always been considered unethical . . . I don't know at all whether I would have had the guts to put it on myself. But it wasn't my decision. It was Herrndorf who had to decide to put it on.''

In other words, were Burke and Macadam projecting their own nagging doubts about whether the programs were airable, onto Herrndorf?

''Right. I don't think either article had the slightest influence on that decision. Herrndorf had made his commitment a long time ago.''

But what about the agenda for the department heads' meeting?

''The story doesn't make sense. The department heads wouldn't have had the authority to cancel. They're there to consult and to give advice, but they can't cancel somebody else's program.''

On the other hand . . . ''there were a lot of questions being asked in other CBC departments about the programs, about all the money that was being spent on something nobody had been allowed to see. Sometimes things will get on the agenda just to embarrass somebody – for political reasons.''

In the event, the shows were scheduled for the evenings of June 12 and 13, 1978, shortly after the appearance of Adilman's *Star* article.

A last-minute screening was held June 5, for Herrndorf, Robin Taylor – a former newspaperman who had succeeded newly-promoted Herrndorf as head of CBC-TV public affairs – and a handful of senior CBC executives. (Herrndorf had moved up another rung on the CBC management ladder, to Vice-President Planning.) Following the screening, Herrndorf sent a long memo to Nielsen, Macadam and Burke, containing twenty-two suggested changes to the programs. They ranged from changes in the order in which the items would be presented to script changes designed to strengthen certain allegations, to a request that reference to an Ontario provincial court judge included in the *Portrait of a Mobster* profile of Paul Volpe be dropped completely.

The decision to drop any reference to the judge was the only order that seriously rankled. Dubro had conducted a long and progressively more inebriated interview with the judge over two bottles of twenty-year-old Scotch at the judge's lavishly furnished home. During the interview, the judge had confirmed what *Connections* already knew – that he was in the habit of socializing with Volpe and other Toronto Mafia figures. The CBC's lawyers had argued long and strenuously that the reference could not be successfully defended in court in a libel action. Although the item was intended, ostensibly at least, merely to show that the judge was indiscreet in his social contacts, the innuendo in the context of the Volpe profile went far beyond that, suggesting serious impropriety. But no impropriety could be proved.

It was one case where the lawyers were clearly correct, and it may be difficult to understand why Dubro in particular fought so hard to keep it in. The answer is clear to anyone who has seriously investigated the workings of organized crime and the personalities of the criminals involved. It is difficult, if not impossible, after such an investigation not to develop a powerful contempt for these criminals, together with an almost physical revulsion for the ways in which they systematically destroy the lives of their victims. One also learns that they operate within moral and ethical structures that are sometimes even stronger than those of ''straight'' society. The difference is that the codes accepted by organized criminals are the creations of psychotic minds.

Criminals like Volpe, Paul Dubois, Violi and the others defend themselves so fervently because they actually believe that there is nothing wrong with what they are doing. Break the legs of a defaulter on a loanshark's loan? Why not? He didn't live up to his end of the bargain. Murder an informer? Of course. And the more brutally, the better. He has committed a breach of trust and clearly deserves the worst.

It is clear to the investigator that no-one with healthy moral and ethical sensibilities can avoid feeling contempt and disgust for these criminals. That a judge, a politician, a senior civil servant seeks out and enjoys their company is *prima facie* evidence of his unsuitability for his job. It is not, however, the kind of evidence that will stand up in court.

A few days before the air date another problem cropped up. Macadam received an unexpected phone call from MP John Reynolds, who told him he had some hot information on a plot to frame him by spreading stories that he had co-operated with Mafia figures. They arranged to meet June 9 at a Toronto hotel restaurant.

Macadam and Dubro, wired for sound, arrived for the meeting to find that Reynolds was accompanied by a lawyer and was more interested in obtaining information than in giving it. He wanted to know if Macadam's interview with him was going to be used on the air, and if so, how and when. He had been told, he said, that the CBC was out to get him. There were many veiled references to the laws of libel.

The verbal fencing went on for forty-five minutes, with Dubro and Macadam trying to discover how much Reynolds knew – whether he knew enough to try to obtain an injunction to keep *Connections* off the air – and Reynolds trying to discover the fate of his interview. Finally, Reynolds decided to lay his cards on the table. He told Dubro and Macadam that he had discovered who "Pat Cala" really was and why he had told Macadam his story. Cala, he said, was an undercover agent for the United States Treasury Department, and his allegations were part of an elaborate smear campaign against Reynolds instigated by aides to the late Howard Hughes and Intertel, an investigative firm they had hired. A year earlier, Reynolds had helped to obtain copies of several thousand Hughes documents seized by Mexican authorities on the billionaire's death. He had done so at the request of a constituent, John Meier, who was a former employee of Hughes' Summa Corporation and was being sued by the company in an action alleging financial misdeeds. Meier had said he needed the documents to defend himself in court. Ever since that time, Reynolds claimed, he had been harassed by Intertel agents who were "out to get" him for assisting Meier. "Cala" was obviously part of this plot, he said.

So far, Dubro and Macadam were more amused than disturbed by what Reynolds had told them. They were relieved to discover that Reynolds did not know the air date for their programs, or the identity of Cala, or even, it seemed, what the program was going to say about him.

Reynolds, apparently believing that he had convinced Dubro and Macadam of the unreliability of Cala's statements, then decided to tell them who had tipped him off. Dubro and Macadam were stunned by what he said.

"It came from Claude Wagner. Somebody, obviously, in your system is a friend of his and said, you know, 'They're out to get you, Claude. They're going to say that Reynolds was your campaign chairman [during the Progressive Conservative leadership convention which elected Joe Clark] and raised some funds in Little Italy and some of those guys might have been Mafia guys and you could have been leader of the country . . .' And he [Wagner] was concerned and that's why he made the suggestion, 'You'd better get yourself some legal advice before they slander you.'"

The information given to Wagner was so detailed and accurate that it could only have come from someone who had actually seen the item on Reynolds.

But with the air date only three days away, there were myriad minor production details to attend to – there was no time to try to track down the leak. And after the programs had been safely aired with no problems from prior injunctions, there seemed little point in checking further into the incident. The source of the leak was never discovered. It was the only serious breach of security during the two and a half years the project had been underway.

One other unwilling participant in *Connections* expressed an interest in knowing the contents of the programs before they went to air.

On the mornings of both air dates, press screenings were held so that reporters could write about that evening's show in the afternoon papers. (The more sensitive, injunction-prone items were carefully deleted for these sessions.) It was during the first press screening that Macadam was called out of the projection room for a telephone call. It was from Paul Volpe.

Volpe first asked Macadam, pointedly, "How's your health?"

Then he told Macadam he knew that he was going to be on the programs because he had seen the newspaper advertisements and heard the television promotions. What he wanted to know was whether or not his wife would also appear. "I don't want to see her on there," he told Macadam. "I will be very angry if she is on."

Macadam told him he couldn't tell anyone what was going to be on the programs, but Volpe was insistent. Finally, Macadam said:

"Look, Paul, I'm standing here completely surrounded by CBC lawyers and they won't allow me to confirm or deny anything. I know it's just ridiculous, but there's nothing I can do. They just won't let me open my mouth."

Macadam was standing alone in his office at the time, but Volpe seemed to accept his explanation. He hung up ill-humouredly, resigned to waiting until the show was on that evening to discover the answer to his question. (Mrs. Volpe was not seen in the program and was mentioned only briefly in the narration as being an executive of an exclusive Toronto woman's clothing store.)

At long, long last, it is 9:30 p.m., Sunday, June 12, 1977, and the television sets of several million Canadians are tuned to the CBC network, as announcer Warner Troyer appears on their screens to introduce *Connections I*.

"Good evening, I'm Warner Troyer. What you are about to see tonight is not a set of pretty pictures. It is the first of two programs on organized crime in Canada. Some of the images are brutal; some of the language is offensive . . . and many of the implications of what you will see may be disturbing. But these are all qualities of the world of organized crime as it exists here in Canada with its close ties to the United States and other areas of the world.

"This program, and the one tomorrow night, are the result of two and a half years of investigative television journalism by a team headed by producers William Macadam and Martyn Burke.

"In order to provide you with a look at just who are the leaders of the organized crime world in Canada . . . and how they gain their power and their fortunes, it was often necessary to employ unusual filming techniques. Hidden cameras, concealed microphones, and night lens equipment were frequently the only means of accomplishing the task. It was decided on several occasions to sacrifice technical quality simply in order to bring the faces of organized crime onto your home screen . . ."

And for the next ninety minutes, and for ninety minutes the

following night, a shocked nation watched as the *Connections* cameras systematically exposed a web of crime which stretched from coast to coast, and which few viewers had even dreamed existed or *could* exist in this country.*

Reaction came almost immediately. Monday morning's Toronto *Globe and Mail* carried a review by critic Blaik Kirby, calling the series "the biggest and most daring TV exposé ever undertaken into organized crime, either in Canada or abroad . . . One of the absolutely must-watch TV shows of this or any other season."

The *Toronto Star* and *Toronto Sun* both ran front-page stories on the program. The *Star* story began:

"It was, above all, a searing family portrait.

"For 90 minutes last night, the CBC zeroed in on the men it described as the nation's leading mobsters. Naming them by name. Showing them on the screen. Filming business fronts. Accusing them of far-reaching criminal activities.

"With a daring that most Canadian newspapers have so far avoided for fear of lawsuits, the CBC special . . . fired at its targets from coast to coast – and fired with deadly aim . . ."

Newspapers across the country carried similar reports, although few were quite so breathless. In Victoria, the *Times* asked British Columbia Attorney General Garde Gardom for his comments on the program, but he refused to make a statement, saying he would have a major announcement to make on the subject of organized crime in the near future. In Ontario, Attorney General Roy McMurtry said he would take a close look at organized crime in his province and was prepared to order a public inquiry if he found the police did not have crime under control. The following day McMurtry met with the heads of the Toronto police, Ontario Provincial Police and Ontario detachment of the RCMP to discuss their reaction to the programs. A news conference on the meeting was scheduled for a day later. Of course, the odds of his finding that police did not have crime "under control" were vanishingly small, but the fact that he called the meeting nonetheless gave some indication of the impact of the programs.

Unfortunately, the programs were broadcast during a period in which the TV rating services were not polling viewers, so there are no accurate figures available on numbers of viewers. It is clear,

---

* For a brief synopsis of all five programs contained in the first and second *Connections* series, see Appendix 2.

however, that the audience for the first program was very large, and that the audience for the second was very much larger: an informal poll done by the CBC indicated that the second-night audience may have been the biggest the network had ever had. In Toronto, certainly, the downtown streets were noticeably barren during the 9:30 to 11:00 period Monday, a phenomenon similar to that produced by the first televised space shots and live coverage of the aftermaths of the Kennedy assassinations. It was difficult to find anyone who had access to a television set who did not see at least the second program.

Press reaction following the airing of the second program continued to be outspokenly favourable and prominently played.

The Vancouver *Province*, in a lead editorial: ''. . . The CBC television programs this week documenting the extent of organized crime in this country, with names and precise information that show deep, concrete research indicate what can be done by a public broadcasting service when it has the will, focus and commitment to do it.

''Indeed the CBC revelations stand as a reproach to both the private broadcasting systems and the newspapers which have failed in their public duty as watchdogs of the public interest. The same information could have been obtained by them but they either couldn't or wouldn't look for it . . .''

The *Winnipeg Free Press* took a similar editorial stance:

''Knocking the CBC is a favourite pastime of Canadians. But the Corporation made up for a lot of past sins in the presentation of its twin-barrelled program on organized crime . . .''

The Winnipeg *Tribune*'s TV critic gasped: ''The CBC made history last night and Sunday with what undoubtedly was the most staggering, shocking and revelatory documentary ever made . . .''

In the Ottawa *Citizen*: ''Thanks to a powerful exercise in television journalism, the myth of a virgin Canada untouched by the ravages of organized crime has been blown to bits . . .''

The Vancouver *Sun*: ''The CBC has dramatically and commendably underscored the fact of organized crime in Canada with its tentacles deep into life in our major cities . . .''

By the morning of June 14, *Connections* had become one of the two or three top stories of the day for virtually every news outlet in the country – radio, television and newspapers. This would continue to be the case for the rest of the week.

CBC Radio's flagship newscast, *The World at Six*, for Tuesday,

June 14, covered the story exhaustively. A few excerpts from the script provide some of the flavour of the reaction, particularly in Ottawa, where the Commons opposition had jumped on the story with a vengeance:

Announcer: "For the second day in a row the CBC television report on organized crime was the hottest topic on Parliament Hill. There was a virtual uproar in the Commons as opposition MPs repeated their demands for a national inquiry. Nearly all of the question period was devoted to the issue, and there will be more of the same tomorrow. The program has resulted in comment from the British Columbia government as well. But first, a report from Brian Kelleher in Ottawa."

Kelleher: "There were shouts and jeers flying back and forth across the floor of the House today for nearly the whole hour of question period as the opposition accused the government of sitting on its hands while organized crime grew in Canada, and the government in turn accused the opposition of holding up legislation that would permit the police to carry out more investigations and prosecutions.

"The leader of the opposition, Joe Clark, says 'Let's have a national Royal Commission on organized crime.' A Royal Commission could subpoena witnesses, names and places could be brought out, but instead, he says, the government is refusing action, pretending that the responsibility for inquiries is in the hands of the provinces. Mr. Clark says that's nonsense."

Clark: "The Minister of Justice tries to hide behind the fact that some of the jurisdiction is provincial. Well, some of it is, but most of it is federal. What we're dealing with here is problems relating to violations of immigration laws, we're dealing with narcotics matters, we're dealing with questions that are clearly in the federal domain, and the federal government can't leave the Mafia to Prince Edward Island. It's going to have to take its responsibilities itself and act itself."

Kelleher: "Both the Tories and the NDP say that RCMP manpower isn't being distributed properly. Stu Leggatt of the NDP says he understands that the RCMP have 600 people looking into political subversion, and that they are being helped by another 500 people in the defence department, but he says that there are only six full-time RCMP members in Ottawa working on organized crime."

Leggatt: "It's our opposition day tomorrow, and that will be on the subject of a Royal Commission, so we're going to have a full-dress debate in the House tomorrow on that particular subject. The second thing we're going to do is continue to accumulate evidence of a lack of prosecution, a lack of effort in terms of those who have been named in this [CBC] inquiry who have been clearly involved in organized crime. It seems to me we've got to have a special department of the RCMP . . . that's got to be their sole jurisdiction and they've got to move – almost like Elliot Ness if you want to put it that way – against these organized criminals."

Kelleher: "But the Minister of Justice, Ron Basford, says that while provincial inquiries into organized crime might serve a purpose, the police aren't so much interested in inquiries as they are in action. He says his Bill C-51, already before Parliament, would broaden wiretapping powers for the police . . . Mr. Basford says that for years the police have been saying they need more power, that organized crime is growing, and the government didn't just discover organized crime two days ago on television; it had new laws ready to go."

Basford: "My position is clearly that we have legislation before the House which has been recommended by attorneys general and police across the country for the past three years, and that Parliament has been warned that they need these amendments, and my position is clearly that this should be dealt with as a priority item and these amendments passed."

Kelleher: "So that's where it stands: the government refusing a national inquiry, saying pass new laws instead, the opposition determined to get an inquiry. Tomorrow, the next round as the NDP touches off its debate . . ."

Duffy: "This is Mike Duffy in Ottawa . . . Not all Members of Parliament were happy with the programs. Last night's reference to the activities of Vancouver MP John Reynolds has prompted the Conservative party leader, Joe Clark, to call Mr. Reynolds to Ottawa."

Clark: "As soon as I got into the office this morning I telephoned John Reynolds in Vancouver. He's on a plane tonight – this afternoon – to Ottawa. I'll be meeting with him tomorrow morning. I want a full explanation from him of all of the activities with which he is alleged to be involved. I understand that Mr. Reynolds has been in touch with his lawyer . . . I really have no further comment at this stage on that matter. I am getting to the bottom of the situation in my party and I want the government of Canada to get to the bottom of the problem in this country by doing its duty and calling an inquiry."

Duffy: "The Solicitor-General, Francis Fox, says the RCMP are not investigating Mr. Reynolds. Mr. Fox says the force has no reason to do so."

Fox: "To the best of my knowledge, there is no inquiry going on in the RCMP concerning Mr. Reynolds . . . I think that there are a number of examples . . . the show focussed on a number of individuals and through insinuation tried to tie them up into the ramifications of organized crime. But we have no evidence of any kind that that is the case."

Duffy: "Another MP who was mentioned in passing in the program, Conservative member Claude Wagner, today announced that he is taking legal action against the CBC. Mr. Wagner said the references to him were amateurish sensationalism and an insult to a man who has spent seventeen years as a jurist and a politician fighting organized crime."

Wagner: "I feel that the CBC acted in a very disgusting manner. Don't you think so? Did you see the program?"

Duffy: "I must confess I didn't see it."

Wagner: "Oh, well I wouldn't encourage you to see it because you'd probably throw up."

Duffy: "What was wrong with it, sir?"

Wagner: "Ask your colleagues. Ask those of us who've seen it."

Duffy: "When will you be taking legal action?"

Wagner: "Whenever I'm ready. Soon. As soon as possible. May God have mercy on their souls, those guys at the CBC."

Duffy: "Mr. Wagner says he has no intention of allowing the CBC to do to him what the Mafia was not able to do in seventeen years."

Other newscasts reported that Charles Caccia, Liberal MP for Toronto Davenport, had made public all his correspondence relatting to attemps to obtain a parole for Domenic Racco. Caccia told reporters he'd had no idea the Racco family was alleged to be part of organized crime. He said he stopped trying to get the parole when Racco was charged with arranging, from his jail cell, to have someone crippled.

Meanwhile, the *Connections* office was being inundated by requests from newspapers and radio stations for interviews with

Macadam, Dubro and Burke. Everyone wanted to know how the shows were made, and who made them. The three were interviewed for CBC's major TV newcast, *The National*. Burke told the story about the United States marshals and the cleaning woman who walked in during the Teresa interview; Macadam talked about tracking down the Vancouver drug stories; and Dubro was asked to explain the office filing system, which he did to the reporter's satisfaction on the third take.

"Someone told me later that I looked like I was selling tooth-paste," Dubro says.

The flood of lawsuits that everyone had been anticipating failed to develop, but there was a trickle. Wagner sued. And the next day John Reynolds rose in the Commons to protest his innocence and announce that he, too, would sue. And he did.

Ontario Conservative MP Allan Lawrence, who, as Ontario Attorney General, had assured the province that the Mafia did not exist in Toronto, threatened to sue *Connections* for having used an excerpt from the speech in which he did so. He did not sue.

Half a dozen other figures mentioned in the programs also sued on behalf of themselves or their businesses: several others announced that they would sue, but did not.

At the time of writing, none of the lawsuits had come to court.

The programs touched off a flurry of interest in Quebec-style crime probes, from newspapers and politicians.

British Columbia Attorney General Gardom said he wanted all the provinces to unite in a fight against organized crime. But, he assured voters, if the other provinces would not agree to co-operate in his proposed all-out battle, "that does not mean under any circumstances that British Columbia will not go it alone." The story ran under the headline: "Gardom Urges National Crime Purge." And that was the last that was heard of it.

Ontario Attorney General McMurtry and senior officers of the three major Ontario police forces held a news conference to say that a crime probe would be of no use in combatting organized crime, and could hinder work they were now doing in the field.

But it was Winnipeg that produced the most entertaining crime probe story of all. On June 15, this story appeared in the *Winnipeg Free Press*, boxed within a longer item quoting the Winnipeg police chief as saying that organized crime has no interest in the city because of the limited profits to be made there. (He was apparently unaware that organized crime traditionally thrives among the poor.)

"A report on organized crime prepared in the mid-1960's by Winnipeg lawyer Maurice Arpin only now is being studied.

"Commissioned by former Conservative premier Duff Roblin, the report went to the Attorney General at the time, Stuart Mac-Lean, but no one seems to know what happened to it after that.

"MacLean couldn't be reached and Roblin had trouble even recalling the report when asked about it Tuesday.

"It was Roblin who called Arpin to his office more than a decade ago to request he prepare the report, and later sent the Winnipeg lawyer to an Ottawa conference of attorneys general and the solicitor general which dealt with the subject of organized crime. But Roblin had to phone Arpin to make sure there had been such a report.

"Attorney General Howard Pawley of Manitoba says he now is studying the report – which he just received. He will decide whether it should be made public after he's read it.

"Arpin wouldn't say what the report contains because it's privileged information. It was work for a client and prepared by counsel, he said.

"Arpin has only one complaint about the document. He said he's never been paid for preparing it."

Meanwhile, the then Manitoba premier Ed Schreyer called on the federal government to hold a national inquiry and promised his province's co-operation.

Several newspapers reported the suspicions of a London, Ontario radio announcer that an actor's voice had been used in an interview with a hooded Toronto mobster. Macadam and Burke refused to confirm or deny the report, saying only that it had been an authentic mobster under the hood and that what was heard was what had been said during the interview.

The voice, they said, had been "altered" to protect the life of the informer. In fact, the voice *was* replaced by that of an actor, after attempts at electronic modification of the mobster's own voice had ended in unintelligibility.

Toronto Sun columnist and author Joan Sutton wrote in her paper that she had known Mrs. Paul Volpe over the years to be a hard-working, industrious businesswoman, and complained that it was unfair of *Connections* to have mentioned her and her place of work simply because she was married to a man the program identified as a Mafia leader.

A St. Catharines, Ontario security company president announced that his company's telephones had been "ringing off the hook" since *Connections* had been aired, with customers asking about de-bugging services. The shows, he said, "underlined the belief that there's a great deal of bugging going on," and pointed out that his company's job, "is to help you find the buggers. We're the de-buggers."

A more serious story appeared a few days later in the *Financial Post*. It stated that since the airing of *Connections*, businessmen across the country had become markedly more concerned about their business contacts. It quoted a lawyer with a large Toronto firm as stating:

"The number of calls from businessmen attempting to check the credentials of clients and suppliers has been increasing daily since the program was aired. Our clients are uptight, not only about those people mentioned in the programs, but other business connections as well."

An executive with a large department store chain said:

"In the past, there has been little reason to check out thoroughly competent suppliers of goods and services. Now we're faced with a situation where one suddenly realizes it could have been your firm's name on the screen. Now the onus is on us to make sure our suppliers and contacts are clean."

"The CBC should be awarded a plaque," said a pulp and paper company officer. "It's going to cost money, but we want to know with whom we are dealing. Two weeks ago, I was indifferent and so were a lot of other businessmen."

The story went on to detail a sample of the business world's reaction to the programs:

• A Montreal banker said his superiors had handed down orders to keep closer tabs on some of the bank's suspected disreputable clients. "We're in a difficult position," he told the *Post*. "We are legally forced to take deposits and provide normal banking services. But some customers are going to have a more difficult time negotiating loans."

• A Toronto stockbroker said his firm was taking a closer look at a few clients with dubious reputations. "These are not people mentioned in the CBC program," he said. "Every salesman in our firm has been told to reconsider whether he really knows his customer."

• A major company in the fast-food business was investigating its suppliers of meat, cheese, pastry and other products. "We can't be caught out on this one,'' an executive was quoted as explaining. ''Our customers wouldn't understand if we became involved in such a mess, no matter if we didn't know who we were dealing with.''

• A Toronto insurance executive had a second look at four contracts with various corporations and he was investigating further. One contract, he said, wouldn't be renewed. ''A program like the CBC production really hits home,'' he said. ''I'm concerned about the miniscule percentage of our business that may be in the bad apple category.''

• A Maritimes club owner said he was checking the credentials of the firm that provided entertainment for his operation. ''I really don't know much about them, but I'm interested enough to spend a few dollars to find out.''

• For construction company executives, dealings with some unions and subcontractors had always created problems. Now, the *Post* reported, many industry leaders were taking a harder look at the subtrades, suppliers and union representatives.

• Real estate and development companies, as well as mortgage lenders, also reported they were tightening checks on some customers since the program had been aired.

''Don't even apply for funds if your reputation is the least bit sullied,'' said one mortgage lender. ''We don't want the aggravation.''

Reaction to the programs from police forces across the country was universally favourable, with the partial exception of the RCMP. Word filtered back to Dubro and Macadam through their sources that some members of the force had felt betrayed by the Vancouver sections, which suggested corruption in the drug enforcement arm of the force. Others were arguing strongly that it was high time the situation was exposed and cleaned up.

That fall, the programs were screened before a meeting of the Association of Canadian Chiefs of Police. At the subsequent annual convention of the Canadian Police Association, Solicitor General Francis Fox praised the programs for ''rais(ing) the national consciousness that Canada faced a problem that was national in scope.'' The message came through to those with other than policing responsibilities that we had to deal with a class and type of crime affecting, directly or indirectly, every person in every area of Canada. Finally, a Medicine Hat, Alberta citizen who previously felt himself remote and unaffected by the ravages of organized

▲ Martyn Burke in Uganda interviewing Idi Amin.

▼ Jim Dubro, associate producer of Connections.

Bill Macadam, co-producer of Connections.

Diagram used on Connections film to show the links between underworld figures in Canada. ▼

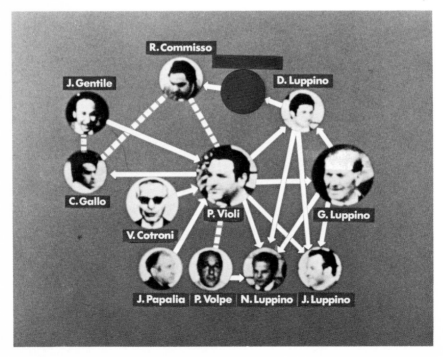

This woman's purse contains
a portable camera specially designed for
indoors surveillance filming. Note camera lens three buttons down.

Inside shot of the Connections van where Francis Granger and other cameramen
spent long hours on surveillance filming.

▼

Former Mobster Chuck Carlo being interviewed and filmed in the middle of a lake in Ontario.

Paul Volpe, the leader of one of Toronto's Mafia families filmed at his home without his knowledge. ▼

▲ Right, Joe Romano and left, Paddy Calabrese, undercover agent working for Connections, discussing the sale of stolen bonds beside the Bayshore Inn pool.

▼ Calabrese leaving Bayshore Inn with Romano who carries the supposedly stolen bond in a folder.

Co-producers Bill Macadam and Martyn Burke interviewing Vic Cotroni who is unaware that he is being filmed.

Vic Cotroni, Godfather of the Montreal Mafia.

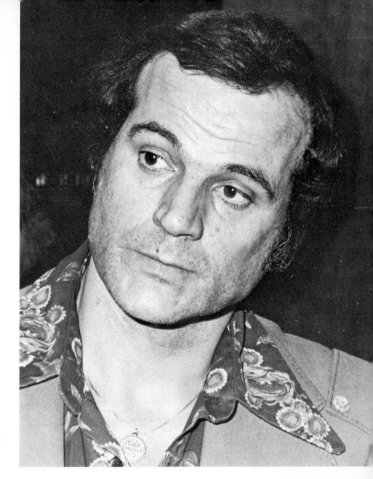

Claude Dubois,
leader of the Dubois
Brothers gang in
Montreal.

Victims of Mafia vendettas in Italy during the filming of Connections.

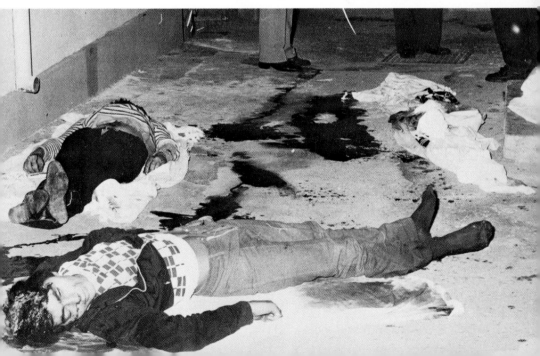

▲ Editing Connections – on screen, Paolo Violi who was later murdered in Montreal.

▼ Screening Connections. Principals involved (l. to r.) co-producer Martyn Burke, associate producer Jim Dubro, co-producer Bill Macadam, executive producer Dick Neilsen, and editor Steve Weslak.

crime in Toronto, Montreal and Vancouver, wrote:

"As a member of this society I demand that . . . [the] government initiate action immediately to destroy this element of gangsters, murderers, and drug peddlers who appear to have so easily infiltrated our way of life. Surely we cannot tolerate this any longer after the evidence that has been presented to us. If it is allowed to continue, it is obvious to me that these animals [will] have succeeded in gaining control and power in our country. Will you please make every effort to have something done for those of us who still have values, [who want to] be able to walk the streets without fear and [who want to have] a future for our children."

In the weeks following the programs' airing, Dubro and Macadam learned that pirated videotape copies of the shows were being used as training films by several United States law enforcement agencies, including: the FBI, the Federal Drug Enforcement Agency, the Securities Exchange Commission, the Federal Prosecutor's Office in New York, the California Organized Crime Strike Force, the Dade County (Miami) Police Force, the Buffalo Organized Crime Strike Force, the Federal Department of Customs and Immigration, and the Federal Post Office.

The programs eventually won the CBC's own Anik, *Prix Wilderness* Award (in May, 1978) for the best documentary of the year; the ACTRA (Association of Canadian Television and Radio Artists) Award for best writing for a documentary (ACTRA does not have a "best documentary" award), and the Press Club of Canada's Michener Award (honorable mention) for meritorious public service in journalism.

The shows were also entered in the International Emmy Awards competition and the Canadian Film Awards contest in several categories. But they were quietly withdrawn by the CBC, apparently because the Corporation feared that public screenings of the films before each award presentation would aggravate any problems in fighting the lawsuits arising out of the programs. (There are no complete public screenings prior to Anik, ACTRA and Michener award ceremonies.)

An angry Telex was fired off to CBC president Al Johnson, signed by Burke, Macadam and Nielsen. It read:

"We strongly object to *Connections Parts I* and *II* being withdrawn without consultation from the Canadian Film Awards and the International Emmy Awards. We cannot believe this is to be CBC policy. The principle here is paramount. If one accepts that because there is a lawsuit against a program – whatever its (the lawsuit's) merits – the program cannot be entered for an award, it will automatically eliminate the best and most controversial programming of departments such as current affairs and drama. We request that you intervene with the Canadian Film Awards Judging Committee and ask that they reconsider the program for entry even though the normal deadline has passed. This should be done on behalf of all those in the industry who have asked us to make certain that these programs are considered.''

It seemed a sound enough argument, but there was no response.

Part II

Connections: The Second Series
A further investigation into organized crime in Canada

Producers: William Macadam, Martyn Burke
Associate Producer: James Dubro
Senior Researcher: Michel Auger
Researchers: Jamie Boyd
              Jane Porter
              Craig Taylor
              Andrea Kolchinsky
              Felix Sulvaran
              One name withheld by request
Consultants: Patrick Calabrese
              Ralph Salerno
Camera: Francis Granger
         Len Gilday
         Martin Duckworth
Sound Score: Bruce Nyznik
Sound Recording: Aerlyn Weissman
              John D. Crawford
              Glenn Hodgins
Senior Film Editor: Steve Weslak
Editor: Oliver Manton
Assistant Editor: Daniel Dutka
Unit Manager: Jim Innes
Facilities Co-ordinators: Casey Kollantay
              Andrew Bell
Production Secretaries: Joan Miller
              Lynn Ackerman
              Mary Silvano
Sound Re-recording: Soundmix
Service Producer: Alf Norris
Narration: Name withheld by request
Executive Producer: Richard Nielsen

The Second Attack

12

" 'My club' is one of the most potent phrases in the English language."

Martyn Burke

It is mid-March, 1979. Spring is in the air. Macadam, Burke, Nyznik the soundman and Steven Weslak and the other editors are holed up like rats over at Soundmix, trying to get the second series finished in time for the March 26, 27 and 28 air dates. They have been working round the clock for nearly two weeks in darkened editing and screening rooms, looking after last-minute edits required by the CBC brass and lawyers, mixing the sound tracks, laying in credits, billboards, supers, fades, dissolves and other optical effects. They will make their deadline, but only just.

I have blown mine – it is now impossible for me to finish this book by March 31. The best I can hope for is April 15. This makes my publisher's editor very nervous, and she does not hesitate to remind me of the consequences of too many delays. She has her own production deadlines to meet, and if she misses them, the book could be held up for months. Deadlines are ugly things.

For Dubro, however, this post-production phase of the operation is a relatively easy period. He is constantly on call for checking script changes for accuracy, and lately has been supplying a lot of information to the CBC's public relations department for the official announcement of the second series. But he still has time to follow the stock market closely and chat with his broker a couple of times a day. Dubro has prospered in a modest way since the first *Connections* series – his salary has trebled, he has had job offers from newspapers and American TV networks, and he has been making a few hundred here and a few hundred there on the market. His biggest headache at the moment is a dispute between Burke and

Macadam over program credits for each of the three shows that make up the second series. The question of the moment is whether the whole embarrassing mess should be dumped in the lap of Dick Nielsen for an executive producer's ruling.

In the nearly two years since the airing of *Connections I* and *II*, Macadam's production company – Norfolk – has grown substantially and now seems poised for an expansion that would make it one of the country's biggest private production houses. It has moved out of Macadam's living room and kitchen to plush new headquarters at a nifty University Avenue address. Macadam is curently negotiating with a large corporation to provide ten hours of prime time network programming – a multi-million dollar prospect. And, as always, there are many other irons in the fire.

Burke's *Power Play*, completed the previous summer, is having a modest success in Europe, and has won him a ''best screenplay'' citation at the Canadian Film Awards. His publisher continues to breathe hotly down his neck for the last few chapters of his Vietnam novel, and he tries to do a few pages a day. He has completed a new screenplay about a TV reporter investigating organized crime (why not?) and sent it off to make the rounds of potential producers. And he has half a dozen other projects in various stages of pre-production. Few who know him doubt that he is on his way to becoming a name to be reckoned with in international cinema.

The reception given by critics and the public to *Connections: The Second Series* will have an important impact on the careers of both Burke and Macadam. Just one more week to wait, and the suspense will be over.

This time, though, the anxiety over possible retaliation from criminals will linger. Both Macadam and Burke are genuinely concerned that some of the criminals involved in this series might just be crazy enough to try something. Until now, the two producers have had the security of secrecy; that will vanish with the corporation's announcement of the series to the press. The motorcycle gangs and the new Toronto Mafia families are especially worrying: both have reputations for mindless violence. Neither will like the way they are dealt with in the second series. Possibly there is another element to their anxiety, too: expose the mob on TV once and get away with it – fine. But do it twice and maybe you're beginning to push your luck. Maybe the mob will begin to see you as a continuing threat . . . something more than one-shot wonders, best ignored. Who knows what goes on in those alien minds?

It seems inevitable in retrospect that a second series would be done, given the reception afforded *Connections I* and *II*. But twenty-one months earlier, it was by no means a foregone conclusion. Burke and Macadam had each sworn a hundred oaths that neither would ever work with the other, and Dubro was fed up with both of them. Burke left Toronto almost immediately after the first two shows were aired, to continue work on *Power Play*, for which fresh financing had been arranged. Macadam immersed himself in Norfolk business, incensed over the losses the company had taken in making *Connections* – losses that Norfolk's accountant had calculated to be in the neighbourhood of $80,000. Dubro agreed to take a job with a Toronto newspaper, as half of a two-man investigative task force.

In the end, it was mainly money that brought it all back together. The CBC's new head of current affairs, Robin Taylor, offered Macadam and Norfolk a contract big enough to make up for some of the losses incurred in the first series: a contract as big as the Ritz. Macadam was thus able to offer Dubro considerably more money than he would get at the newspaper. And for Burke, it was to be a nice, tight eight months of work that would tide him over between feature film projects. Nielsen would once again be executive producer.

Then, too, there was all that research compiled for the first series, all those stories there hadn't been time to go into, all those leads that hadn't been tracked down . . . it seemed a shame to let it all go to waste.

The budget for the new series was set at half a million dollars. As with the first budget, when all the hidden costs were taken into account, the actual cost was far above that – a cool three-quarters of a million, more than the CBC had ever before spent on a current affairs special. The production was assigned a suite of offices on the fourth floor of the Film House building. Macadam's quarters alone were bigger by far than some of the offices that had housed the entire staff of the first series. There was enough money to woo crack reporter Michel Auger away from his job covering organized crime for *La Presse* to work full time for *Connections* as Montreal researcher. There was even money for a top-secret "special project" which Macadam had planned, and which would be perhaps the most ambitious single investigation ever undertaken for television. That money was hidden in the $100,000 travel budget for the series.

The cover name for the new series was "Housing Crisis." Research was to begin late in September, 1977 and carry on through to April, 1978. By that time Burke would be finished with *Power Play*, and he could begin filming for *Connections*. The tentative air date was fall, 1978. There was to be a one, two-hour-long program.

Research got underway on schedule in September with several weeks of travel for both Dubro and Macadam. Old contacts were renewed in Washington, New York, Miami, Los Angeles, Buffalo, Detroit and most major Canadian cities. The Commissioner of the RCMP was once again asked for the force's official co-operation: he replied that his senior officers were split on whether they should co-operate in the light of the accusations of RCMP corruption in the first series, but he nonetheless enclosed in his letter a list of officers in cities across the country who could be approached for guidance. The extent of their co-operation was left to individual officers.

In Buffalo, Dubro was told by a reporter for the *Evening News* about a new conscript in the Justice Department's Witness Protection Program, and he began the long process of arranging for an interview. The man was Chuck Carlo, an unusually intelligent soldier in the Buffalo mob who had become so sickened with his life that he had switched over to the government side.

In Toronto, a police source put Dubro in touch with an associate of the mob who might be willing to provide information. Dubro assigned him the code name "Lou" and arranged a restaurant meeting.

Macadam meanwhile was negotiating with a firm of industrial security consultants who offered training programs in surveillance techniques, taught by ex-Canadian Armed Forces intelligence specialists. This would be stage one in the "special project."

Burke took time off from editing *Power Play* in London for several research trips to Rome, where he was to lay the groundwork for filming Italian connections of Canadian Mafia families. He was delighted to discover that a United States Drug Enforcement Administration agent who had been extremely helpful in the first series had been transferred to Rome from Washington, and was willing to help out once again. A tip from the agent led Burke to Italian police files on the kidnapping and ransom of young John Paul Getty III, where he turned up a link between the kidnappers and Montreal's Paolo Violi. He also learned that only about $40,000 of the $3 million ransom had ever been recovered, and that fact was later to provide the financial background for an elaborate plan to hoodwink the Toronto mob into confirming its involvement in Atlantic City real estate.

But there was little of the excitement of discovery that had marked the first series' research. The breakthroughs had all been made; the research techniques had been learned, the sources had been located and contacts solidified. Investigating the mob had become a matter of routine. The filing system continued to grow apace, and Dubro and Macadam were confident that it would provide answers to virtually any question asked of it.

Their confidence was not entirely justified. Neither had made sufficient allowance for what may be called the law of diminishing returns in research. Simply stated, there is a point in the continuing research into almost any subject when it takes more and more effort to unearth less and less information. It is like exploring for oil: the big, accessible fields are located and exploited with relative ease, but as they are used up, the exploration and development effort must go farther and farther afield, into the remote and hostile regions of the world. Theoretically, a point can be reached when the energy expended in locating, developing and arranging transportation for a remote field exceeds the value of the recoverable energy it contains.

Connections, because of the thorough research for the first series, was now exploring remote and almost inaccessible realms of investigative journalism, areas of investigation where huge effort would be required to develop significant new information. The increased budget for the program, the huge travel allowances, the hiring of Michel Auger, the elaborate training planned for the "special project" . . . none of these was enough to permit the initial objectives of the second series to be met.

It was Burke who first raised the alarm. He had returned to Toronto in March, 1978 to begin working full time on *Connections*, and when he saw the program outline that Macadam and Dubro had prepared after their initial six months research, he was seriously concerned.

The outline proposed dealing with twenty separate organized crime topics: the movie industry, banking, unions, lawyers, cheese companies, legitimate businesses used as mob fronts, pornography, arson, cocaine, dope smuggling in the Maritimes, the structure of the Vancouver mob, a profile of a mob moll, corrupt politicians, trucking companies, Canadian criminals operating in Miami, the Italian roots of the Canadian mob families, organized robberies, life in the mob from the point of view of some of its members and former members, motorcycle gangs, and a day in the life of a selected mob figure.

Seen in retrospect, the list represents a hopelessly ambitious undertaking, given the limited time and resources at *Connections'* disposal. And in fact no-one really expected that *all* twenty topics would be covered. But in the end only the last five items were dealt with in the three and a half hours of the second series.

"I guess the success we'd had with the first series made us overconfident," explains Dubro. "We were convinced we could do just about anything." They had, in other words, fallen into the trap of believing their own reviews.

It was a trap that Burke's longer experience had trained him to avoid.

"It was a scattershot approach," Burke says. "When I got back we had a meeting with Nielsen. We went through everything. That was when our troubles really began, because I started yelling at Macadam, 'Show me the research material. Show me the back-up for the stuff.' The classic case was pornography . . . I went crazy when we were talking about pornography. All Macadam would say was 'It's all in the files. Look in the files.' And I would say 'No, I want to know what you've got right now.' But there were never any specifics. It really became very fractious. The fact is, though, that that was a connection that really fell flat . . . I mean, it bit the dust totally. All this stuff like the business connection and the union connection, they just utterly crumbled in our hands after we looked at them."

Burke has his own idea of what went wrong with the research, which, in the end, may say more about his relationship with Macadam than it does about the problem:

"We all have our strengths and weaknesses . . . I have a good case of street smarts, I think. But I cannot go into the clubs that Bill can go into. He has access to that world. 'My club' is one of the most potent phrases in the English language. On the first show, what we did was mainly an overview of organized crime . . . it was mainly information that was in some way or another initially gleaned from little leaks that we got at the old boy level. In this recent *Connections*, the outline and the intent were more street-oriented, more activity-oriented, and it was a place where the old boy way of operating didn't work as well."

Be that as it may, both Dubro and Macadam admit that they tried to do too much, thereby dissipating their resources.

"For instance," Dubro says, "we had this list of about fifteen politicians whom we knew for sure had mob connections – one of them we think is actually a member. But every time it came up at a meeting we'd say, 'We've got that information pretty well nailed down already . . . we should concentrate on other things.' Of course when it came right down to it, we didn't have enough. We had maybe ninety per cent of what we needed. And finally we reached a point where there wasn't enough time to go out and get the remaining ten per cent that we had to have to put something on the air. The same was true of unions and pornography and the movie business and several of the others. There's an enormous amount of research that we didn't use."

There came a time, in June of 1978, when it became clear to everyone concerned with the project that the research effort was not going to meet its objectives; that they would have to concentrate exclusively on their strong suits and let the others go.

The decision was a happy one from the point of view of the public's understanding of the mob. For it meant that rather than repeating the first series' fact-oriented approach in which viewers were told who, what, when and where, the second series would concentrate on the more meaningful of the traditional journalistic questions – why and how. In other words, the second series would be more concerned with the process than with its results. The techniques that would be used – the confrontation interviews with mobsters, the scams in which mob figures were lured into demonstrating how they do business, the in-depth interviews with former and current Mafia members and mob associates – required relatively little research and were more manageable in terms of the hidden-camera filming involved. But they held the potential for teaching the public a great deal about the mob, for once the process is understood, the results can be predicted and thus should come as no surprise. A public that knows, for instance, the facts of organized crime's involvement in legalized gambling in Las Vegas and the Bahamas might be persuaded that the mob can be kept out of legalized gambling in another location, like Atlantic City. But a public that understands how and why the mob conducts its business – a public that understands the *process* – will know that the mob will find a way, regardless of "safeguards."

But I am getting ahead of the story here, for the decision to shift gears was not taken until after Macadam's "special project" had flown, and crashed, in a large Canadian city that must remain unnamed. It was an audacious attempt to push back the limits imposed on investigative journalism by the technology of television, but it ended instead in defining those limits.

The Special Project

13

"Now I am cat 2 . . . I have been cat 1 and cat 4 already. I am beginning to have identity problems."

From Jim Dubro's 'special project' diary.

On a sunny afternoon late in April of 1978, eight city police prowl cars swarmed into the parking lot of a robbery-prone suburban shopping plaza and surrounded two suspicious vehicles. One – apparently empty – was a light blue van with smoked glass windows. The other was a rental car, whose two occupants had been observed chatting with the driver of the van as he lounged against their front fender. Inside the car, the police noted a pair of super-8 film cameras, walkie-talkies, recording equipment, binoculars and a sophisticated VHF communications set. The truck was locked, but had the police peered closely into the smoked glass, they would have seen a wood panel dividing the cab from the rear of the truck, heavy blackout curtains, black vinyl covering all the interior surfaces, a sixteen-millimeter camera mounted on a heavy tripod, a bean bag chair, a walkie-talkie, a portable toilet . . . and a nervous cameraman. It looked for all the world like a mobile S&M parlour.

Dubro, Nyznik and Craig Taylor, a freelancer working under contract to *Connections* for the special project, were questioned closely by the police, who apparently suspected them of casing the plaza bank in preparation for a stick-up. But their cover story had been carefully prepared: they worked, they said, for an out-of-town film-production company, and they had the credentials to prove it. They explained that they were in the city shooting a commercial for television. They would not tell the police the truth – that they were working on the second series of *Connections* – because they had

129

been warned that the local mob had informants inside the police department.

Connections' surveillance vehicles had been investigated by police so many times in the past several days that it was beginning to seem like an orchestrated campaign of harassment. It was a pain in the neck, because each time a vehicle was "burned" by the police or spotted by one of the criminals under surveillance, it had to be returned to the rental agency and exchanged for a fresh one. But that was just one of a host of unforeseen problems encountered during the ill-starred special project.

The project had begun with a tip given Macadam months earlier by a high-ranking law-enforcement source. The contact had told him that one of the city's respected public figures – a man who had for more than a decade held one of the loftiest positions of public trust to which a citizen can aspire – had knowingly or unknowingly for years maintained friendly relations with two disreputable characters: one, a notorious associate of the local Mafia and the other a wealthy businessman involved in loansharking.

"If you had the ability to follow them around for a few days," the source assured Macadam, "you'd be sure to catch them all together. They meet all the time."

It seemed an ideal opportunity to illustrate the ways in which organized criminals use social contacts to gain respectability and Macadam decided that *Connections* would develop the necessary surveillance capability. They would re-create on film a day in the life of a mobster, tracking his every movement with stop-watch precision, recording his meetings with respected members of society. It would far surpass anything that had been achieved in the first series.

In January, 1978, Macadam negotiated a $10,000 contract with a firm of private security consultants to provide five days' training for a *Connections* crew in the finer points of tailing and surveillance, and to provide a consultant who would work as full-time co-ordinator of the operation. The scheme was cloaked in secrecy from the beginning – almost obsessively so – and it would become a kind of fun-house looking-glass image of the kinds of operations undertaken routinely by the world's counter-espionage agencies.

It was flawed from the start. Such operations need a rigid chain of command and strict obedience to orders from above if they are to succeed, but no-one on the *Connections* team was likely to conform successfully to military discipline – least of all Macadam himself.

Moreover, the team had access to only a few of the techniques employed by professional investigators. It could follow its subjects and film them surreptitiously – it could even interview them using body-pack tape recorders, but it could not use wiretaps, audio surveillance, mail intercepts or most of the other tools that are the backbone of professional investigations undertaken by government agents.

Connections went into the project with one hand tied behind its back. It was one thing to park a surveillance truck outside a banquet hall or real estate office or some other known mob hang-out for a few days and grab footage of criminals entering or leaving. It was quite another thing to select three targets, follow their movements over a period of several days and capture their meetings on film. All of that, however, is obvious only in hindsight.

The training program organized by the security consultants commenced April 17, shortly after Burke had returned from Europe. For the stocky, crew-cut ex-Army intelligence officer who conducted the program, it was to be an abrupt and uncomfortable introduction into the self-centred, undisciplined world of current affairs television and to the colourful characters who populate it.

The team consisted of Macadam, Burke, Dubro, Nyznik, Taylor, secretary Jane Porter, researcher Auger and cameraman Granger. They were as motley a crew as has ever plagued a serious-minded field commander, whom most insisted on calling "Uncle Don."

Uncle Don was uneasy about the compromises he had had to make in setting up the program. He had made an initial surveillance trip to the city to check the locations of houses and hangouts of the three subjects and generally get a feel for the lay of the land, and he was convinced that at least fifteen people would be needed to do the job. As they would all be amateurs, he had calculated that a minimum training period of five to six weeks would be necessary, before the actual operation could begin.

But Macadam had in mind a crew of only five or six, and anyway the $30,000 cost of such a lengthy training program was out of the question. They compromised on a crew of nine, including Uncle Don himself, and five days of training in Toronto followed by ten days of actual operations in the target city. At that, it seemed an extravagantly expensive proposition, especially since there could be no guarantee that it would succeed. Burke was particularly dubious, Dubro only slightly less so.

Dubro recalls Uncle Don's first day at the secret *Connections* office: "He thought we were extremely unprofessional. I mean, he walked in here for the first time, looked at the [suspended] ceilings, the metal desks and so on and he said, 'This is the most insecure office I've ever seen.' He said there were fifteen or twenty places where you could easily plant a bug. He looked at the sofa in Bill's office, for instance, and he said, 'My God, that tubular metal frame is the worst possible thing . . . those hollow tubes really conduct sound.' It became quite a big thing, he really thought we should de-bug the place . . . have it swept. He was in a terrible state . . . the locks on the doors, the doors themselves, everything upset him.

"We all thought it was very strange indeed. He said, 'Now I want the windows closed and the blinds shut all the time, lights out when they have to be opened, no papers on the desks because they can snap photos from the building across the street; get rid of all the stuff with hollow tubing . . . we need new ceilings . . . and you'll have to get rid of these phones.

"I just had to laugh, you know . . . there was no way we could do all of that stuff," says Dubro. "In fact, we didn't do any of it."

Training began with two days of boardroom lectures in which Uncle Don, with the help of flipchart and blackboard, described the techniques of concealing a walkie-talkie or super-8 movie camera, of sitting in a parked suveillance car without becoming conspicuous, of following a car without being noticed, of the use of correct radio procedures and codes . . . much of which *Connections* crew members had picked up on their own through trial and error in working on the previous series.

"He told us," Dubro recalls, "that the key was to be flexible . . . to be ready to change your plan when it became necessary. He said you have to have a lot of patience and physical stamina.

"When you're on surveillance, you park the car facing the quarry, and have a toothpick ready to jam the door switch for the courtesy lights. If it's dark you use a penlight under the dash for maps or notes, and you don't smoke unless you do it under a blanket. Make notes on plain white paper with a thick felt-tipped pen so that they can be read in any light. You keep the windows open to keep them from fogging up, and you always watch for counter-surveillance. Always use code on the radio. If you're going to follow a car, it helps if you can put a piece of scotch tape over one of its tail lights – the tape sparkles and you can spot it a block and a half away.

"If you have to go into a restaurant, get your bill right away, because you never know when the guy you're following is going to leave, and you don't want to attract attention to yourself by rushing up to pay. For the same reason you should always use cash. And you should keep a pocketful of dimes for phone calls.

"It was just like being back in school . . . he was up there writing on the blackboard, and we were all sitting up taking notes in our notebooks."

Uncle Don also showed them a large-scale map of the target city and pointed out the locations they would be most concerned with: the homes and hang-outs of the three subjects and rendezvous points for the surveillance crews.

He described the organization of the operation itself: there would be a base station equipped with maps and radio equipment, four surveillance cars and two camera vans. Each car would be equipped with a VHF radio set and two lower-powered walkie-talkies that could be used away from the car if necessary. Each vehicle would also have a city map, a clip board, a penlight, a watch, a set of binoculars, writing materials and a list of code words. The cars would be manned by teams of two.

The function of the base station, he said, would be to oversee the entire operation, give directions and keep records. He warned everyone to keep radio messages as brief as possible.

It was when the question of code names came up that Burke finally flipped out completely and began to rant about the silliness of it all. Uncle Don had prepared elaborate code lists for radio communications, which were to be destroyed at the end of each day and replaced by a new code. Surely, Burke erupted, this was overkill. Surely, if a code was necessary at all, it would evolve naturally during the operation. Uncle Don was not accustomed to such insubordination. His face flushed as he insisted on the importance of the code. The argument continued for several hours; Dubro's weary suggestion that they use pig Latin was ill-received. Finally, a compromise was reached in which a few key words would be encoded and that code would be used throughout the operation.

The respected citizen would be referred to as "Lightning," the wealthy businessman woud be "Thunder" and the Mafia-associate would be "Rain." A surveillance sweep would be a "weather report." Filming was "anchor"; to move out quickly, to "float"; danger, "lamplight"; observing, "sandbar"; moving surveillance, "sailing." The surveillance vehicles were to be referred to as "cat 1", "cat 2", "cat 3" and so on. Other vehicles were "skates." Rendezvous points were numbered and referred to as "boxes." Someone doing counter-surveillance would be a "supervisor"; if it was the police, it was an "official supervisor." All numbers would be preceded by the word "water" and inflated by one, so that the number 3 would become "water 4."

"You can imagine what the *original* code was like," Burke says sourly.

By the end of the formal lectures, Burke had decided to wash his hands of the special project. He used, as his excuse, the fact that he was moving to a new house. He would have to remain in Toronto to supervise the movers, he said. After the disruptive scene with Uncle Don, Macadam was not sorry to see him out, but in retrospect he feels that Burke's absence crippled the operation. There is no doubt that the episode seriously undermined the morale of the rest of the crew and increased the tensions that developed naturally once the operation got underway. It certainly did nothing to improve the already dodgy relations between the co-producers. (To replace Burke, Macadam immediately hired a freelancer who, still fearful of mob reprisals, has asked that his real name not be used here: I'll call him Dave Atkinson.)

The three days of Toronto field training which followed consisted mainly in attempting to tail a chase car driven by two of Uncle Don's colleagues. The base station was set up in the kitchen of Macadam's house – a room which was already doing double duty as an office for Norfolk's long-suffering secretary and bookkeeper, Joyce McEwen.

The trick was to get close enough to the chase car to film its occupants – without being noticed. If the occupants did notice, they were to smile into the camera as proof that the tail had been burned. Each few miles the tail car would be pulled off and another would slip into position. Uncle Don would plot the operation carefully on his Toronto street map, assigning positions to cars and setting up opportunities to grab footage with the super-8 cameras.

When the time came to fly to the target city, security was maintained at Uncle Don's suggestion by splitting the crew among several different flights. Once there, they booked into four different suburban motels.

Craig Taylor and Uncle Don were to leave a day early, to make last-minute preparations. Taylor had already done two weeks of groundwork in the city: on Macadam's instructions, he had rented an apartment in which Uncle Don's command centre would be located. It became known, inevitably, as the "cat house." He had also rented two window vans and prepared them with blackened interiors, curtains, smoked glass, phony identification signs and even a couple of portable street barricades with flashing yellow lights. Four surveillance cars had been rented from different agencies, using credit cards supplied by Taylor, since Macadam had insisted that none of the rentals be traceable to the CBC or Norfolk. This was to be a leakproof operation.

The first two days were devoted mainly to identifying the various cars parked outside the three target homes, although the businessman/loanshark was tailed briefly until his pursuers lost him in traffic.

Dubro kept a somewhat cryptic diary of the period, which conveys some of the flavour of the enterprise. We pick it up here on the third day – the day of the police bust at the shopping plaza:

"Thunder (the businessman/loanshark) was the target.

"*9 a.m.* T7 [one of the seven cars normally parked outside Thunder's house] pulled out. Bill was talking on the radio in one of his long-winded conversations, so we lost it. Drove around looking for where he might have gone.

"*12:00 noon.* A meeting at Box C [the shopping plaza parking lot]. We accidentally parked right next to licence number – , which was T1. We got out of there in a hurry and parked in another spot. Called in all the troops. Cats 2, 3 and 4 sat on the T1 in the plaza lot for 2 hours, when the police moved in on us. They had us surrounded – the entrances and exits were sealed off. We showed ID and used our cover story. They thought we might be robbing a bank. We all left leaving [cameraman] Francis in the blue van. We were tailed by the police.

"*3:00.* A rendezvous with Bill in Cat 1 at the Holiday Inn. We went to pick up Francis, who had filmed the whole thing.

"*3:30.* Box A rendezvous [another shopping plaza] to discuss what had happened and how to proceed. Me, Bill, Craig, Jane, Michel, Dave, Bruce. Walked endlessly through the plaza, looking for a safe place to talk. Everyone very paranoid, thinking we are being followed either by Thunder's men or police or both. We went outside behind the plaza and that wasn't safe enough and then we went into the woods beyond and [one of the less experienced members of the group] thought that the trees might be bugged. It got ridiculous. And it started to rain. So everyone was pretty down, because of the police. We thought Thunder was on to us and had called in the police.

"*8 p.m.* Meeting at base with Uncle Don, Michel, Bruce, Bill. Paranoia galore. Michel ready to take next plane back to Montreal because of how things are going. Discussed tomorrow's plan. Decided to go after Rain [the mob associate]. I am switched from cat 4 to cat 1 – they all want me to join Bill to make sure he doesn't talk too much on the radio. Bruce is a tower of strength, as Bill might say, really holding things together."

The operation also had its lighter moments. Picture Dubro decked out in unaccustomed sweat suit jogging down the street toward the home of Rain. His early-morning mission is to check the licence plates of cars parked outside the home so that their owners can be identified. Before he reaches the home he is overtaken and engulfed by an entire high school class jogging down the same street. This would be marvellous cover, with perspiration-drenched Dubro hunching along in the midst of the athletic teenagers, except that he is so near-sighted that when the group passes Rain's home he has to drop out, slip on the *pince-nez* he uses occasionally for reading the fine print in dusty eighteenth-century tomes, and peer at the plates. He does not trust his memory, so he must pause to fumble for a scrap of paper and a pencil stub with which to record the numbers before jogging on down the street, his heart on the threshold of fibrillation.

Another sample: Cameraman Granger is being rocketed around inside the blacked-out van being driven wildly through the city streets by Craig Taylor, who is intent on following radioed instructions from Uncle Don. The yellow construction barricade, which Granger despises as an example of Macadam's wretched excesses in putting the whole operation together, is bouncing around with him. Finally it rips a hole in the bean bag chair, which, it appears, is not filled with beans at all, but rather thousands of polystyrene pellets highly charged with static electricity. The pellets cling like magnets to everything they touch. It is like a plastic blizzard in the back of the truck and when Taylor finally stops and opens the rear door, Granger emerges looking like a snowman and breathing fire. Sorted out and underway again, en route to some sensitive surveillance filming, Granger finds that the yellow light attached to the barricade has somehow become activated and cannot be turned off: each time if flashes, it illuminates the inside of the truck for all on the street to see. Can he be blamed, in his near-apoplectic state, for destroying rented property?

But mostly it was a time of rising tension and depression as the wearying crew watched the days tick by, approaching the ten-day deadline on the operation imposed by the budget and by other filming commitments. The businessman's wife had now been admitted to hospital, and instead of making his usual nightly rounds, he was spending much of his time at her bedside. And the mobster and respected citizen remained elusive – in fact the mobster had yet to leave his house.

Day 6 as recorded in Dubro's diary was typical in most respects, except that it welcomed a first small success:

"Now I am cat 2, with Craig. I have been cat 1 and cat 4 already. I am beginning to have identity problems.

"*11:15 a.m.* In position at Thunder's.

"*1:06 p.m.* T7 spotted proceeding south and we are all in pursuit. We followed him successfully – and this was our first real success – to the parking lot of the hospital. We had sandbar on the skate. Cats 1, 2, 3, 4 and cat 6 [the camera van] in position at hospital at 1:45.

"*2:20.* Thunder came out of hospital. We had him surrounded, and we got him on film. I hope we use that film!

"*2:25.* Thunder back in position at home.

"*3:05.* Skate count. T2, T3, T7 in place. We radio to base to have hospital checked and discover that it is Mrs. Thunder who is the patient.

"*4:15.* Cat 4 went to do a weather check.

"*5:05.* T5 out and does U-turn on street: possible supervisor. Cat 4 reports official supervision.

"*5:20.* R1, 2 and 3 at Rain's.

"*6:15.* T2, 3, 4, 5 at Thunder's.

"*6:20-7:00.* Took a break.

"*7:15.* T7 was out again. We pursued. East on 16th St., down W 12th Ave. He was dressed casually. Proceeded to hospital again. We blue-finned him with skate at hospital. [Blue-finned means he was in direct line of sight.] Get establishing shot of skate in parking lot.

"*8:15.* Thunder out of hospital.

"*8:30.* T1, 2, 3, 5, 7 back at Thunder's.

"*9:20.* Two new cars in at Thunder's. There is a party for the kids going on.

"9:40. T5 leaves. Cars in and out for the party.

"11:30. Called it a day. This was our first big success, to be able to follow T7 to the hospital, film him leaving the building. It wasn't much after six days of working round the clock, but it was something.''

By Day 8, the situation was getting desperate. With only three days to go, all the operation had to show for its enormous efforts was the film of Thunder, which was supplemented by more footage shot at the hospital on the day following the first success.

And then, early in the evening of Day 8, Auger and Jane Porter made a routine check on Rain's house. The entire team was electrified when Porter radioed her ''weather report'' to Uncle Don. Lightning's car was parked in Rain's driveway. They had the two of them – the mobster and the respected citizen – together.

The film truck was at that moment parked outside Thunder's house, on the wrong side of the city, and Uncle Don ordered it back to Rain's house as quickly as possible. As Taylor and Granger fought their way through heavy traffic, the other surveillance cars took up pre-arranged positions on the streets adjacent to Rain's, ready to give chase if Rain and Lightning should leave the house.

As the minutes passed and Taylor continued to bully his way through the stop-and-go traffic, the others struggled to contain their inpatience. Some good footage of Lightning and Rain together might just pull the whole enormously expensive operation out of the fire. At least it would not have been a complete waste of time.

''We got there rather later than everyone had hoped,'' Taylor remembers. ''I parked the van within filming distance of the house, got out and locked up and sauntered away as casually as I could to rendezvous with one of the other cars some blocks away.

''It was all done according to a pre-arganged plan, of course, but it does become a bit frightening after a while. It's frightening for Francis locked up inside the van . . . and you're leaving in full view of the house and [Rain's] bodyguards are not nice guys. We were sure we'd been burned in that van already, and were taking, really, a desperate last-ditch gamble. And you're never sure if the vehicle with which you're supposed to rendezvous will be there or not, so you're just sort of walking into the wild blue yonder, hoping like hell somebody's there to pick you up.

''This was just at dusk . . . it's terribly difficult at the best of times when you're parking the van for a shoot, to get it at just the right angle and position – you don't have time, and there are cars parked on the street and whatnot . . . and Francis is shouting and screaming, 'Not yet, don't leave yet! Move forward two feet!' and I'm yelling, 'I can't, Francis, for God's sake, I'll smash into a car!'

"When we arrived, we were very excited, Francis and I, because the drapes in the front window were open and I could see the whole lot of them sitting in the living room – Rain and his wife and Lightning and his wife, and it just seemed so perfect.

"But somehow I managed to park the truck so that a hedge I hadn't noticed partly blocked that view and shortly afterward the drapes were pulled.

"Francis was there in the truck for about two hours. And he finally did get some night-lens footage of Lightning saying good-bye to Rain who was in his pyjamas, on the front porch."

Dubro's diary picks up the story:

"10:30. We had a champagne party with the crew at base. We discussed the Lightning/Rain meeting and the film. It was odd that Rain was in pyjamas. We were very happy. Eight days of round-the-clock work and finally we had it – the meeting of Lightning with Rain."

It was the visual record that would be essential if they were to put the story of a mobster's lofty social contacts on the screen.

In the euphoria of the moment, Macadam decided that the next day they would take a gambler's risk to make the most of their changed luck. Rain's car had so far defied their attempts to trail it from the ground, so they would rent a light aircraft the following day and track it from the air. The necessary arrangements were made: Dave Atkinson would accompany the pilot as a spotter and Granger would go along as cameraman. Communications would be complicated: the pilot would have to radio messages to his base at the airport, from where they would be relayed to Uncle Don, who would pass them on to the surveillance cars on the ground.

On the morning of Day 9, Dubro and Macadam had breakfast with a police source, as they did most mornings. It was then that they learned why they had been unable to catch Rain on his rounds, doing business. Rain, the source had learned, had been released from hospital only a few days before the *Connections* crew arrived in the city. He had undergone open-heart surgery, and was con-valescing at home. It was a staggering piece of bad luck, and a major failure of *Connections'* normally responsive intelligence network. Had they known in advance, the whole project would certainly have been delayed by several weeks and its chances of success would have increased enormously.

It was by now too late to cancel arrangements for the aircraft. It took off on schedule at 9 a.m., and at 11:30 it spotted Rain's expensive foreign sedan pulling away from the house. The plane successfully tracked it all the way into the canyons of the downtown core, managing to put the ground surveillance cars into good position during two stops it made on the way. But the car, it developed, was occupied by two women, who were apparently on a grocery shopping trip.

And neither were there any successes on Day 10. The exhausted crew returned to Toronto, on separate flights, the next day.

It was not until many weeks later that they learned that the precious night-lens film of the meeting between Lightning and Rain had been ruled by the CBC's legal department and senior current affairs administrators to be legally suspect. To use the film in the context of the rest of the program, the lawyers argued, would be to imply strongly that the respected citizen, Lightning, was involved unethically or even illegally with organized crime figures, and *Connections* could produce no evidence that this was so. Not an inch of that film was ever to appear on the television network.

14

The Paddy Scam

"Okay, fine Joe. Now listen, Joe, this is what I look like, alright? I'll have a straw panama hat on and a three-piece beige suit with checks on it."

Paddy Calabrese, on the phone setting up his first meeting with Joe Romano

Within days of their return to Toronto, Dubro and Macadam had plotted the outlines of yet another audacious scheme to document the daily wheeling and dealing of a prominent organized crime figure. This time the target would be Vancouver mob associate Joe Romano. The special project had demonstrated the extreme difficulty of tailing a subject with hidden cameras . . . so they would have their target come to the cameras and do his dealing there. Once again, *Connections* would be breaking new and potentially controversial ground in TV journalism.

The plan had grown out of an idea proposed by Paddy Calabrese, the former Buffalo Mafia soldier who had put Macadam on to the John Reynolds story in the first series. In the intervening months, Dubro and Macadam had kept in close contact with Calabrese, who was now operating a private detective agency in the western United States, and the relationship had developed into one of strong mutual admiration and friendship. The two often asked him for his expert advice in planning undercover operations.

Dubro and Macadam telephoned Calabrese to discuss details of the new plan. The idea was to demonstrate, through Romano, how organized crime operates in dealing with stolen securities. Calabrese, they decided, would offer to sell a bond he would represent as having been stolen, to Romano – and the *Connections* crew would be there to film the ensuing negotiations.

For Calabrese, there would be an obvious element of risk in the operation. His previous work in the Vancouver underworld as "Pat Cala" had resulted in the breaking up of a large counterfeit operation and the conviction of two mobsters, Carlo Gallo and Franco Magasoni. Calabrese had good reason to expect an attempt at revenge. And during that operation, too, Calabrese had been introduced to Romano: although their meeting had been brief, there was still the chance that Romano would recognize him.

So it was necessary for Calabrese to carefully prepare a new identity for himself, one which would lull Romano into believing he was dealing with a bona fide member of the organized crime fraternity.

Early in June, he met with Macadam and Dubro in a hotel in San Francisco to discuss strategy. The plan that emerged from that meeting worked as follows:

Calabrese, using the name Frank Angelo, visited the offices of a San José, California cheese company, posing as a buyer for a chain of pizza parlours in the north-west United States. He discussed prices, quality and delivery services at length with a company salesman.

The company – California Cheese – is owned by Angelo Marino, a notorious West Coast Mafia figure and a man whom Calabrese had learned from his earlier work in Vancouver had ties with Joe Romano. The sole purpose of the visit was to use the company's telephone to place a call to Romano's home and leave a message while Romano was at his office. The message relayed to him from his home would ask him to phone Frank Angelo at a number Romano would recognize as being that of the California Cheese Company. At the cheese company Calabrese asked that any call from Romano be transferred to the Fairmont Hotel, in San Francisco.

Calabrese then took another step to establish his "credentials." He had heard that a retired West Coast Mafia figure he knew from an earlier investigation of mob activities in Alaska was in hospital in San Francisco awaiting heart surgery. He paid him an afternoon visit.

"It's me, Frank Angelo," he told the ailing mobster.

The mafioso strained to clear his mind of the fog induced by sedatives:

"Who?"

"Frank Angelo. Your cousin," Calabrese replied. "How are

you feeling? I came to see if there is anything I can do for you."

The old man could not remember having a cousin by that name, but he was delighted to have a visitor. Yes, there was something he would like to have. Calabrese had to bend over the bed to hear the feeble request.

"I would like a pear," the man said.

Calabrese recalls the outcome of the meeting with an uncomfortable chuckle:

"He was pretty dopey from the drugs and what not . . . I brought him up a big basket of fruit and some cigarettes, and he would have done anything I wanted after that."

Calabrese made sure to leave a "Frank Angelo" calling card in the fruit basket.

If Romano called to check, Calabrese would expect the mafioso to tell him, "Frank Angelo? Sure. He was just up here to visit me. Brought me a basket of fruit. He's a good boy."

Back in his hotel room, Calabrese and the *Connections* film crew waited for Romano to return the call from the cheese company. At six, the phone rang:

"Hello, Joseph. This is Frank Angelo. You don't know me, but we have some mutual friends. Listen, I'm flying up to Vancouver. Could we get together for a couple of hours up there? I'm going to be staying at the Bayshore."

Romano: "Sure. When are you going to be here?"

They arranged to meet at the hotel, and then Romano asked: "You want to tell me anything else?"

Calabrese: "Ah . . . you want to parley on the telephone?"

Romano: "Well, I mean . . ."

Calabrese: "It's just something that maybe you could give a right direction, that's all."

Romano: "Oh, okay. But I mean you'll have people that we know each other?"

Calabrese: "Yes. I'll have the right credentials. Okay?"

Romano: "Okay, fine."

Calabrese: "My cousin here in San Francisco [here he named the hospitalized mafioso] knows one of your friends up there."

Romano: "Oh, okay. Your cousin is there. Okay, that's fine."

Calabrese: "And I called you from San José today, okay?"

Romano: "Well, I saw that. I got that."

Calabrese and Romano met the following day at the Vancouver hotel. Knowing that Romano would not have had time to thoroughly check his references and would therefore be unusually alert, Calabrese did not wear a body-pack for this meeting, even though the encounter was recorded on film from a hidden camera. He was interviewed by Macadam immediately after the meeting:

". . . I sat down and I gave him two cards, one from the salesman at the California Cheese Company and another one from a [Mafia] espresso place in San Francisco he knows about . . . I told him that I would like to talk to him regarding a bond that I have . . . that we need some direction in which way to go with these bonds. He was a little hesitant in the beginning and then he starts softening up a little bit and giving me a little advice . . ."

"Weren't you a bit nervous when you met him?" Macadam asked.

"No, no. Once he came up to me and took off his sun glasses and I took off mine and we looked each other in the eyes, I knew he didn't recognize me . . . Anyway, I explained to him that we had 250 of these $5,000 municipal non-registered bonds and I gave him the copy to look at, and he looked at it briefly and then he put it on the table and said, 'Okay, tell me the whole story.'"

The story Calabrese and Macadam had concocted was that the bonds, worth about a million and a quarter dollars, had been stolen from the secret stash of a mob member somewhere in the American mid-West. The criminal had assumed they had been stolen by an estranged wife, and in any case could not report them to the authorities as having been stolen without bringing down the wrath of the tax department.

Calabrese said the price he and his associates were asking was half the face value of the bonds. Romano told him he thought he might be able to get him forty percent. But by the time he had taken his own cut, and given a cut to a middleman and to the banker who would eventually take the bonds – a banker in Europe, Romano said – Calabrese and his associates would be left with about twenty percent of the bonds' face value.

As the camera crew watched apprehensiely through binoculars and the telephoto lens, Romano and Calabrese got up from their table and walked to the hotel parking lot, where they climbed into Romano's Mercedes convertible. Romano, in an gesture of hospitality, had offered to show Calabrese a bit of Vancouver. During the ride, the two idly discussed such topics as the development of Vancouver's Italian district and the relative merits of law enforcement agencies in Canada and the United States. Romano told

Calabrese that Canadian police were years behind those in the States; that few important arrests were made. Romano was carefully testing Calabrese, probing for holes in his "cover." He apparently found none.

A week later, another meeting between Calabrese and Romano was arranged, and this time Calabrese brought one of the actual "stolen" bonds for Romano, so that it could be checked by Romano's banking contacts. Once again the venue was the poolside terrace of the Bayshore Inn, and once again the *Connections* crew filmed the meeting from a hotel room window overlooking the pool. But this time Calabrese was wired for sound.

Calabrese and Macadam had spent several hours discussing strategy for the meeting, rehearsing, elaborating emergency plans. Obviously, a real bond would have to be purchased and handed over to Romano if the scam were to continue.

"He wants that bond," Calabrese told Macadam. "I said to him, 'Look, it's $5,000.' And he said, 'No, its only $2,500 [at a 50 per cent selling price] and if you're worried about me for $2,500 when you're dealing in four, five hundred thousand, you shouldn't be here right now.'

"That's right, too, you know. If I was really dealing with the guy I would trust him enough to say, 'Here, here's the bond. Take care of it.' Because he would know I would come back and kill him if we're connected with people . . . "

"Okay now," Macadam replied, "let's think this out. If we were willing to buy that bond if necessary . . . if we lost it, if we can get him on film taking it and then he doesn't give it back, then maybe we can have a charge of theft laid against him."

It was an audacious idea, even for Calabrese:

"Oh you're brutal. You're bad, let me tell you. Not only do you want to nail this guy . . . salt in the wounds it's called. Oh my God, that would be . . . Jesus, that would be outrageous, honest to God. I think that would be . . . fantastic!"

Their conversation turned briefly to other tactical questions before returning to the problem of the authentic bond.

Macadam had another suggestion.

"Why don't you get a receipt from him? Just . . ."

"A receipt?"

"Yeah. Just have him write a little note."

"Just a little note for this bond? Well, what am I going to do . . . wait a minute. Crooks don't ask for a receipt."

Calabrese paused to consider the idea further.

"[I could tell him] 'just give me something that I could show my partners that you received it, with your handwriting on it. They told me they were going to kill you, too, [if it's not returned].' Something like that."

He was warming to the idea.

"That's right! A receipt. What's this world coming to?"

But despite the hours of planning, the actual meeting took an unexpected and, for Calabrese, frightening turn.

Calabrese occupied the poolside table the camera crew had selected a few minutes before Romano was due to arrive for the meeting. He ordered a breakfast of a poached egg, orange juice and coffee for two.

Romano appeared before it could be delivered. After a friendly greeting, he got right to the point. He was still concerned about Calabrese's references, he said. To mollify him, at least temporarily, Calabrese gave him the telephone number of another California mob aquaintance, but he asked Romano not to call him for two days, until Calabrese had had a chance to meet with him and explain the bond deal.

Romano agreed: "From my point of view, then I will be more comfortable."

"That's exactly what I'm doing it for," Calabrese assured him.

Calabrese then showed Romano the authentic bond. "Now I got to ask you a couple of questions . . . I'm going to give you this one . . . what are you going to do with it, can I ask?"

"I'm going to verify whether or not it's a legitimate piece of paper . . . And whether or not they are reported stolen. That's a very simple thing. From the stand-point of dollars, it means fuck-all to me from one point of view – the bottom line is $1,500 and the top line is $2,500."

"Right," confirmed Calabrese.

"For the kind of deal we're doing, if I was going to do something up front [myself] . . . I'd look at the score and I'd say 'Listen, tell you what. Give me $10,000, give me $25,000 – give me something so that I know my work ain't bullshit. At this point, like I said before, it was sort of an insult to me. I felt that if you want to do business with me . . . for a G-note, or $1,500 or let's call it $2,000 at the most . . .

"I mean, we spend more than that for dinners and parties together, partying it up . . . I gave one of these guys we're talking about a thousand dollars' worth of cigars for a birthday gift.''

To have a good recommendation from a mob connection was not always enough, Romano advised Calabrese. When doing business with a stranger, he said, ''. . . I see what he drinks, what he smokes, what he wears . . . I'm sorry, but I'm materialistic. I'm dealing in money . . . I mean some people notice the watch I got on. It doesn't mean fuck all, but the right people know what it costs. The right people know what it costs. Same thing with cars. It don't mean fuck all to me 'cause I've got 'em in the garage. Some people know that it's a Rolls-Royce. Other people – I don't make a big thing out of it. My wife's got a Mercedes. What the fuck. All I'm saying is that if there's something we can do, fine. But there's got to be a certain amount of trust. I realize that you've got to develop it and I've got to develop it. We earn it. It's not something that's given.''

Romano went on to complain that he had already spent several hundred dollars making telephone calls to contacts in Canada and bankers in Europe to find out whether they might be interested in the bonds.

But Calabrese was no longer listening. He had just seen death walk past in the person of Carlo Gallo. Gallo was the mobster he had sent away for dealing in counterfeit money, the man who would now be looking for revenge.

Upstairs in the hotel room, the cameraman was changing film. Macadam peeked through the telephoto lens. He saw a waiter approach Calabrese's table with the breakfast he had ordered, and saw Calabrese, whose appetite had vanished, brusquely refuse to accept it.

''What's going on?'' he asked cameraman Len Gilday. ''He's sending back his breakfast.''

''Maybe the toast was burned,'' Gilday ventured.

Now another man was approaching the table. Calabrese seemed very tense . . . and then the camera was rolling again. Macadam made a mental note to use a radio mike to back up Calabrese's body-pack in any future meetings of this sort. It was agony not knowing what was happening.

''What are you doin','' Calabrese said to Gallo.

''You're lookin' good, Paddy.'' And to Romano: ''How ya doin'.''

Romano repeated Calabrese's question: ''What are you doin' in this place?''

"Talkin' business." He glared at the two for a moment and then walked back into the hotel.

Calabrese struggled to maintain his composure.

"Let me tell you something," he said to Romano. "He's connected with a couple of people that I know. Alright?"

"Alright."

". . . He just made a bad move."

"Oh? All he said was 'Hello Paddy,' instead of 'Hello Frank'. . ." Romano observed.

"Frank, Paddy, Frank . . . they call me both. But this is the fucking deal. I'm going to tell you. He just made a bad move, unless you brought him around – I don't know."

The menace in Calabrese's voice surprised Romano. Instead of pursuing the question of names, he confessed what Calabrese already knew: that he had been investigated by police in connection with the same counterfeit deal for which Gallo had served eighteen months in jail. He hadn't seen Gallo since that time. It was clear that Romano and Gallo were not on good terms, and that Romano had been just as shaken by the encounter as Calabrese. Thanks to the mistrust that is widespread inside the mob, and to Calabrese's resourcefulness, the scam could continue, for the moment.

"Joe, let me ask you something. How soon, if we turn [the bonds over] to you – how soon could I get it? What are we talking about timewise?"

"From the day let's say everything is tickety-poo . . . it depends on how fast you can travel or someone can travel to a bank out of the country and make a presentation."

"What are we talkin' about? What part of the world?"

"I won't tell you now. Okay? Sorry. I'm not going to tell you now."

"Okay, that's fine."

"Let's say you need a passport. Okay? . . . I'm saying to you it doesn't matter where it is, it would be done at a bank. It would be a simple thing of where a man walks in and makes a delivery and says 'I'm here to deliver,' and the man checks the things and on the basis of that the bank says 'How do you want the money?' . . . And they make out a bank draft or a series of drafts, however you want, in whatever name you want. Generally speaking, it's done through a company or companies, because that way, it's easy to dissipate. Some of it is sometimes cashed . . . You will know who the agent is that you got to see. Let's say you got to go see Mr. Smith. Smith is not there, but Mr. Brown is there. Then you can't make the fuckin' deal. You say, 'Excuse me, I'll wait for Mr. Smith to come back from lunch.' You know what I'm trying to get at? It's as simple as that.''

At that point, Calabrese handed over the bond, in a manila folder.

"I don't want to insult you," he told Romano, "but you got to understand something. I got people . . . as far as this goes I'm giving you about $1,500. Big fuckin' deal. You got more than that in phone calls when you're done with the thing . . .''

It was a delicate question. How to explain that the CBC's accountants would go berserk if they knew he was handing over $5,000 of the corporation's money to a mobster.

"Fifteen hundred dollars. Big fuckin' deal. I realize that. But, tell me something . . .''

Romano anticipated his question:

"Will your people get it back?''

"Yeah.''

"Oh, they'll get it back. No question about that.''

"Alright, that's what I'm saying . . . Will you do me a favour?''

"Yeah.''

"On a napkin – somewhere – just sign the fuckin' thing that you got this thing from me – whatever.'' Calabrese tossed a napkin across the table to Romano.

"I don't care if you put it on a sugar package . . . just say I got this thing from so and so this date and that's all I want for this thing.''

Romano seemed to be hesitating.

"Not for any particular reason,'' Calabrese added lamely.

"No, I'm just trying to think how to word it. Just let me think . . .''

"Any words you want to put it in, I don't give a damn . . . Here, put it on this piece of paper.''

Romano was still holding back.

"I'm just trying to figure out . . .''

Calabrese kept up the pressure: "You want the pen or the pencil? Just put down number nine bond. So we know it's number nine.''

"From Frank Angelo?''

Calabrese watched breathlessly as Romano made out the receipt and signed it. When it had been completed, he sat back in his chair, took a long look at the pool, the ocean in the background, and said: "This is a *nice* place."

"Oh, it's beautiful," agreed Romano. And the meeting ended.

Back inside the hotel, Calabrese's body-pack was still running as he approached the room from which the camera crew was operating. He knocked impatiently on the door, and Macadam asked, "Who is it?"

"It's me, that's fuckin' who."

The door opened and he burst into the room.

"Didn't you see Carlo Gallo coming up to me? Did you see that?"

"I didn't know who it was," Macadam replied, startled by Calabrese's obvious distress.

"What do you mean? That was Carlo Gallo!"

"Holy shit," was all Macadam could think of to say.

"He come up and he says, 'Hey, Paddy.' . . . Did you see him? Do you have him on film? That's Carlo Gallo. What's the matter with you? You could get me fuckin' killed out there, you know? He was with another guy and they are making their moves right now . . . I better check out of here real fast. In fact right now. He's going to make his fuckin' moves right now."

Calabrese left the hotel almost immediately, and Macadam and the crew removed his luggage later.

The level of risk was getting uncomfortably high. Romano was still suspicious of Calabrese's credentials, and now he had heard Gallo refer to him as "Paddy." It was only a matter of time before Romano connected that name with "Pat Calla," the government agent who had blown the whistle on the counterfeit deal. And who knew what Carlo Gallo was up to?

But the scam could not be called off . . . not yet. Romano still had the CBC's $5,000 bond. There had to be a third meeting, to get it back.

It took another series of phone calls to set it up. Sensing Romano's growing reluctance to continue dealing with an unknown quantity, Calabrese and Macadam decided to raise the ante. If this deal went through, Calabrese told Romano, there were others in the immediate offing. In fact, his London banking contact would be in town the day of their meeting, and Romano would be able to meet him. The "London contact" would be Macadam.

There was a second reason for Macadam's involvement in the

meeting – Calabrese and Macadam both felt that there was a real risk of a hit man showing up for the meeting, instead of Romano. So long as Macadam was with Calabrese as a witness, the risk of a "hit" was reduced. If Romano appeared on schedule, the risk would be reduced further, and Macadam would be able to leave the two to talk. But Calabrese could no longer be left alone, even in the hotel lobby.

Once again, there were elaborate preparations for the meeting. It was thought unlikely that they could meet again within camera range on the hotel terrace without further arousing Romano's suspicions, so arrangements were made to shift the camera crew from the hotel room to the surveillance van if that should prove necessary. (It didn't.) Calabrese would, of course, be wired for sound. They decided that he should offer Romano a cigar, in return for one he had given Calabrese.

"That way we won't have an obligation to him," Calabrese said.

Macadam purchased a handful of Monte Cristo Crystal Mansions as the two passed through the hotel lobby and gave one to Calabrese.

"Thank you," he said, and lit up. "Oh, what a beautiful cigar . . . Ahhh, that's good . . . These fucking things cost two bucks a piece! I mean, this is like putting perfume on a pig giving me this. This is Romano's style." He stuck another in his jacket pocket.

As they waited for Romano to arrive, the two ironed out a few last-minute details. Calabrese spoke to the hotel doorman, to whom he had been introduced by Romano.

"Hello, Doug. Remember me?"

"Yeah. Frank."

"Has Joe pulled up yet?"

"No, I haven't seen him."

"Do me a favour, will you? Here, put this in your pocket." Calabrese handed him two two-dollar bills. "Tell him that Frank's up by the pool. Any kind of cops around?"

"No, nothing as far as I know . . ."

"Let us know if any come in – on that [pool] phone, will you?"

"I will."

Calabrese was also concerned about Macadam's near-sightedness. A recent article on Macadam in *Quest* magazine had been illustrated with a full-page photo of him staring imperiously into the camera lens through his aviator's glasses. By removing the glasses, he thought he would make himself less recognizable to anyone who had seen the photo.

"You're going to be blind as a bat," Calabrese warned.

"No, no. I can see."

"You told me you don't need them. My God . . . how are you going to see Carlo if he walks up . . . I can see it: [here, Calabrese thrust his arms forward, palms outward] 'Frank, Frank, where are you . . .' You're like that guy with glasses in the cartoon, that can't see worth shit."

And they were still trying to decide on an alias for Macadam as Romano pulled up in his Rolls.

"Is it 'Fisher' or 'Foster'?" Calabrese asked. "Eh? Charles Fisher? Charles Foster? Ah, fuck. I might call you Bill McCann, I don't know . . .

"Here he comes now. He's coming now . . . once you're introduced you say, 'You guys have some business to talk about . . . I'll be available for a call.' Okay? We'll do it that way . . ."

"Joseph."

"Morning."

"How are you doing? Charles Foster – Joe Romano."

"A pleasure," Romano shook Macadam's hand, with the limp, damp handshake that is unaccountably almost universal among mobsters.

"I'll be available for a call if you need me," Macadam said, and he returned to the hotel room.

Calabrese leaned over the table to Romano. "Remember I told you about the guy from London, doing the thing with the other bonds? That's who he is alright. He wanted to talk to you and see what you could do and if not, he doesn't have to be in on the conversation. The receipt and everything else – he's the one who's got it."

"He's got it?"

"Yeah."

"Because I want to give him back the bond and I want the receipt back. Has he got it now?"

"Yeah, it's in his luggage. About 2 o'clock his luggage will be in. He just got in this morning."

The plan was to force Romano to return that afternoon for a

fourth meeting so that the crew would have an opportunity to film him entering and leaving the hotel from the surveillance van. The shots were necessary for continuity.

"Oh," said Romano. "[The receipt] is not here, then."

"No, he just got in from back east. He's got to get his luggage. What's the story with the bond?"

"It's fine. My people discussed it. One guy is right there now. He took the trip. The percentages seem to be settled. Someone's gone there now to discuss it. I gave him the copy of the bond and I verified that the bond is legitimate and he said there was no more need for it, so I said, 'Fine.' As far as I'm concerned, what I want is basically to get the receipt, give him the bond and take the thing and then I'll tell you where to make the delivery or whatever the case may be."

"Okay, let me ask you something. After these other things, could you possibly make a move with these [new bonds]?"

"I'd have to know what the inventory's like."

"The legitimacy of the bond is there," Calabrese pointed out.

"Yeah, I'm not concerned with that. I'm concerned now with inventory. What we're talking about. How much of this and how much of that – you know what I mean?"

Romano explained what he meant through a kind of underworld parable:

"Let me tell you something. There's a very famous story in this town – every town has a famous story – a guy came with a diamond. Beautiful diamond . . . unbelievable. It was worth in those days $15,000 and the guy sold it for $5,000. Now, when he came he said, 'Listen, instead of one I got three. Will you take three?' 'Of course we'll take three.' So they bought. One good stone and two lumpies. All for the same price so they paid $15,000, which is what the stone was worth."

He did not intend to be hustled, in the same way, into buying phony stock certificates, he indicated.

Romano expressed concern, too, about Macadam.

"Where do I check him out? . . . He's not Italian."

"You know that, you know that," Calabrese confirmed.

"There's nothing about him that's Italian . . . If he started talking Italian to me then I'd be impressed, but so far, I don't know who he is."

"Alright. He's an accountant. He's a lawyer and he's an accountant. But when we turn over the rest of the shit you'll know everybody. Period. The hedging part . . . it'll be over with," Calabrese assured him.

Their discussion continued for another twenty minutes, and Romano agreed to return in an hour for the exchange of the bond for the receipt. As he pushed his chair away from the table, Calabrese remembered the cigars.

"Want a cigar? I asked Charles to go and get some. The best ones. That's what he smokes. This any good?"

"Number one," Romano commented approvingly. "Yeah, this is very good. Tom Jones smokes these."

"Tom Jones?"

"Yeah, the be-bopper. This is his cigar. Alright. I'll see you at noon."

Back in the hotel room, the body-pack once again recorded Calabrese's excitement as he fumbled to unstrap it:

"Bill, if this thing isn't on . . . if this thing isn't on I am going to go fucking bananas. See if it's on. We got everything. We got a shot at 12 o'clock. He wants the receipt. Okay, please tell me it's fucking on please . . ."

The noon meeting was brief and to the point. Macadam gave Romano his receipt, and received the bond in return. He assured Romano that at their next meeting, he would have references prepared:

"I will get you those credentials, " he said. "There will be no question in your mind."

But there were no further meetings. The scam had been stretched to the limits of credibility, and it was time for Calabrese and Macadam to get out of town.

During the course of their research into the activities of Joe Romano, *Connections* had learned through law enforcement sources that despite his criminal associations Romano had managed to maintain a long-standing friendship with Angelo Branca, a newly-retired senior justice of the British Columbia Court of Appeal. Intrigued by this bit of information, Macadam was to return to Vancouver to interview Branca. The subject of the interview, Branca was told, would be "ethics and the judiciary." Romano was not mentioned for fear the former judge would then refuse the interview, and Macadam believed it was important to try to shed some light on this relationship. How was it that Romano had managed to conceal his unsavory connections from a man who had been both an excellent criminal lawyer and a senior member of the B.C. bench? *Connections* research had turned up several cases of contacts between mob figures and respected members of society, notably , those targeted in the "special project." Here at last was an opportunity to openly explore the whole question.

The encounter took place in Branca's office at the law firm he had joined on his retirement from the bench and it included the following exchange:

Macadam: "Do you know this individual, sir?"

Branca: "I know Joe Romano, yes."

Macadam: "Do you know him well?"

Branca: "I don't know him well . . . I know him fairly well, let me put it that way."

Macadam: "Do you know him well enough to go to his house, or . . ."

Branca: "Oh yes, I've been to his house."

Macadam: "Would his . . . questionable activities in the past, would that be at all a problem . . ."

Branca: "No, I was never aware of any questionable practices on the part of Joe Romano at all. Matter of fact he's . . . he has a family of five or six children – it is one of the finest and best regulated families that I have ever visited. Bar none."

Macadam: "The reason I mention him is that some people of Italian extraction have told us that he is a very bad example of organized crime and they feel he is not a credit to the Italian community."

Branca: "They must know far, far more about him than I do. Far, far more about him than I do. I have never seen anything wrong with Romano's conduct over the seven or eight years that I have known him casually, that would create any suspicion in reference to Joe, other than his being a good citizen. Nothing at all."

Macadam: "So you know him well enough to say that you think he is a good citizen."

Branca: "I think he is a good citizen."

Macadam: "He was charged on a . . . uh . . ."

Branca: "I think he was charged with some securities matter, pending before the court, and I think he's charged now with, uh, extortion."

Macadam: "And I think he had some income tax . . . uh, conviction."

Branca: "Yes, I think he has some income tax conviction."

Macadam: "Well, would somebody like that . . . on the bench, would that create a problem in terms of associating with him?"

Branca paused for several seconds before replying:

"It depends on how you associate with him. I could see nothing wrong with going to his home with other friends, you see, and talking to him, partaking of his hospitality, and things like that. Nothing wrong with that at all."

Macadam: "Even after he's charged."

Branca: "Well, that didn't happen . . . I've never been to his home after he was charged. He's only been charged recently."

Macadam: "Well, he was charged with this Seneca [securities] thing a few years ago, I mean . . ."

Branca: "That charge was only laid a little while ago . . . that was only laid in recent months."

Macadam: "December of '77." He checked his notes to confirm the date.

Branca: "December of '77?"

Macadam: "That's right."

Branca: "That may be so."

Macadam: ". . . In a case like that, if it's someone you know that's been charged, would that make a problem for you as a judge?"

Branca: "I don't think so. I still think I would accept him as a man in whose favour the presumption of innocence applies. In other words, a man is innocent until he is found guilty."

Macadam: "Well, yes, I accept that of course. A man is innocent until proven guilty. The question, though, is really about what you were saying earlier. You have to be like Caesar's wife . . . you cannot associate with somebody who may appear not to be pure."

Branca: "Now, I don't say that I would go to his home two times a day or three times a day. But despite the fact that he has been charged, if an occasion arose where I would have to go to his house I would have no hesitation . . . none at all. And I can't see how anybody could say my going there in those circumstances is suspicious, is doing something that I shouldn't do . . ."

Macadam: "But anyway, you have said that you have never seen him since he was charged . . ."

Branca: "No, I've seen him . . . but I've never been to his home."

Macadam: "But you've never been to his home for the past two years."

Branca: "That's right."

15
A Visit to Calabria

" ... schools closed, all of the municipal administration went to the funeral, the cinemas were closed for two days ... this is showing respect for the deceased person but most of all it is fear of what could happen later in case you do not show respect toward the family of the assasinated boss."

Undercover agent describing a recent Mafia funeral in Southern Italy.

On his return to Toronto, an exhausted Macadam had just enough time to have his laundry done, pick up a fresh crew (sound recordist Aerlyn Weissman and cameraman Granger) and catch a plane for Rome. There, the three met Burke, who had arrived a few days earlier to do some advance legwork. The next two weeks, during which they traced the roots of the Canadian Mafia among the towns and villages of southern Italy, provided some of the most soul-chilling experiences of the entire project. It was there that, for the first time, they began to understand the true nature of the fear that is the Mafia's most effective weapon.

When the group left Rome on the sunny southbound Autostrada, they had recruited a flamboyant Italian ex-narcotics agent named Nicola Longo, as their translator and guide. They drove two vehicles: a German Opel sedan and a Ford Transit van rigged out for surveillance filming. Walkie-talkies provided communications between the two.

Longo, the translator, had a small reputation in Italy as having been a Kojak-style cop - a sensitive cowboy type whose spectacular career had provided him with dozens of anecdotes about wild gun fights, hair-raising chases and spectacular drug busts. It was rumoured that he was no longer in the business because he had been too efficient - some of his busts had harmed the interests of corrupt superiors. He had since married an American and was negotiating the sale of movie rights to his life, with a Hollywood producer.

On the way south from Rome, the group traced the route followed by the agent who had delivered the $3 million ransom in the sensational Getty kidnapping, at a transfer point near the town of Lagonegro, south of Naples. Burke had located the agent through American law enforcement contacts in Rome, and after a long series of clandestine meetings had talked him into doing an interview in which he described the operation. The interview, combined with the film shot along the route provided the backbone for the Getty item. A spectacular supplement was *Connections'* surveillance film of one of the kidnappers who, despite the fact that most of the ransom money is still missing, had been released from jail and was living in Rome. (Young John Paul Getty III, readers may recall, was held for many weeks and had an ear amputated by his abductors before his ransom was paid and he was released.)

The next day there was filming further south, in Rosarno, where a corruption-ridden superport project provided an object lesson in the way Mafia influence can cripple an economy. The corrupting influence in this case was Momo Piromalli, reputedly the most powerful Mafia boss on mainland Italy until his death early in 1979. Piromalli and the Mafia of his Calabrian home town – Gioia Tauro – was known to have exerted considerable influence on the Mafia in Montreal, through blood ties.

"When we got into Gioia Tauro," Macadam dictated on his taped diary, "it was about two in the afternoon. We filmed various shots, including a John Deere dealership which had been owned by Longo's brother, and which had been shot up quite extensively when he refused to pay protection. Finally the police advised him that he was going to be killed by the Mafia, so he had to leave town . . . Then we went to the police station and presented our letters of introduction from the government and asked them if they could tell us where Piromalli's house was located.

"They all seemed nervous about doing this – certainly everyone here is extremely nervous about the fact that we are involved in doing a film of this kind. It's another example of the power of the Mafia here. They [the police] have all said that if the Mafia find out, they will kill us for certain, and there is a certain amount of apprehension [among the police] that by assisting us they might also put themselves in danger.

"Finally, however, we got one of the police officers to ride with me and Longo in the car while Aerlyn and Francis followed in the van, which Martyn drove. I pointed locations out to them over the walkie-talkie as we drove by the three Piromalli brothers' houses . . . which are certainly more impressive than the types of Mafia houses we have been filming in Canada.''

The brief stay in Gioia Tauro ended abruptly on their return to the police station. Burke and Macadam were told to leave the town immediately, and not to return without an armed escort. The police also expressed astonishment that the film crew would involve a woman. ''If they [the Mafia] get hold of her,'' one policeman warned, ''she will no longer be a virgin, so to speak.''

Macadam's diary resumes:

''We left with a very weary crew on the Autostrada for the drive to Reggio di Calabria . . . We were high up in the mountains as we approached Reggio, and we could see the lights of Sicily across the Straits of Messina.

''We found our hotel, the Grand Excelsior, and persuaded them to keep the dining room open late for us for dinner. The crew then went to bed, exhausted. We were rather concerned that Nicola was very frightened at this point. I spent a few hours talking to him over cappucino and it seems to have made a difference. He is very conscious of his image of bravery and fearlessness. I explained to him that we are all scared at times and there is no bravery without fear; that doing the film was a way of challenging ourselves. That appealed to him. This morning we are back in gear and he seems enthusiastic and cheerful.''

Indeed, so thoroughly recovered were Longo's spirits that later in the day, when the vehicles had pulled off to the side of the road for a quiet afternoon siesta, Longo crept up beside a dozing Macadam, drew his pistol and fired a shot into the air a few inches from Macadam's head. Macadam does not record his reaction in his diary. Nor did Longo explain his motives for the little prank, but the two seem equally predictable.

Macadam's offerings of moral support were not always appreciated by Canadian members of the crew, either.

Burke recalls, ''Aerlyn would go nuts. She had worked on everything from riots in Chicago to the Middle East war in 1973, but Macadam would say to her, 'If anything goes wrong, don't worry. I'll be right here.' And she would say, 'Big deal! Who the hell is he to tell me when to get nervous and when not to. I can decide for myself when it's dangerous and when it's not.' ''

Weissman herself has an interesting perspective on Longo's apparent trepidation: "We were all pretty frightened by that time. It was clear that if anything went wrong we wouldn't be able to rely on the police for help. If somebody was hassling you and you called the police, the cop who would show up would be probably be the guy's cousin. Even at the hotel, we could be sure that if anybody wanted to get at us it would be no problem – they would know everybody on the staff and would be able to walk right in.

"The thing about Longo was that he came from that area of Italy, and he knew what was going down . . . it's not really fair to say that he added to our paranoia. When I looked at his reaction, it simply confirmed my fears . . . I knew we were right to be frightened."

Perhaps because she was the only woman on the crew, Weissmann often found herself mediating disputes between Burke and Macadam. The arguments were sometimes spectacular.

"We were in a town outside Reggio one night and they started yelling at each other right there on the street – I think Bill had said, 'It will take us this long to get to such-and-such a hotel,' and Martyn said, 'How the hell do you know' and that started it. And finally Bill yelled, 'That's it, I've had enough! I'm leaving!' God only knows where he thought he was going to go, but he stomped off to the van. ['I was simply going on to the hotel,' Macadam recalls.] And Francis the cameraman said, 'Hey, wait a minute, you're not going without me – all my equipment's in there.' And I figured I'd better stay with the car because that's where all *my* equipment was. Our loyalties were to our equipment.

"Anyway, it finally got smoothed over. I said to them, 'Look you guys. I'd rather be doing something other than this stuff,' so we went in and had dinner instead. It was ridiculous . . . here we were scared to death about blowing our cover and we were shouting at each other in the middle of the street."

Macadam's diary resumes the following morning:

"We had a good breakfast at about 11:30 and Martyn and Nicola and I walked up to the police station where, of course, none of the senior officers had arrived. But finally they began to trickle in and we were able to discuss a number of things.

"We learned that Paolo Violi had come here [to Reggio] five years ago, and that he was very close to people here. The police kept mentioning him with Sera Mommolitti here, and also the Naples group. They all talked about 'the Canadian group with connections with Siderno' [the Racco/Commisso group in Toronto]. They said Violi had been here to see Mommolitti to buy land for buildings and restaurants. It is also generally believed that the Violi-Cotroni organization laundered some of the Getty ransom money for organized crime people here. The police files, which they showed us, listed Violi as a prime associate of Mommolitti, who helped mastermind the Getty kidnapping, and they also indicated that the two are related. They say here that Cotroni [Montreal's godfather] was born in Mammola, near Polistena, and not in Reggio as we had thought . . .

"I am recording this while Francis and Martyn are a few feet away filming a shot of Reggio and panning over to Sicily and back. We are, I believe, in a sort of police parking lot: it is 4:05 in the afternoon and everyone is out for their afternoon snooze, so no-one is bothering us. We have a great view of Reggio, Mount Etna and the island across the strait – Sicily. As soon as they are done we are moving on to Santa di Polsi, which is a hairy climb through the mountains, we are told. There we should find the Calabrian Mafia's special shrine to its patron saint, the Madonna di Polsi."

The drive through the Aspromontes provided Burke and Macadam with what both describe as the most intense single experience of their four years' involvement with organized crime.

As the little convoy climbed the tortuous switchbacks into the desolate mountain range, possibly the poorest, most primitive, region in all of Italy, Burke recalls that "everybody in the crew was in great spirits, and we were laughing and comparing notes and so on.

"But as we got further and further into the mountains, we all fell utterly silent. It was the spookiest place I have ever been in my life. We would drive into these little towns where quite literally hundreds of people have been killed over the years in Mafia feuds, and where scores of people, including Getty, have been held for ransom in caves, and all the people in the towns would stop whatever they were doing and stand there silently watching us. And there was not a friendly face among them, or at least so it seemed to us. And as we went further and further in it got more and more primitive.

"For the first time, we all understood the Mafia in a 'gut' sense. It was like experiencing a kind of malevolent *Legend of Sleepy Hollow*. You could feel the fear and suspicion. It was palpable, in the air. Before that we had all understood the power of the Mafia intellectually, but there we *felt* it for the first time . . .

"The only other time I have experienced anything like it was in

Vietnam, when I was on a convoy that was going into territory that we knew was enemy territory. You couldn't tell, obviously, who were Viet Cong and who were the 'friendlies'. Everybody you looked at as you were riding on the Jeep seemed to have the potential for great evil. You began to see things in terms of great evil . . .''

For Weissman, the experience of the Aspromontes was summed up by a stop made late in the afternoon of that day at an isolated *taverna*. They needed to ask directions to the shrine, and they were ravenously hungry.

It was a small fieldstone building, probably several hundred years old. The ceilings were low, and the floor was of hard-packed earth.

''There were two old, old men in there playing cards . . . they looked like they'd been there a hundred years. And then the proprietor came out and he really blew my mind. He had a round face and fat, sensuous lips and little satyr's eyes. It was the kind of face that comes from generations of inbreeding, like you sometimes see in isolated places in the world. We saw a lot of people like that. He had an incredibly evil, sensuous look about him, something very primitive or elemental. He looked just like Pan. But he was not stupid by any means. He looked at us in a way that people there often did: how scared would you be with a knife to your throat, how would you react? That's their whole trip – death and dying. They're so into it . . . that's their big moment. That's how they size you up.

''Whatever is weird about you, whatever is in your darkest nature, your inner violence . . . those people could look into you and hook into it; pick up on your confusion or your anxiety and control you through it.

''This is going to sound weird, but that building had a smell about it that I had experienced only once before in my life – in the monastery in Romania where Dracula is buried. It is an indescribable smell of dampness and earth . . . and I don't know what . . . animal sacrifice, death . . . very spooky.

''He served us huge sandwiches made of home-made bread and home-made cheese, and *prosciutto* made from wild boar and home-made wine. And he told us it would take at least four more hours to get to the shrine and that the road was even worse than the ones we had already been over.

''It isn't that we decided not to go on and try to get there while there was light to shoot . . . we didn't take a vote or anything. There was just an unspoken consensus that we would not go on, and we just got into the car and truck and headed back out of the mountains.

"But after that I really began to understand the whole trip these people are into . . . after being invaded and occupied over and over since before the Greeks, they finally said, 'Okay, you say you're the boss and this is the law and this is what we are supposed to do . . . but we have our "own thing" (*cosa nostra*) and it is based on blood ties because that is all that can be trusted. It is a very, very primitive thing they are into . . .

"We stuck out like sore thumbs there with our new van and car with Rome plates – and we all obviously looked like foreigners . . . we were outsiders and it seemed to us like, if our cars were to slide off the road in one of the spots where it was crumbling away down the side of the mountain, we couldn't expect help. What we could expect was a band of who knows what to come and finish us off and strip everything bare. And that would be the last anyone would ever see or hear of us because it is so rugged there that you'd never find the remains unless someone took you to them."

Over the next few days the *Connections* crew travelled back and forth through those mountains a number of times, filming the towns – Gioisa Ionica, Sinopoli, Oppido, Mammola – where the Canadian Mafia bosses had been born and raised. The feeling of primal fear never really went away.

The towns were like little walled fortresses on the slopes of the mountains. Despite the fact that you could often see one village quite clearly from the outskirts of its neighbour, there was very little communication between them. Macadam recalls:

"We would tell the people in one place that we were going into the next one and they would say, 'Oh, don't go there, they'll kill you for sure.' And when we got to the next town and we told them were we'd just come from, they would say, 'You mean you just came from there and they didn't kill you?' They would be completely incredulous."

In Siderno, Burke and Macadam wanted film of the home of Antonio Macri, the Mafia don who until his recent death had exerted a significant influence over organized crime families in Toronto. A meeting was arranged with the local police chief but, as Macadam's diary records, "unfortunately we got very little information from him. Finally I asked him if he would take us to the Macri house and he said 'no.'

"Martyn and Francis proceeded to film photographs of criminals posted on the police station bulletin boards . . . I must say, the security at these police stations is unbelievably poor: all the windows are left wide open and they all talk at the top of their lungs, so you can hear everything they say out on the street. No wonder the Mafia knows exactly what they are doing.

"Like everyone else here, the police are terrified, but we finally persuaded them to be a bit more helpful by offering to assist them in getting information from Canada – they said they had no information about the Canadians at all. We asked them once again if they would show us the Macri house, pointing out that we had a surveillance vehicle and that no-one would ever know it had been filmed. One of the officers then agreed to guide us there: he stayed in the back of the van, hidden there with Francis and the camera."

The Calabrian shoot ended on a typically schizophrenic showbiz note. With two days of filming yet to be done in Rome, it was essential that the guide Longo remain with the crew. But Longo was due in Hollywood to discuss his life story with producer/ publicist Joe Hyams, husband of Elke Sommer. Burke agreed to phone Hyams to promise him that the ex-policeman would be in California within a few days.

"It was a ridiculous scene," said Burke, shaking his head at the memory. "It's midnight in this creepy little town in Calabria, we're up to our asses in Mafia, and here I am on the phone to Joe Hyams in Hollywood, California assuring him that our translator will be there on time to discuss his screenplay."

16
Angels and Outlaws

"They're punks. They're animals. They give a lot of beatings for no reason at all. They terrorize a lot of people. A lot of people are afraid of them, and they have a right to be."

Montreal mob member on motorcycle gangs.

Throughout the summer of 1978, Macadam snatched time whenever he could find it to work on what was to become *The Biker Connection*. It was an area he had taken almost entirely unto himself, and one that the other principals involved in *Connections* were happy to leave to him. Unlike the Mafia, long since well-entrenched in the social structure, the bikers were true outlaws in the sense that they had nothing to gain from preserving a veneer of respectability. There were virtually no internal social restraints on their inclination to use violence to solve problems. While the Mafia has traditionally been reluctant to commit mayhem outside its own community for fear of "bringing down heat" from the police, the bikers were already under such intense pressure from police that it was difficult to see how it could get any worse.

Moreover, there is a primitive wild-west concept of honour among bikers – one which scorns discretion and makes revenge an imperative of pride and dignity. Bikers who wish to retain the respect of their peers do not take challenges lying down.

In preparing *The Biker Connection* Macadam, perhaps for the only time outside the Italy of the Calabrian Mafia, had reason for genuine concern for his own safety and for the safety of his crew. Nonetheless, he was able to get close enough to the motorcycle gangs to film them without hindrance at funerals and on "runs," and even at a meeting in western Canada during which they strengthened their expanding network of drug distribution, prostitution

166

and other crime. In a sense, his infiltration was too successful, for the film shot for the bikers' sequences (mostly by Martin Duckworth) had a polish and a lyricism that belied the real danger involved in obtaining it.

"The trouble with the bikers," Macadam says, "is that you never know when they are going to turn ugly." But the lush beauty of Duckworth's film tended to obscure any real sense of that ugliness from the viewer.

The bikers' story was one that had been known to the police for several years: two rival gangs – the Hell's Angels and The Outlaws – were involved in a vicious, continent-wide battle for North American supremacy. At stake was a big share of the lucrative illicit drug distribution business. Despite their rivalries, each club had prospered, and as the founding members moved into middle age, they took on more and more of the flavour of traditional Mafia-style organized crime bosses. The chopped and chromed Harley-Davidsons and Wehrmacht helmets were now reserved for the occasional weekend run: during the week they were replaced by suit and tie and Cadillac and Corvette or Mercedes. The leaders had moved into lavish homes which were often protected by elaborate electronic devices, and some clubs had even set up real estate investment companies (under arms-length ownership, of course) through which to channel the huge profits obtained from illicit drug dealing.

The Hell's Angels, it was rumoured, had an organized "hit" squad, known as "The Filthy Few," composed of a handful of members who were willing and able to kill on contract, their fees ranging from a few hundred to as much as ten thousand dollars.

Macadam chose to make contact with the Hell's Angels' chapter in Montreal, and to do this he simply walked into their clubhouse one afternoon, and told them he wanted to make a film about them. The film, he said, would deal with police harassment. (And it did, though not from quite the point of view the bikers had been led to expect.) The members agreed to discuss the idea and a time was set for Macadam to return. This time, he met with one of the chapter's leaders (I'll call him Steve Robertson – not his real name.) Robertson was, as a tattoo on his forearm proclaimed, a member of "The Filthy Few." Once again the discussion was inconclusive: Macadam left his home telephone number and asked Robertson to call him once they'd made a final decision.

When the call finally came, it could scarcely have been at a worse time for Macadam. It was the day before the crucial meeting at Vancouver's Bayshore Inn between "Paddy" Calabrese and Joe Romano to discuss the phoney bond deal. And Burke was already in Italy, and therefore unable to assist.

Murder had prompted Robertson's call. A Hell's Angel had been shot to death by a member of The Outlaws, and his funeral was to take place the next day in Drummondville, Quebec. Hell's Angels from across North America would be there to demonstrate their solidarity, and Robertson was expecting heavy police surveillance and possible harassment. The presence of a CBC camera crew, he felt, would help to keep the police in line.

Hours later Macadam was aboard the overnight red-eye special from Vancouver to Montreal. At the airport he picked up a station wagon and sped to Drummondville to meet cameraman Duckworth and soundman Niznik at the church where the funeral was being held. Macadam located Robertson in the hairy throng of bikers and their blue jean-clad wives and girlfriends, and was given permission to film proceedings from outside the church. He asked Robertson for a driver for their station wagon and that request was granted, too. With an eager Hell's Angels novitiate at the wheel and Nyznik wedged in the open rear doorway, the vehicle sped alongside the cortege of scores of chromed and lacquered Harley 74's and chopped Sportsters with Duckworth teetering precariously on the roof and Macadam hanging on to his waist to keep him from sliding overboard. Two of the bikers captured on film by Duckworth themselves became victims of Outlaw guns within a few weeks.

On the return run to Montreal, a roadblock set up by the Quebec Police Force, the RCMP and the St. Hyacinthe police gave Macadam a further opportunity to establish his credentials with the bikers. While Duckworth filmed the operation, Macadam made himself conspicuous by demanding to see the officer in charge and then loudly berating the policeman for interfering with the bikers' civil rights.

One of the Hell's Angels was taken into custody by police and driven to the St. Hyacinthe police station. And within the hour there, too, was Macadam, demanding to know what the biker had been charged with and, on discovering that no charge had been laid, pressing for his immediate release. Back at the Hell's Angels' clubhouse, he was delighted to discover that his vocal concern for the bikers' rights had paid off; he was greeted like a minor hero and heartily thanked for his support. The barriers were coming down.

And later that month, Macadam was in Montreal on a shoot when a police contact told him of an impending raid on a Hell's Angels' farm outside the city. Macadam was there to report back to the Angels' clubhouse that one of their leaders had been arrested, and to offer his assistance in getting him sprung. His help was not needed – the biker had already been released. But his offer was appreciated.

Late in the summer, Macadam felt confident enough to approach his Angel friends with a problem. He needed contacts, he said, with other motorcycle gangs across the country to fill out his film. Could they help?

He had asked at just the right time. The Montreal Angels had been planning to meet with the Grim Reapers in Calgary and Satan's Angels in Vancouver: Macadam offered to pay Robertson's air fare to Calgary if they would take him along, and the trip was on.

The *Connections* crew met Robertson and two other gang members at the Toronto airport for the flight to Calgary. All three Angels wore their colours – the sleeveless denim jackets with the famous winged death's head emblem on the back. In Calgary, they were met at the airport by a member of the Grim Reapers, and the group drove to the posh Calgary Inn where Macadam had made reservations for them. He had deliberately reserved only three rooms; since each of the rooms had only two beds it would, he hoped, force one of the bikers to share his room.

"I thought that under those circumstances I might be able to get him to relax and talk a bit more openly," he explained.

But all three politely declined his offer. Macadam gave a spare key to his room to Robertson in case he changed his mind.

The businessmen populating the hotel lobby looked on as though the hotel had been invaded by rats as Macadam and the bikers signed the hotel register. Desk clerks stammered and fumbled with credit card forms.

"It was a fairly bizarre scene," Macadam recalls with a chuckle, ". . . nobody at the desk knew quite what to do. They had never had a party of Hell's Angels staying there before."

Late that night the room shared by the three Angels was visited by Calgary police officers wanting to know what the bikers were doing in town.

"We're on holiday," the Angels told them.

The police also visited the room occupied by the cameraman and soundman, to check their identification. Macadam, however, was left undisturbed, possibly because the hotel staff recognized him from previous stays. He learned about the police visits only when he was awakened by an aggravated Robertson appearing at his bedside to give him the news.

The following day was spent filming a motorcycle run organized by the Grim Reapers in honour of their guests from Montreal. It was a long, tiring day, and a successful one. Duckworth had shot film that later proved to be of feature film calibre. Some of it showed the Montreal Angels in earnest discussion with the Grim Reapers' leaders, in a bottle-strewn gulch that was the destination of the day's run.

Back at the Calgary Inn that night, Robertson decided he would accept Macadam's offer to share his room: there seemed less chance of being disturbed in the night by curious police. Macadam, exhausted, turned in early and fell asleep almost instantly. The next thing he remembered was being awakened once again by Robertson:

"Hey, man, turn on the TV, quick."

Macadam blinked his eyes into focus: "You turn it on. The switch is right there, for God's sake."

The television came to life, and there filling the screen was a chaotic scene of noise and dust and motorcycles and police and . . . Hell's Angels, fighting it out.

Macadam's heart sank: this must be the national news and he had somehow that day missed the biggest biker story of the year. There were dozens of them there – it looked like a full-scale riot.

"What the hell is this?" he demanded of Robertson.

"It's *Hell's Angels on Wheels*," the excited biker replied. "It's on the late show. Fantastic, isn't it?"

There was a pause, as all of this registered, and then Macadam said with measured irony: "If you ever wake me up in the middle of the night again, I'll kill you."

Robertson merely laughed.

While there was the normal amount of disagreement between the producers of *Connections* as to the merits of the biker item as it finally emerged from the cutting room a few months later, no-one connected with the project disputes that getting close enough to the bikers to film them openly was something only Macadam could have done.

Macadam credits this to the fact that he alone among the team was unattached, with no family responsibilities. But this is clearly not the whole explanation for the special kind of courage that was required to take risks no-one else was willing to take.

I asked executive-producer Dick Nielsen about it. It's the kind of problem he enjoys ruminating over.

"There are different kinds of courage," he said. "For instance, I have two friends, both of whom served in the army for most of World War II. Both of them went through a lot of the grimmest combat, slogging their way up through North Africa and Sicily and Italy. One of them has the kind of courage I can relate to: he was a foot soldier and he did everything that was asked of him, but he was the kind of guy who would always leave his bootlaces undone so that when an officer told him to do something he would always have those extra few seconds to assess the situation for himself, because he could always say, 'Just a moment while I tie up my boots.' He was scared most of the time, but he did his job alright, and he also survived in one piece.

"The other friend was completely different. I once said something to him about how terrible it must have been, going through all that combat, month after month. And he said to me, 'You know, for the first few weeks it really was horrible – I was petrified half the time. But then something inside me snapped and from then on I actually enjoyed it . . . I thoroughly enjoyed it for the rest of the war.' He was wounded a couple of times, but he somehow survived it all, too."

Neilsen paused to light his pipe, and I asked him, "Well what happened to the second guy? Did he ever 'snap back' to being normal?"

"No, I don't think he ever did."

"Good grief . . . what's he like now?"

"He's *one* of the strangest men I know," he smiled.

17
Family Life

"For me, Violi was not a leader. You know why? For me, too many times he used too many punks. Suppose your daughter is about to get married . . . he tells some guy to go and steal the gifts at the wedding . . ."

Montreal mafioso on why Paolo Violi was murdered.

The murder of Montreal Mafia boss Paolo Violi in 1978 left an obvious gap in the leadership of the city's organized crime family. *Connections*, naturally enough, was interested in finding out who was going to fill that gap. Research by Dubro and Auger turned up three likely candidates: Nicola Rizzuto, Nicola DiIorio and Joe DiMaulo.

"We decided to cover the whole thing like a campaign for the leadership of one of the political parties," says Burke. "Just find out who the candidates are, and go and talk to them." They also interviewed Vic Cotroni, the aging and increasingly infirm god-father of the Montreal family, who had resumed leadership pending the selection of a new boss.

Rizzuto was in Caracas, Venezuela, but Auger's superb contacts within the Montreal police made it relatively easy to find the other two. Each was constantly being watched by the police, and the *Connections* crew was able to predict where each would be at any given time of the day. Then it was simply a question of placing the surveillance van in position, wiring Burke and Macadam with body-packs, and setting them loose. As an added precaution, another crew member was assigned to a radio-equipped car. He would occasionally check the interview location to keep an eye out for any activity that might pose a threat to the interviewers or the cameraman inside the van. (This had been a routine since the near-fatal gassing of cameraman Granger during filming of the first series.)

A number of refinements had been made to the surveillance truck itself as a result of the experience gained in the first series. While the windows were still covered with a thin film of reflective plastic, the curtains and cardboard cutouts used to prevent back-lighting of the concealed cameraman had been replaced with an indoor "tent." The frame was made of aluminum tubing and was adjustable. Almost any rented window van could be converted into a proper surveillance vehicle in a matter of hours by installing the tent, applying plastic film to the windows, carpeting the floor to deaden sound, and installing a plywood partition between the front seat of the truck and the space in the rear.

Granger had by now painted all the metal parts on his camera, lenses and tripod with flat black paint, and would sometimes don black gloves and a black hood to complement the dark clothing he routinely wore during surveillance shoots. Any light that might leak into the van would thus be absorbed by the dark cloth rather than being reflected back outside through the smoked windows.

Ventilation remained his biggest problem: in making the rear of the vans light-tight it was also necessary to make them virtually air-tight as well: certainly, there was no way to open a window to let in a little breeze. On a warm day, Granger would be bathed in sweat. During these Montreal shoots, the outside temperature hovered in the nineties and Granger manned his camera stripped to his skivvies.

"Whenever I opened up the van after a shoot to let him out," Burke says, "I thought of that scene in *Bridge on the River Kwai* where Alex Guinness is finally let out of the little tin hothouse. I half expected Francis to come out marching stiffly to 'Colonel Bogey'.

"Usually, though, he'd just say something like, "These fuckin' punkoolos . . . I'm sick of this business. Let's get out of here.""

(For Granger, the erratic hours, constant travel and emotional and physical stress involved in his work with *Connections* resulted in considerable personal sacrifice: he began the series with a wife and a family and a home in north Toronto – he ended it, two minor breakdowns later, living alone in a tiny bachelor apartment.)

The interviews did not produce much useful information, nor had they been expected to. They did, however, prove to be highly entertaining. Without exception, the Mafia men were astonished to be confronted by journalists, and they showed it. They were not accustomed to such open interest in the selection of a new boss for the Mafia family.

Cotroni was approached as he left his sister's house in the Italian section of Montreal. It was quite an experience for the old man: he had never before been interviewed by reporters, and at first he seemed to think it might be a set-up for a hit.

Burke called out to him as he approached his car:

"Mr. Cotroni. How do you do, sir."

"How do you do."

"We're from the Canadian Broadcasting Corporation."

Cotroni is fumbling with the key to his car door. He clearly wants to get away. "Yes . . ."

"You know, CBC television. And we're just wondering if . . ."

Cotroni now notices Macadam approaching. He's cornered. "What is it? What do you want?"

"No, no. It's okay." Burke has seen the fear in his eyes. "We don't want anything. We just want . . . Mr. Cotroni, it has been alleged that you are the head of the Montreal Mafia."

"Oh, no. I'ma head nobody. I'm head myself, that's all."

"Well, they've said that you are the godfather of the Mafia," Macadam interjects.

"Oh, ho. Godfather, eh?"

"It's not true?" Macadam asks.

"No, me, I just came to see my sister, that's all."

Burke is feeling cocky. "Yeah. We wanted to ask you if you knew who killed Mr. Violi."

"I don't know."

"What is the situation on that?"

"I don't know nothing about that."

"Really?" Burke says. "You don't know anything about it?"

"Nothing. That's it. No."

"Well, we heard about someone by the name of Mr. Rizzuto. Do you know anything about Mr. Rizzuto?"

Cotroni, of course, denied knowing Rizzuto. However one of the men convicted of conspiracy to murder Violi was Domenico Manno, Rizutto's brother-in-law and *Connections* sources had told them that Cotroni must have known about it in advance.

Rizzuto and Violi had, a decade earlier, been joint contenders for the leadership of the Montreal mob: the selection of Violi had ultimately been made by the New York head office – the Mafia family of Joe Bonnano. Rizzuto had had to console himself with an assignment in Caracas to handle the mob's business there. But under Violi's leadership things had gone from bad to worse for the Montreal mob, and it is presumed that Rizzuto was able to convince the New York family – then under the leadership of Carmine Galente – that Violi had become a liability. In any case, the problem was eliminated with Violi's shotgun murder in December, 1978.

Rizzuto could thus logically be considered a fourth contender for the leadership in Montreal. *Connections* hired a private investigator who was familiar with Caracas to try to track down Rizzuto and learn something about his movements. Although the investigator had come highly recommended, Macadam and Burke began to have their doubts about him from the moment he telephoned his first surveillance report from the South American city. The message he dictated to Norfolk secretary Joyce McEwan read: "The baseball is at home plate but there is a spitball in the bullpen."

Macadam looked at the message: "What on earth is this supposed to mean?"

"How should I know?", McEwan replied.

Macadam phoned Burke and read the message to him. Burke had no idea what it meant.

The investigator had not told them he would be relaying his reports in code, much less what that code would be. Macadam phoned him back at the Caracas Hilton and spoke to him in plain English. (He has since forgotten what the mysterious message meant.)

The investigator eventually located and photographed Rizzuto's Caracas home. But in the few days budgeted for the task he was unable to learn enough about Rizzuto's movements to provide a reasonable assurance that a crew flown to Caracas from Toronto would be able to find him quickly. The plan to cover the Caracas connection had to be scrubbed.

But if Rizzuto was indeed a candidate for the leadership, one man who would know would be Vincenzo Randizi, a friend and a fellow Sicilian, who runs the Montreal coffee bar where Violi was murdered. After clothing worn by the killers was found in the basement of Randizi's coffee bar, police charged him with the murder. But he was to be acquitted after the crown prosecutor admitted there was no evidence against him.

Macadam and Burke paid a late night visit to the bar, while a cameraman filmed them through a special light-intensifying lens.

"Excuse me, are you Mr. Randizi?" Burke asked him.

"Yes I am."

". . . we would like to find out some information about what happened here a few months ago, you know, with Mr. Violi, when he was killed here . . . this is where he was killed, right?"

"Now the . . . listen to me. I have too much headache already. I don't wanna still have no more, believe me."

"You've got headaches?"

"Yeah."

"I understand that you were one of the people that . . ."

"You don't understand me. Forget about it. Have a coffee, if you want coffee. I don't want to talk about it."

". . . somebody said that Nick Rizzuto was coming back to take over from Violi."

"Like I said, I don't want to talk about it. I don't want to know nothing . . ."

The next candidate on the *Connections* list was Nicola DiIorio, who has been involved in loansharking and gambling for the Cotroni mob. He served time with Violi in prison, and was often seen with Cotroni himself. A *Connections* surveillance team led by Burke finally cornered him in a downtown Montreal parking lot at mid-afternoon, as he tried to climb into his car:

Burke: Mr. DiIorio, Mr. DiIorio . . . I'm from CBC. I wonder if I could talk to you for a minute . . . who's going to be taking over from Paolo Violi?"

"You."

"Me? I don't want the job. I was wondering about you."

"Don't worry about me. Forget it."

". . . How is your business, Mr. DiIorio, can I ask you that?"

"Very quiet. It hasn't moved up, it hasn't moved down. It's very quiet. I don't know . . ."

"What is your business, Mr. DiIorio?"

"Ah, see, if you don't know, then don't ask me."

"Well, it is true that you're in loansharking?"

"What?"

"Is it true that you are in loansharking?"

"You gotta lotta nerve!"

"Well no . . . I'm not asking . . ."

"You got a lotta nerve! . . ."

Once again, the interview continued for several minutes, but DiIorio refused to admit any knowledge of the leadership problems facing the Cotroni family. As he drove away from Burke, the hidden camera zoomed in for a through-the-windshield close-up of DiIorio shaking his head incredulously.

The interview with Joe DiMaulo (he was caught sunning himself on the balcony of his first-floor Montreal apartment) was no more informative than the others. Although the FBI lists DiMaulo as the acting chief of the Montreal family since Violi's death, Canadian authorities aren't sure: the belief in Canada is that he could have the job, but doesn't want it.

But if the interview gleaned nothing about the leadership contest, it did produce one brief insight into the life of a child of a Mafia figure. Knowing that DiMaulo had only recently returned from a long sojourn in Florida, where had fled to stay out of reach of subpoenas from the Quebec Crime Probe, Macadam asked him how the crime probe had affected his wife and children.

"Very much," DiMaulo answered. "Very much . . . I don't think I need to tell you that if you were a father of a child and you were accused in the papers all over of being a member of the Mafia . . . I mean how is the child supposed to react? So they are going [to school] with hate. They are going together to school to fight and protect themselves because of being accused every day of certain names."

"How many kids do you have?"

"Two . . . twelve and four."

"The twelve year old was quite aware of the . . ."

"Well, yeah, sure, sure, sure. And she's getting a big reaction out of this. You know, sure, she's very hurt about that . . . we brought her to a doctor yesterday and we were recommended very highly to go and see a psych . . . psych . . ."

"Psychiatrist?"

"Psychiatrist, yeah. I mean he [the doctor] came out, like he said the kid is hurt about something. You know?"

"Do you think it was the crime probe?"

"Sure. What else? It wouldn't be no other way because we are a good family . . . and they get all the love that they deserve and that's the way things should be. That's the only place that she got hurt . . . A mother one day sent a newspaper with a kid that's going to school with my kid. She said, 'There. Bring this to your girlfriend you're going to school with. This is her father. A member of the Mafia.' My kid comes home with the piece of paper and she says, 'Dad, is it true?'"

"How do you explain it?" Macadam asked.

"How did I explain? . . . I try to give her all the best explanations I can . . . what else could a father do? Try and make her understand that it's not right to believe in these false things – these things that are in the papers all the time, you know? But it is up to her to try to understand and see what their parents are, really. In the future she will understand better, have better judgement of her parents . . . What kind of explanations do we give the kid? The best explanations we can."

If the DiMaulo interview had provided a brief glimpse into the sordidness of everyday life within the mob, another interview later that fall threw a far more intense light on the subject.

Dubro had known about Chuck Carlo for months, and had spent a great deal of time during the spring and summer of 1978 trying to arrange an interview with him. Contacts in the United States Justice Department, the United States Marshal's Office, and Lee Coppola, a reporter at the *Buffalo Evening News* who knew Carlo, were all pressed into service. But in the end Dubro was told that Carlo had refused to be interviewed.

It was a serious disappointment, for the articulate Carlo was believed to have a depth of understanding of the workings of the mob that was perhaps unique. A former soldier in the Buffalo Mafia, he had in 1975 decided for the sake of his family to get out, and had offered his services to the FBI in return for a place for himself, his wife and his children in the Witness Protection Program. To fulfill his part of the bargain, he agreed to masquerade as a "fence," buying stolen goods from criminals. After nearly two years of constant tension, during which Carlo's dealings with criminals were recorded and photographed by the FBI, the operation was wound up with the arrest of two dozen burglary and robbery suspects and the recovery of half a million dollars in stolen property. Now, at 34, Carlo was a fugitive from the mob's vengeance, having been provided with a new identity, round-the-clock protection and a new job by the Witness Protection Program.

On a typically hectic day in October, two months after he had been told there would be no interview with Carlo, Dubro received a phone call from Carlo himself.

"I understand you've been making inquiries with Lee Coppola," Carlo said.

Dubro recalls, "It had been so long that I'd given up on the interview. I'd forgotten his name completely. It was quite embarrassing. I was very suspicious until I figured out who he was, because he sounded just like a mob guy.

"When I finally did get straightened out, I said, 'Oh, I thought you had turned us down,' and he said no, that was something U.S marshals [who provide his protection] had made up on their own, and he was furious about it. He said he'd called because he'd figured they'd done something like that. He asked what we were doing, and I described how he would fit in. We discussed the possibility of an honorarium – I said that we would pay his expenses. And then he chose a location for the interview. He said, 'I like to fish . . . I used to do a lot of fishing up on the French River [near Sudbury, Ontario]. We could go up there for a few days and talk and get to know one another. I'd feel secure there and we could go over everything.' I said 'Fine.' That was two o'clock in the afternoon and he was in Toronto the next day."

By then Carlo had contacted his favourite fishing lodge and persuaded them to re-open for three days and lay on a guide. Dubro had organized transportation from Sudbury to the lodge for himself, Carlo, sound recordist Weissman and cameraman Len Gilday. Macadam flew directly to Sudbury from Montreal, where he had been filming a Hell's Angels funeral, and arrived at the lodge in the small hours of the morning.

It was an unusual location for a *Connections* shoot, and Weissman remembers that, "Len Gilday and I were wondering if Jim would be wearing a tweed coat and tie; in fact we were curious to see what both he and Bill would wear because we weren't sure whether Brooks Brothers made thermal underwear." (They were disappointed when both arrived clad in nondescript nylon and wool.)

As had been the case with "Paddy" Calabrese, the entire crew liked Carlo instantly.

"Both of those guys are simply amazing," Weissman said. "Very attractive and incredibly charming. They can function extremely well in social situations . . . they can be whatever they have to be just like putting on a costume. But underneath that they know exactly who they are and what they are capable of doing, and that makes them very straightforward people. I wouldn't hesitate to put my life in the hands of either of them because I know that whatever the situation, they would know exactly how to handle it.''

After a day of successful, if chilly, fishing, the group moved several miles to a cottage on a lake, where the following day's interview would be conducted. To provide an interesting visual backdrop for Carlo, Macadam decided to sit him in a canoe tied to a swimming raft in the middle of the lake, and the camera and sound equipment were set up on the raft. The location worked well enough, although Macadam later wondered whether the trouble of setting it up had been worthwhile: when the equipment was being ferried ashore afterwards, he slipped from the raft and fell fully clothed into the near-freezing water.

This interview and another two days later in Toronto, for which Carlo donned his ''mob suit'' – a dark, three-piece affair with padded shouders – provided some of the most gripping, emotionally wrenching material in the entire *Connections* experience. Carlo's disgust at what he had been in his youth was almost palpable, and his presence on the screen, even though the lower part of his face was covered with a bandana, was riveting. But beyond that, his description of life as a soldier in the mob was perhaps the most complete, authoritative and convincing ever to be filmed. The brief segments used in *Life in the Mob, The Robbery Connection* and *Death in the Mob* made them memorable.

A transcript of the original interview with Carlo, cut slightly for editorial purposes, appears in Appendix 1.

18
Bonnie's Canadians

" . . . they have to be absolutely, scrupulously clean. Or we front it . . . in the beginning we front it in such a way that it is clean."

Bonnie's guidelines for potential Atlantic City casino investors.

The Bell installations man finally came in February 1979 to take out the special red telephone that had been sitting on Dubro's desk for the previous six months. It was no longer of any use to anybody, and its mere presence had become annoying. Whenever it rang, it was like a 3 a.m. knock on the door. A woman had to answer it, and she had to know what to say: "Hello, Frank Angelo Investments . . . I'm sorry, Mr. Angelo is out of town. This is his answering service. May I take a message?" The last time it rang, a couple of weeks before it was removed, there had been a mad scramble to find the production secretary (who'd gone for coffee) and tell her what to say when she picked up the receiver. The caller was a salesperson from the Yellow Pages wanting to know if Frank Angelo Investments would like an advertisement in the new edition.

Fat chance. Not only was there no such company as Frank Angelo Investments, there was no such person as Frank Angelo. Both had been created by Burke and Macadam as part of an elaborate scam designed to tell *Connections* who really was behind some suspicious-looking investments in Atlantic City, New Jersey, real estate. It was a scheme that was not – could not have been – plotted in advance. Rather, it evolved, on an hour-by-hour basis as Burke and Macadam worked to stay one step ahead of fast-moving events.

It was the last major story for the *Connections* crew. Appropriately, it turned out to be a breathtakingly successful demonstration of the skills developed by the team over the previous four years:

its research expertise, its ability to adapt quickly to changing circumstances, its covert filming and recording techniques, as well as its attention to detail and ability to operate successfully under pressure.

When the voters of Atlantic City approved gambling casinos in a referendum in 1976 the moribund, debt-ridden city of saltwater toffee and Monopoly became a boom town almost overnight. The crumbling Moorish hotels with their peeling concrete minarets and gargoyles were suddenly attractive investments, for this was to be Las Vegas East, just a day's drive from Manhattan. Gamblers and speculative investors were euphoric. But there were also those who feared a mass invasion by organized crime, for nowhere in the Western hemisphere has casino gambling been able to avoid infiltration by the mob.

The ambivalent feelings surrounding the developments were summed up by New Jersey Assemblyman Steven Perskie, who said: "We may be selling a piece of our soul, but we're putting a high price on it."

New Jersey Governor Brendan Byrne made an impassioned speech in which he said: "Organized crime is not welcome in Atlantic City. And I warn them again, keep your filthy hands out of Atlantic City; keep the hell out of our state."

And a New Jersey priest, at a public ceremony following the passage of the referendum, called on the power of the Almighty in this grotesque invocation:

"Give us Thy grace, O God, to always put the value of human life above the value of the dollar lest the blessing of casino gambling become a curse."

The big money moved in to the city's new-booming real estate market, of course, but it was difficult to connect any of it with the mob: it was all on the up-and-up, all strictly legitimate. Nonetheless, the *Connections'* team was convinced that by far the surest wager to be made in Atlantic City was that a substantial portion of that money was the freshly-laundered profits of organized crime.

As an American, rather than Canadian story, it was not one that would normally have been pursued by *Connections*. However, during months of investigation into the affairs of Toronto real estate investor Angelo Pucci, Dubro had turned up records of real estate investments by Pucci in Atlantic City amounting to well over a million dollars.

Pucci seemed to have obtained his investment capital quickly and mysteriously. Ten years earlier, he had been a waiter at Toronto's King Edward Hotel. Since then he had picked up large interests in substantial tracts of expensive downtown Toronto real estate. He may have been a frugal man, hoarding his tips, or he might have acquired a silent partner.

Here, *Connections'* superb contacts paid off. A source inside the Toronto mob (code-named "Lou") told Dubro that Pucci had indeed taken on a partner – none other than Toronto Mafia boss Paul Volpe. He said, moreover, that if *Connections* watched an office building recently acquired by Pucci, they would see Volpe there frequently, taking a proprietory interest in the renovations.

It was a tenuous link, at best, but it seemed worth pursuing. Researcher Daniel Dutka was dispatched to Atlantic City to do an initial reconnaissance of the Pucci properties. One, he discovered, was in an expensive new residential development – a $155,000 condominium – which neighbours referred to as "the Canadian house." Dutka reported his discovery to Toronto, and began watching the house.

Burke, already in New York with cameraman Gilday and sound recorder Weissman to film an interview, booked tickets to Atlantic City on the assumption that the house would be in use, either by Pucci or perhaps Pucci's clients or partners. When a second day of surveillance reports from Dutka continued to be negative, he was in a dilemma. The shooting schedule for the second series had been almost completely used up, and yet the series was weak on Toronto material. This could be exactly the kind of story they needed. On the other hand, there seemed little justification in sending an entire crew to Atlantic City for a few feet of film of an empty condominium, particularly since it was not even clear that there was a story to be told about it.

With the crew packed and ready to go and the scheduled departure time drawing near, Burke waited impatiently for one last telephone report from Dutka. It, too, was negative.

Burke had to make a decision, and he decided to gamble; the crew rushed to the airport to make their flight to Atlantic City.

Burke had a plan of sorts. He and Weissman would pose as husband and wife looking for a townhouse in the range of $150,000 in the neighbourhood of "the Canadian house." That would at least give them an excuse to prowl around and ask questions, and perhaps they would be able to learn more about the house and its occupants.

They struck pay dirt almost immediately. Strolling past the house on the evening of their arrival, they noticed a young woman enter a side door carrying an armload of groceries. When she emerged moments later, Burke and Weissman approached her and struck up a conversation, introducing themselves as Mr. and Mrs. Ed Burton. The woman, a pert blonde named Bonnie, told them she was the real estate agent in charge of the new development, and that she was looking after "the Canadian house" while its occupants were out of town. When Burke and Weissman explained that they were interested in buying in the area, Bonnie invited them to talk about it over dinner in her home, just a few doors away. It became clear that Bonnie knew a great deal about Atlantic City real estate and who was buying it, and in particular, about Canadian investors. She called them "my Canadians." Before the evening was over, Burke had planned his next move and had arranged a second meeting with Bonnie for the following day.

The meeting took place in a bar in Somers Point, New Jersey, late in the afternoon. During the day, Burke had been on the phone to Toronto working out the details of his plan with Macadam and Dubro; when he arrived at the bar, he was wearing a body-pack, and he checked to see that the surveillance vehicle was in position in the parking lot. He would delay Bonnie outside with small talk long enough for Granger to capture her on film.

The body-pack tape begins, "This is sound roll SN-13 on machine A. This is going to be the interview with Bonnie in New Jersey. It will take a few minutes before anything happens."

The next voice was Bonnie's: "How are you?"

"Oh God," Burke replied, "the car's out of gas. I had to get another car . . . the car I had just packed it in – wouldn't start."

"You're kidding. Where's the car? Can I help?"

Burke sweated out more small talk as they moved inside. He complained about his heavy business schedule, the need for him to be in New York that evening, the constant trips to Rome and London . . . all the hassles, as he imagined them, of a Big Time Operator. For his plan to work, he would have to impress Bonnie with his connections.

They ordered drinks and after a few more minutes of idle chit-chat Burke became more businesslike:

"Let me come right to the point. Here's why I wanted to get together with you . . . I've spent a lot of time the last few years in Europe – London and Rome – in a variety of things. One of them being getting money out of Italy, another thing is investments out of London. I got my training in a certain kind of investment area . . . I am not really the end person: I am kind of a front person, an advance man for certain people over there and here on this side of the Atlantic who have a fair amount of money. Some of the money has already gone into Miami Beach, North Miami Beach. A lot of the property there – the hotel property is now completely Canadian. It's Canadian on the front – it isn't on the end.

"I'm familiar with that," said Bonnie, "because we are actually doing the same thing." [That is, setting up fronts to conceal the true source of investments.]

Burke continued to build his story, brick by brick:

". . . We have a fair amount of money that should be coming out of Italy at some point in the future. How much, I don't know, but I can say it's in the millions and there's a lot of it . . ." [this was meant to be a veiled reference to the immense proceeds of the booming Italian kidnapping racket.]

"You can be very open with me, okay," Bonnie suggested.

"I'm being very open with you – very open with you."

"I'm obviously involved in exactly the same situation," she repeated.

"Well, the money that we – all I can say at this point is that . . . there is a fair amount of money that will be coming out of Italy in one form or another and how it gets out is a bit of a problem at this moment. And they want to bring it out through Canada again. I wanted to meet with you again because last night you mentioned your Canadians, and we are trying to establish a conduit through Toronto."

"That's easy."

"Well, we are about to find out just how easy it is . . . our problem right now is getting money out of Italy into Canada and it's a technical problem and if the snags are ironed out there should be a fair amount coming out."

The conversation then turned to some of the reasons why her Toronto people had taken such an interest in Atlantic City:

". . . And I think, my Toronto connections feel that by 1990 we'll have sawdust casinos. . . which is what they're really waiting for . . . real casinos . . . that kind of situation . . . They can't go into casinos obviously, so we buy buildings for them."

Burke, picking up on this last point, asked what the rules were for investment in casinos. Did one have to be an American, or . . .

"No, not necessarily, but they have to be absolutely, scrupulously clean. Or we front it . . . in the beginning we front it in such a way that it is [clean]."

Burke then raised the key question: would Bonnie be willing to put him in touch with her Canadians?

"My Canadians," Bonnie said, "are a company which is in exactly the same situation that you're talking about, which is what I'm chuckling about . . . since it [the money] is coming directly out of Italy through Toronto."

"It's coming out of Italy through Toronto, eh? If we have trouble, would your people be interested [in helping out]?"

"Yes."

"If we have a problem getting the money out . . ."

"We move it through Toronto very well."

"Without revealing any secrets . . . I'm not asking you any secrets . . . but just how do you move it through Toronto?"

"They've established a bank in Toronto through which they move it . . . not a big bank."

"Really. That would be ideal. The big ones . . . we stay away from them. We have had some problems with a couple of banks before, and we want to stay away from them in terms of, like, asking too many questions about certain things that we just don't want to talk about."

"That's not a problem. I mean, they have been moving money very successfully into the Atlantic City area."

Burke then played his final card. If her Canadians were so successful, he would like his own boss – a Mr. Frank Angelo – to meet with them to discuss a topic of mutual interest: money.

Bonnie agreed to talk with her Toronto clients and Burke said he would have Angelo phone her about times and places for a meeting within the week.

By the following morning, the *Connections* office in Toronto was busy creating "Frank Angelo" and his company "Frank Angelo Investments," with headquarters in Rome and a newly-opened office in Toronto. "Paddy" Calabrese was called in to play the role of Angelo. Business cards were printed with a Rome address. The red telephone was installed in the "Toronto office," on Dubro's already crowded desk.

After a briefing in Toronto during which he screened the Atlantic City film of Bonnie and listened to the tape of her conversation with Burke, Calabrese flew to Los Angeles for one phone call. For him to have telephoned Bonnie from Toronto might have awakened suspicions and caused serious complications in arranging the meeting with her Canadians. Calling her from the posh Beverly Hills Hotel eliminated that danger and reinforced the aura of vast, illicit wealth that Burke had tried to establish in her mind.

The phone call was duly made through the hotel switchboard:

"This is Frank Angelo calling from Los Angeles."

"Hi! How are you?"

"How you doin'?"

"You got my message okay?" Bonnie asked.

"Yep. Listen, I was talking to Ed, and I understand we have some mutual interests."

"That's correct."

"What I'd like to do is get together with you, if you can make it to Toronto. I understand it's a better area to meet in because your people are there."

"That's true . . . that's fine."

"Did Ed fill you in on anything as far as, uh . . ."

"Uh, very little, but I'd prefer not to discuss it . . ."

"Okay."

"We can talk about it when we meet."

"Fine."

The meeting at which Calabrese would meet Bonnie and her Canadians was set for four days hence, a Sunday. He gave her the phone number of the new Toronto "office" so that she would be able to contact him.

It was not until Saturday that the red telephone rang for the first time. A man wanted to speak to Ed Burton. He said he was calling at the request of Bonnie in Atlantic City. The man was Angelo Pucci.

Burke, posing as "Burton," spoke briefly with Pucci and the following day's meeting with "Frank Angelo" was arranged for four o'clock at the courtyard cafe of the Hampton Court hotel, by coincidence directly across the street from one of the CBC's largest production centres. Bonnie, Pucci said, wouldn't be there.

It was now obvious that one of Bonnie's Canadians was Pucci. That was no surprise. Who the others were, and whether any of them would be at the meeting, was the subject of intense speculation as the *Connections* team scrambled to prepare for the encounter.

Three rooms had to be booked at the hotel, and it took a small front-desk confrontation to get what they needed – one on the third floor for "Frank Angelo" and two on the second with camera positions facing the courtyard. Camera and sound equipment had to be smuggled in as ordinary luggage by *Connections* researchers and crew members posing as husbands and wives: a bellhop balked at carrying one suitcase stuffed with a camera, tripod, film and various accessories. The suitcase weighed as much as a small motorcycle.

Calabrese's credentials were put in order. He would have relatives in the New York garbage business – a field notorious for its Mafia connections. He was also given a manila folder containing a small-arms catalogue and several sample stock certificates from notoriously disreputable Caribbean banks: he would be leafing through the file when Pucci arrived.

By three o'clock Sunday afternoon, everything was ready. Cameras had been set up in two of the rooms and the sound equipment, including a tiny radio microphone to be worn by Calabrese along with his body-pack, had been tested. The surveillance van and a radio-equipped car were standing by in case Calabrese was asked to leave the hotel to continue the meeting elsewhere.

Two researchers occupied the courtyard table selected by the camera crews as giving them the best filming opportunity. They would leave as soon as Calabrese walked into the courtyard, so that he could then sit down at the chosen table.

At 3:45 p.m., Calabrese strolled into the courtyard and sat down at the table vacated moments earlier by the researchers, to wait for Pucci and whoever might accompany him. Five minutes later, the red telephone rang in the *Connections* office and a secretary took a message. It was Pucci – he said he was sorry, but he wouldn't be able to make the meeting.

Burke groaned when he heard the news, and there were howls of outrage from the crews. It looked as if the story had collapsed. What had gone wrong? Had Pucci somehow picked up their scent . . . somehow sensed that something was wrong with "Ed Burton" and his story? If so, how much did he know?

That evening, Burke and Macadam discussed strategy to salvage the operation. Given the elaborate security precautions they had taken in setting up the scam, it seemed unlikely that Pucci could be on to their game. His misgivings about meeting with Frank Angelo could only be explained in terms of routine underworld paranoia. If that were the case, then there might still be a chance to save the operation.

What would Mr. Big do if he had come three thousand miles from Los Angeles to Toronto for an important meeting, only to have it cancelled at the last minute? Macadam answered his own question: he'd be angry and he'd demand a new appointment. Okay, then Frank Angelo would be angry, and so would Ed Burton. Burke, as "Burton," called Bonnie in Atlantic City to bitch.

The next morning, Monday, August 21, the red telephone rang for a third time: it was Pucci again, and he re-scheduled the meeting with "Frank Angelo" for 2:00 p.m. that day, at the same location.

Once again, the crews tested their equipment, occupied the prime table in the courtyard and wired an understandably jumpy Calabrese for sound. After Pucci's cancellation of the previous day, all bets were off: no one knew what to expect. The tension was excruciating.

At two o'clock Pucci and another man approached Calabrese's table, and the cameras began to roll. Burke, watching from his hidden vantage point, let out a subdued whoop. The man Pucci had brought to the meeting was none other than Paul Volpe.

Calabrese, now a long way out on a limb, managed to maintain an appearance of relaxed affability as he stood to shake hands with the two.

"Would you like some wine?"

"No, coffee," Pucci replied.

"Annisette?"

"No."

Pucci sat next to Calabrese in the shade of the table's beach umbrella. Volpe sat opposite the two, brusque and ill-at-ease, the bright sunlight bouncing off his balding pate.

It was alarmingly clear that neither Pucci nor Volpe was in any mood for small-talk, so Calabrese got directly to the business at hand.

"Bonnie was talking to Ed about something that we're involved in and she said that maybe there was something you guys could do for us or something as far as . . ." Calabrese glanced at Volpe's face and as a result of what he saw there, immediately changed tactics.

". . . before you do anything I want you to check out where I come from . . . my uncle is in San Francisco." (Here Calabrese dropped the name of a mob member who was willing to give him a reference, to return an old favour.)

Volpe asked, "Real estate?"

"No, he's not in real estate."

"[His number] is on the card?"

"It's on the card with mine . . . the number is here, the number where you can get hold of him."

As Volpe pocketed the newly minted Frank Angelo Investments card with the San Francisco phone number scrawled on the back, Calabrese returned to business:

"Let me ask you about this . . . I don't know too much about what they discussed in Atlantic City about this . . . we've got some money and she expressed an interest – said she had somebody in Toronto who took some money out of Italy . . ."

"Out of Italy?" Pucci seemed surprised.

". . . and put it somewhere here and in Atlantic City."

Volpe seemed intensely suspicious as the explanations continued:

"I don't believe this. You came three thousand miles for this conversation?"

Calabrese replied, "Uh, yeah. I was supposed to see somebody that maybe could help us with, uh, our little venture."

"Great. How much money we talking about?"

"How much money? Oh, about five or six."

"Hundred million?"

"No, just million."

Volpe laughed derisively. "We talk with people who got two or three *hundred* million from Italy that want to invest."

"No use talking to me then," Calabrese said, "I mean, because . . ."

"It doesn't make sense here, five or six million . . . to take it out of Italy . . . it's no problem to take it out of Italy if someone wants to stick their ass out . . . if it's in American dollars."

"Well, I realize that, but so what? It . . . It's coming out of there but, uh, there was an outlet, uh, a little easier than I . . . from what I understand Paul, uh, this is the way . . . you know, this is why I came out."

"I'll give you the easiest outlet in the world," Volpe laughed. "Send it to me . . . that's all, give it to me."

"Send it today, right?" Calabrese chuckled politely.

"Send it to me, that's all . . . I mean, this broad, is she nuts, this girl, or what? She got her head screwed on? This guy comes three thousand miles . . .''

Volpe wanted to return to the question of "Frank Angelo's" credentials.

"What does your uncle do?"

"He was in the garbage business in New York. He had, uh . . ."

"In New York?"

"Yeah, in Manhattan. Yeah."

"In Manhattan?"

"Right. And, uh, he's retired . . ."

"He's alive today?"

"He's alive, he's . . ."

"He's your uncle through, uh . . ."

"My mother's side."

"Your mother's side."

At this point, Volpe ordered Pucci to telephone Bonnie to get confirmation of the Ed Burton story, and Pucci left the table for the hotel lobby.

Burke, eavesdropping via the wireless microphone concealed inside Calabrese's shirt, became seriously worried. Volpe was too suspicious, too belligerent.

Burke grabbed the room telephone and called Macadam, who was standing by at his home.

"Volpe showed up, and he's too suspicious. Something's going to happen here. Something could happen . . ."

Macadam, detached from the pressure-cooker atmosphere of the hotel room, but understanding it from his own experience, sensed that Burke might be on the verge of over-reacting . . . of perhaps trying to pull Calabrese out before it was necessary. He urged Burke to remain calm, and to telephone immediately should the situation deteriorate. As he hung up the phone, he wondered briefly whether to alert police contacts of a possible need for protection for Calabrese, but he decided against it for the moment.

Calabrese had meanwhile managed to switch the topic of conversation back to money:

"It's sittin' in Italy now."

"And is it available in Italy now, or is it in a bank in Italy?"

"No, no, no . . . some is in a bank, some of it . . . uh, a couple of people got it."

"And they're afraid to take it out?"

"Lemme . . . from what I understand, from what I've been

getting, they're getting it out and they're getting it through two of the banks in, uh, the West Indies or the Caribbean, wherever the fuck it was, alright?''

"Right. This is . . . [here, Volpe stops and shakes his head] We're dealing, Frank, with the biggest construction guys almost in Canada here, we're dealing with . . . and everything's above board. I mean, we're never going to hide nothing. And I just don't understand it . . . out of the clear blue sky, uh, to bring in money from Italy . . . If I had money here and I wanted to bring it somewhere I'll get it out.''

"Yeah, me too.''

"You know? I mean, by hook or crook, I'll get it out. It's a natural thing.''

"They want a legit . . . from what I understand . . . Can I talk to you?''

"Yeah.''

"Alright, from what I understand, I'm going for a finder's fee . . . If I can find an outlet . . .''

"Right.''

". . . I'm going to make money and I don't have to touch a damn thing, alright?''

"Well, Frank, I'm going to be honest with you. I'm going to find out about you. I'm going to get somebody to reach your uncle.''

"That's no problem.''

"Yeah. But it's just too bad, you know . . . it could have been done a bit better.''

Volpe's next question caught Calabrese off guard.

"Does your uncle know anybody in New York . . . anybody else?''

"Uh, you talkin' about people?''

"Yeah.''

"Well, yeah, he . . .''

"He knows somebody?''

"Yeah, he knows somebody.''

"You want to give me a name? Can you give me a name?''

"Well, you want to give *me* a name, and I'll tell him to call. You want to do it that way? Who do, uh, who do you want for him to call, and he'll make a phone call.'' But Volpe was not about to be lured into disclosing his New York contacts to a stranger.

"I'd like a name from him, alright?'' he insisted.

"Alright. You want me to have him call you?''

"No, no. Not me. I don't even want to talk to him . . . I just want him to give me somebody in New York that . . ."

"That can say who he is, right?"

". . . I can send somebody to New York and, uh, find out about you."

At this point, Pucci returned to the table, and Volpe greeted him expansively, as if wishing to blunt the edge of his suspicion.

"Well," he told Calabrese, "you got the best guy in the world right here . . . He's the best guy in the world. I'm his partner. Best guy in the world for real estate."

From Pucci's subsequent comments about his conversation with Bonnie, it was clear that she had confirmed the details of her meeting with Ed Burton, but that she remained unable to answer Pucci and Volpe's most urgent questions: Who *are* these guys, Burton and Angelo? Can they be trusted?

"I want you to get me a name," Volpe reiterated. "A name in New York."

"Maybe, uh . . ."

"One thing about it," he interrupted, "you hit the right thing, whoever you are, Frank. The garbage business. You hit the right one, the garbage business."

"Wh . . . wha . . . do you . . . you think I'm, uh, do you think I'm lying to you?"

"No, I don't think you're lying."

"Alright."

"But one thing about it, you hit the right thing, the garbage business . . . couldn't be any stronger, the garbage business. You know, Frank, if it's on the legit you happened to strike the right pair, believe me . . . If it's on the legit you can buy that broad a new car for a gift, because you couldn't get a better guy for real estate than this guy here."

"Just for the introduction, huh?"

"That's right . . . you could buy her a brand new Cadillac. Because if you've got people that want to invest money, you could not get a better real estate man than this guy here."

Pucci added: "And I'll tell you, there's not a better place in North America right now."

"Atlantic City?"

"It's tops. It's tops."

The meeting wound up with an agreement to meet again the following day, after Volpe had had an opportunity to check Calabrese's credentials. But the increasing risk to Calabrese made a further meeting out of the question. And anyway, *Connections* had all it needed: Volpe had been linked to Atlantic City real estate investments, and to Pucci and his growing Toronto real estate empire. As a bonus, they had Bonnie on tape talking of "fronting" dubious money as a matter of routine practice in the city.

"Frank Angelo" telephoned Pucci's office later that day to say that he had been called out of town on urgent business. He would be in touch again in a few days, he said. But contact was never resumed.

19
The Conclusion

" . . . they are saying that someone should have a talk with some people from the CBC."

**Toronto mob associate reporting the street
reaction to the second series.**

There were the usual (for *Connections*) delays in editing, once filming had been completed. In September, 1978, CBC current affairs chief Robin Taylor granted Macadam a two months' extension of Norfolk's contract. And then there was another extension, to February. Burke and Macadam, of course, fought more or less continuously over everything from the length of items to the wording of credits, which did not make life easy for the post-filming technicians. Senior editor Steve Weslak summed up the tenor of the times for me when I met him on the subway one morning early in March:

"If I ever have to work with either of those sons of bitches again," he said, "I'll kill myself." (Three months later, however, Weslak was back working with Burke on another film project.)

The material had been packaged in one ninety-minute and two hour-long programs, which were to run on three consecutive evenings. This meant enormous headaches for network programmers: arranging for three and a half hours of prime time pre-emptions is not an easy task. Their proposal that the ninety-minute program be run last instead of first to ease their problems was responded to by Burke and Macadam with a Telex to CBC president Al Johnson which began: "We wish to register our strong opposition to the compromises now being forced upon a second *Connections* series on organized crime . . . to begin this year's series with anything less than the same 90-minute format for the first show will simply confirm that scheduling rigidities now take precedence over the most important programming and audience considerations . . .''

Johnson, only dimly aware that a second series was being produced, sent a demand for information rattling down the chain of command, with the result that Robin Taylor, a harassed man at the best of times, was driven close to distraction with inquiries from CBC bureaucrats who knew even less about the shows than Johnson. The schedulers, amid loud complaints, were sent back to their drawing boards, and eventually came up with a satisfactory 90-60-60 slot for March 26, 27 and 28, 1979, with all three programs ending just before the 11:00 p.m. national newscast.

In other words, it was a more or less routine post-production period, except perhaps for the fact that the lawyers had been able to find relatively little to concern them. Apart, of course, from the night lens footage gleaned during the "special project."

Working out of the *Connections* office for three or four months, in constant contact with the people who produced the shows, seems to have sharpened my powers of observation. If I am at lunch with Burke or Dubro or Macadam, I am aware of the people at the next table, particularly if there are no women in the group. Walking up the stairs to the office, I watch men rush past me, heads down: most of them don't even see me, but I know what they look like. To swarthy men driving expensive cars I graciously concede the right-of-way at crosswalks and intersections: a few months ago I wouldn't have noticed either the car or the driver. This experience has been shared in greater or lesser degree by everyone associated with the project.

And so, when I arrived at the *Connections* office on the blustery morning following the airing of the first of the three programs of the second series, I noticed two men on the street outside the building who seemed somehow out of place. One was in the phone booth in the parking lot next door, and the other was standing in front of the post office across the street. Neither seemed particularly threatening and I promptly forgot about them. When Dubro arrived in the office an hour later he walked over to the window and, parting the venetian blinds, looked out across the street:

"There was a guy standing across the street when I came in . . ."

"I noticed him," I replied.

"I guess he's a cop," Dubro said.

"Yeah, I think he is."

And that was that – the full extent of the excitement following the airing. Police placed a similar, discreet watch on Montreal members of the production staff for a few days, but nothing happened.

Dubro's contact inside the old Toronto Mafia telephoned to tell him that the word on the street was that "some people are very upset . . . they are saying that someone should have a talk with some people from the CBC." But nothing happened.

The House of Commons in Ottawa, which had generated so much of the news following the first series with members' questions, plaudits and protests, had been dissolved for a federal election the night of the second series' debut, and was therefore not sitting. Although Toronto and Ottawa newspapers gave the series front page news coverage, those in most of the rest of the country did not. (In Vancouver, both major dailies were on strike.) The reaction of the TV critics and columnists, however, was no less outspoken in its enthusiasm than it had been for the first series. Once again, critics were willing to ignore questions of production values, focussing instead on the programs' outspokenness and the gutsiness of their producers. The fact that the series was perhaps an hour longer than it needed to be, that it was sometimes confusing and sloppily written, sometimes badly paced, and often repetitious, went completely unnoticed. This undoubtedly says a lot about normal television fare: flawed though it was, *Connections* was nevertheless far, far superior to the overwhelming mass of television programming to which viewers are subjected. It was, in fact, "epic" television, as the *Toronto Sun* described the series, complete with most of the classical flaws and redeeming characteristics peculiar to that ancient literary genre.

This time the television rating services were on the job when *Connections* was aired: the audience for the second series ranged between 1.7 million and 1.8 million over the three nights. It was, by Canadian standards, a huge audience – almost double what network programmers consider satisfying for public affairs programming – and it was remarkable for its consistency over three nights of programming. It seems doubtful, however, that it was as big as the audience for the first series, which was not measured.

Spokesmen for Toronto's half-million strong Italian community were quick to express outrage and indignation, and they soon received predictable support from politicians. The anger of the Italians was – though misplaced – understandable.

The president of the National Congress of Italian-Canadians called the programs "discriminatory, insulting and degrading" to Italian-Canadians, and demanded the resignations of the president of the CBC and the Toronto chief of police – who had ventured the opinion that the shows had done a service in alerting the public to the threat of organized crime. Toronto newspapers received a flood of mail from irate Italian-Canadians, many of whom denounced the series as "racist."

And then, in the Ontario legislature, the Minister of Culture and Recreation, Reuben Baetz called the programs "garbage," and said he agreed with spokesmen for the Italian community who felt the series had tarnished the community's image. Baetz later admitted he had seen none of the three shows.

Toronto's Metro Council rose to the occasion, acting on a resolution presented by a councillor, Joseph Piccininni to censure the CBC for airing *Connections*. The motion passed by a vote of thirty to two. On the same day's agenda was a motion calling for disciplinary action to be taken against policemen who had permitted publication in the Metro Police Association's *News and Views* of articles defamatory of Jews, Blacks, Pakistanis, Maritimers, women and homosexuals. Council decided to take no action on that motion, referring it instead to the Police Commission.

In his interview for the first *Connections* series, American organized crime expert Ralph Salerno made some relevant comments. He was speaking of the parallels between organized crime in Canada and the United States.

". . . The one distinction that I would make is that perhaps Canada is just a little bit behind us, in a very rapidly catching-up stage. We've had and dispelled the myth of the need for an Italian civil rights group . . . right here in New York. [Salerno was referring to the sad experience of the Italian-American Civil Rights League led by Mafia figure Joe Columbo until he was shot during its second annual rally.] We knew that way back in the 1930's Al Capone and criminals in Chicago infiltrated a bona fide fraternal organization called the *Union Sicilian,* and perverted it to their uses.

"You have the Italian clubs in Canada displaying the same kinds of sensitivity . . . 'Don't malign Italians,' and 'Don't pick on Italians' and they are getting angry with people like Ralph Salerno or law enforcement people who are talking about criminals in Canada. They're not getting very angry about the criminals who have formed an organization which requires that you be Italian, which uses Italian terminology in its operations . . . And very, very sadly you have not profited from our mistakes and your government in Ontario is very sensitive to five hundred thousand possible [Italian] voters . . . You're restricting your policemen in what they can do, you're ignoring the fact that those five hundred thousand people are and will be the first, the foremost and the principal victims of Italian criminals. And therefore in thinking of their sensitivities and voting power, your government is going to do very little to protect those people. Your police know that. They know that the veil of silence falls over the Italian community. That means that five hundred thousand people in the Toronto area are in fear, if they know that something is an organized crime matter. You see nothing, you know nothing and you say nothing to the government or any constituted lawful authority because . . . what all those people are saying is that they fear the power of organized crime more than they fear any sanctions the government might impose upon them for not living up to the obligations of good citizenship.

''The fact is that you have an Italian segment of organized crime which is a very important one, and the fact that people try to do something about that group has absolutely nothing to do with sensitivity or insensitivity to the feelings of all citizens who are of Italian extraction. It certainly is not impinging upon their civil rights . . . What is required is not that we stop saying ''Mafia,'' but that we define it better. I think people should understand that anybody who is in the Mafia is in organized crime, but not everybody who is in organized crime can be in the Mafia. I think we have to understand that what we call 'Mafia' is part of a much greater whole.''

The real reaction to the series came in the United States, where the Atlantic City item made front page news in several dailies, including the *Miami Herald* and the *New York Times*. Late in April the *New York Times* told its readers in a front-page story that as a direct result of the *Connections* investigation into Paul Volpe and Angelo Pucci's Atlantic City investments, the New Jersey state government was setting up a special inquiry into organized crime's links to Atlantic City real estate. The state probe is proceeding. (This fact, incidentally, makes *Connections* eligible for a Pulitzer Prize, as having performed a public service in the United States.

Whether the CBC would permit the program to be entered was not known at the time of writing.) CBS's prestigious current affairs show *60 Minutes* screened the series with a view to perhaps picking up one or two of the items, but backed away when it discovered that virtually all of them were over fifteen minutes in length and impossible to cut: *60 Minutes* likes its items to be under fifteen minutes, which the producers judge to be the maximum attention span of the program's viewers. ("Great show, though," they told Dubro.)

And now that the shows are over and the dust has begun to settle, Macadam has left for a holiday on the family's sprawling estate in England and Dubro has gone to New York to screen the series for groups of journalists and other interested parties. Burke is off vacationing in the Bahamas . . . I am left to draw some conclusions about *Connections* on my own. I have avoided asking Dubro, Macadam and Burke for theirs . . . one should never ask a reporter to draw too many conclusions about his or her own stories. The minute a reporter begins analyzing his material in terms of its effectiveness in causing change, he becomes involved in the insidious process of telling the public how to think. This is not part of the job, which is simply to provide the public with information.

The ethical questions posed by some of the techniques used in gathering material for the series – the use of hidden cameras and microphones, the setting-up of interviews under false pretences, the "entrapment" employed in the Atlantic City and Bayshore Inn scams – remain unresolved. Do men and women whose careers involve a continuing conspiracy to break the law have the same rights to privacy as ordinary law-abiding citizens? Or have they, by deliberately living outside the law, forfeited those rights?

These are not new questions, but there is an increased need to explore them, given the coming-of-age of investigative journalism on television, a medium where most investigators are, by training, filmmakers first and journalists second, and where the ratings game provides intense pressure to pay heed to audience numbers and reactions. Audience reaction to the initial *Connections* series was an important – perhaps the *most* important – factor in the decision taken within CBC current affairs to make the second series. The fact that in this particular case there was also strong journalistic merit in that decision does little to relieve one's anxiety over the kinds of non-journalistic "showbiz" considerations that loom so large in the process.

Ironically, although it was *Connections* that most forcefully raised these issues for investigative journalism on television, the two series do not provide a particularly useful framework for their analysis. Few, I think, would disagree that given the degree of public ignorance of the machinations of organized crime in Canada that existed in 1975, and the degree to which that ignorance worked to make possible the continuing expansion of organized criminal enterprises, there is considerable merit in the contention that the making of *Connections* constituted a "special case." The rationale for, if not actually suspending, then at least bending traditional journalistic standards in respect to the privacy of individuals is extremely difficult to deny.

In preparing an item on organized crime's involvement in union activities for the first series, Macadam interviewed an Ottawa union leader who had resisted the mob's attempts to take over his local of a construction union. Despite threats of violence against himself and the beating by mob enforcers of his son, he refused to knuckle under to their demands. In chatting with Macadam while the cameraman and soundman set up their equipment, the union leader told the story behind his decision.

"I asked him," Macadam recalls, "whether he wasn't really scared about taking the position that he took and he said, yes, he had been scared, but he had carried on without telling his family anything about it. They of course could see that he was worried, but they didn't quite know what the problem was. Finally, he said, he had to take them into his confidence, and he told them, 'Look, I went to fight in the war and you accepted that and you understood that I might have to give up my life for my country. If I don't stand up now against these thugs, if I'm not willing to risk my life again, there is no point in having gone to war in the first place – it would mean it had all been futile. You must understand – I have to do this.'

"He said his wife went into the kitchen and had a cry and then came back to him and took his hand, and he knew then that he had been foolish not to have talked to her sooner.

"I was tremendously moved by the story, and I asked him if he would repeat it on camera. And he said 'no.' That it would sound self-serving, and it would make him feel silly . . . that he had only done what anyone is obliged to do in those circumstances."

For that union leader, Jean-Guy Denis, for the untold numbers of other victims of the mob for whom life has been made a waking nightmare of fear and pain and for the policemen and women who are sometimes able to help them end the nightmare, the idea of a society at war with organized crime is neither metaphor nor hyperbole – it is bleak reality. *Connections*, for all its flaws, deserves I think, to be judged within this context.

But it is an uncomfortable irony – one of which Macadam, Burke, Dubro and Nielsen are all acutely aware – that when society gets around to handing out its rewards for meritorious achievement in waging that war, those rewards will go to the filmmakers alone.

Appendix I
Transcript of Bill Macadam's interview with former Buffalo Mafia soldier Chuck Carlo.

Q: Chuck, you're a made man. You were a member of the mob at one time.

A: Ahh . . .

Q: No?

A: Yes, no . . . [no comment]

Q: Did you ever go to the initiation thing yourself?

A: No.

Q: Did you ever hear about what went on during that?

A: Yes.

Q: What did you hear?

A: Well it's a ceremony for the most part. I don't think it's used like it was used in earlier years, and that's due to the surveillance of the FBI. They are kind of on top of things all the time and so you can't have a gathering of the people that are involved in that particular family, to give their blessings, so to speak. You know, it's something that's celebrated. Today they'll send one guy out and he'll go to different members and get their vote and report back to the old man. It's more or less done that way.

Q: The old man – you mean the Mafia don?

A: Uh, huh . . . I was with the Buffalo outfit, which consisted of about thirty-five to thirty-eight people. That extends into Toronto, Montreal, Hamilton, with ties in Florida, Vegas, California, New York, Rochester, all sorts of spots. When you're going to get "straightened out" [enlisted] you're under one guy's wing so to speak, and he more or less sponsors you. Of course, it depends upon his influence as to the outcome of your status. If he's very influential, the time can come quickly. When I say 'the time comes' – that's the time when somebody has to be taken care of and that's one way of initiating you, to take you on a trick. Maybe you'll put the rope around some guy's neck, maybe you'll kill him with a gun, with a knife, whatever – or maybe you won't do anything but just be there. Sometimes an opportunity such as that, and I say 'opportunity' – it's looked upon as an opportunity – comes quickly and sometimes it doesn't. In the old school they made you wait years and years and years but in the new school, the new group, there's no long waiting periods anymore. It's kind of like a watered-down type of thinking.

Q: How about Magaddino – you must have known and worked under Magaddino in Buffalo. [The late Stefano Magaddino was head of the Buffalo Mafia.]

A: Well, when you say 'known' you're talking about a man who was known from one end of the country to the other and respected. Well, I shouldn't say 'respected'. I should say 'feared'. You would be considered fortunate to be in his presence and that was a rather rare thing. He was of the old school. He never spoke directly to you. He spoke to this one and this one spoke to that one and that one spoke to you. They always insulated themselves. You still have that today in the New York mob. But you don't have that in the rest of the country. That's kind of broken down, that chain of command.

Q: What sort of man was he?

A: Well how do you . . .

Q: Why did people fear him so much? How did he get this aura of power and fear?

A: Murder. Just that simple. Murder . . . There's a story that when he first came to the area he had an argument or something and somebody slapped him in the face. They found that fellow a couple of weeks later, dead. So that kind of speaks for itself.

Q: Is there any sort of characteristic that one could apply to the Mafia leaders or the mob leaders – is there anything that . . .

A: Well that usually depends on their own stature – their standing. Most of the guys, they give the impression of being very worldly, very sophisticated, a little arrogant . . . sort of stand-offish. They are choosy of their friends and their associates – that's of course an understatment. They're very, very well dressed, impeccable manners and mannerisms. Of course they're not exactly accustomed to dirtying their fingernails either.

Q: I thought from watching Cotroni when we filmed him that he was almost regal, almost majestic in the way he carried himself.

A: Right, right.

Q: He had a quality of leadership which was very unusual.

A: Well that's a better description than I gave. Of course, that's the characteristic you find in some of the older people. They're from a different world altogether than the group that's in today. The guys today are knock-around guys. They're vulgar, they're profane, they don't have any class. The oldtimers were quiet and low-keyed. They didn't have to shout at you to get a point across.

Q: Tell me what it was like to be in the organization . . . Was it exciting – was it . . .

A: Well it has an undercurrent of excitement, you see. It's according to the way you carry yourself. For the most part most wiseguys – whether they're made guys or fringe guys or rounders or whatever – they tend to have certain mannerisms. The way they dress and the way they talk, the way they carry themselves, the attitude that they have towards other people and so on – that in itself kind of makes you exciting. You tend to pick up these characteristics from other people as you are growing, especially if you are . . . born and raised in an Italian neighbourhood. You see Joe the tailor and Joe this and Joe that carrying a lunch bucket to work and then you see Don Capino – he's got a nice Cadillac and there's always a couple of guys standing around him and they're all well-dressed. They always smile at you and say 'Hey, how ya doin' and so you tend to move toward that direction. You pick up on their mannerisms.

Q: What did you do in the mob?

A: Everything and anything. Whatever was available.

Q: Can you give me some examples?

A: Burglaries, arson, extortion . . .

Q: Were you asked to do this [by mob leaders] or were these things that you yourself initiated?

A: It depends on the man. If you're an ambitious guy and you've got connections here and there, it's something that you develop. You kind of take it from there. Most of your work you develop yourself. But of course whatever work you develop, you go to the person that's responsible for you, for your actions, and you okay it with him first. There's a chain of command . . .

Q: [The bosses] have a stranglehold on people that work with them?

A: There's no question of that. No question of that. You'll hear a lot of wiseguys – made guys – say, 'I'm not a pimp.' They're the biggest pimps there are because the mob bosses take the people that are under them and they take a piece of all the action. And what service do they supply to these people? Nothing. They're giving you permission to steal. Think about that. You. If you get caught you do ten years in the can. While you're in the can they're someplace partying. And you've got to pay them for the privilege of stealing, arson or whatever.

Q: How does that work? How does that work if you do a job – say you do a robbery?

A: Well it depends upon where you do it, first of all. There's families in most of the cities and if you're going to go into a different city you have to get permission from that family. Usually from one family to another there's *piasanos* – these guys may have been born in the same town in Italy. One guy wound up in New York and the other guy in Detroit and another guy in Miami and another guy in Buffalo, wherever. So maybe some information comes along that there's a good score in, say, New York, and whoever's territory it's in, you've got to go and get his permission. And naturally his permission means only one thing – money. They give you permission for anything . . .

Q: You pay a piece to the people who are in the town where you do the job?

A: Well you don't take it upon yourself to do anything, this is another part of the mob. You don't do things like that. You go in and you make a score and it's under so-and-so's jurisdiction. Whatever money you take, or jewels or whatever, when you come back you put everything on the table. And then he does what he has to do and he don't explain it to you.

Q: What does he have to do?

A: Well he takes whatever he feels he should take. They use a lot of excuses. You know, 'After all, I got to take care of so-and-so, so-and-so's got to get ten percent, the other guy fifteen percent the other guy ten percent . . .' By the time they get through whacking it up you're lucky if you wind up with a half a dollar on the dollar. And then maybe you got your partner and then you got to split that with him. How sweet it is. Wouldn't you like to have ten guys like me to share your money with?

Q: Do the soldiers make a lot on money? Did you make a lot of money?

A: At times I made a lot of money. Yeah, when I could keep their hands out of my pockets I could make money. Sure. It depends upon your own abilities. Some guys are real sharp, some guys aren't. Some guys have got the right connections. Some guys don't. It depends on a lot of things. But they always get a piece of you . . .

Q: Can a victim stand up to the mob and if he does, what happens?

A: It depends who you are and where you live. If you're an Italian-Canadian or Italian-American, no you can't stand up to them because the pressures are too great. First of all – social pressures. Second of all, it's inbred, you're taught from the time you're a child to show a certain amount of respect for certain types of people and never to be offensive, or talk back or cause problems. But if you're, say, the average citizen, yes. They don't dare fool around with you. They don't need the headache. They don't need the publicity. They only extort and shake down their own people for the most part, and they know they can get away with it. But the American people or the Canadian people, they know they can't get away with that. They don't dare. But people don't know that, so naturally they're afraid and they may go along with them, which is the worst thing you can do with the mob.

Q: Would you say the main power of the mob is fear?

A: Absolutely. Absolutely.

Q: And if you're not scared of them? . . .

A: They can't do – I mean, what are they going to do to you? Are they going to kill you? What do they win by killing? They cause an investigation and eventually it's got to point a finger towards them. Do they need the headaches? Again, the name of the game is to make money, not to cause waves . . .

Q: When you were in the mob did you ever have a case of anyone as John Q. Citizen standing up to you?

A: Yeah, there was a couple of occasions.

Q: And what happened?

A: Well it's usually a follow-up with a threat. Maybe you bend a car, or you throw something through the windows in the middle of the night, or slap him around or whatever. But if they show no signs of weakening and they show signs of inner courage and strength and they're going to go to the authorities, what am I going to win then? I'm going to wind up in the can: twenty years for extortion if I pursue it. So I have two options. Either I back off or I kill the guy. And ninety-nine percent of the times they back off.

Q: In those two cases where someone stood up to you . . . can you describe what happened?

A: Well, they just weren't going to take the abuse.

Q: What were you trying to do?

A: I can't go into specifics, but they weren't going to put up with it. It's just that simple. They'd say, 'You can beat me up, hurt me, but I'm not going to do it.' So what do you win in a case like that? You don't stand to win nothing. They're not afraid and if they are afraid they won't admit it. And I respect and admire them for their courage.

Q: So you backed off?

A: Absolutely.

Q: Do you think that if people'd stand up to the mob they'd back off?

A: I know they would. If people'd stood up to Hitler, there wouldn't have been a Hitler.

Q: Can you describe a typical mob robbery?

A: Well you've got to do a lot of research. First of all you have to consider the source – that's what we call tipsters. They're the people that give you the information about the party to be robbed, and you have to check him out. If he's a solid guy and his information has been good in the past, then you start to do your investigation. You'll check out the family, you'll check out the house, you'll check out the type of work that the people in the house do, what their hours are, when they're home most frequently, when they're not home, what kind of restaurants they dine in, the kind of cars they drive. You get their licence plate numbers, you run them through the motor vehicle bureau, get a rundown on them in case there's some other type of information that comes into play. You watch them leave the house in the morning, you watch them come home at night, you watch which bedroom lights are turned off first, which light is turned off last, which lights are left on when they leave the house so that you know their pattern. You find out about burglar alarm systems, dogs, kids, how old they are, are they living at home, are they in college – all that kind of stuff. You make no mistakes. There's no room for error.

Q: You have it pretty well under surveillance, do you?

A: Oh yes. It depends on the score itself. If it's a big score you spend a lot of time because you don't want to blow it.

Q: How long is a lot?

A: Anywhere from six months to two years.

Q: Keeping the house under steady surveillance?

A: Well, from time to time. What you do is you have several scores at one time. And you watch each one. They could be in different areas of the city and you'll check one this day and you'll check one the next day and on and on so that when one is ready you can pop it right on the spot.

Q: When you actually decide the time is right for a robbery, what happens then?

A: Well, you've got to go and get your tools. Usually the tools are set aside at a certain point. You got two cars. One man carries the tools and the walkie-talkies. He drives alone. He's got to be a clean guy, no police record. This way there's no reason for him to be stopped and if he is stopped it can't hold up in court because he has no police record if they should search his car and find these tools. And then yourself and whoever you're working with is in another car and then you start to make your 'in', which is already pre-planned. You know exactly which way you're going in and exactly where you're going. It's just a question of four or five minutes and it's finished, it's all over with.

Q: And when you go in, how do you go in?

A: Again it depends. It depends upon the type of structure and how it's locked up. There could be a burglar alarm system. If there is, it depends on how sophisticated it is. You might have to go through the roof. You might have to go through the second floor. If there's no burglar alarm system, you make the 'in' where you can't be noticed, or where there is the least amount of exposure to neighbours. You make it quickly and cleanly.

Q: Alright, having made the 'in', where do you normally go to?

A: Directly to the bedroom.

Q: To the bedroom – why is that?

A: Because people love to be where their money is as often as they can, whether it's jewels, coin collection, stamp collection, whatever. They want it next to them as much as possible. They don't feel secure unless it's next to them.

Q: Have you ever had a close call when you've been in the midst of a robbery?

A: There's no such thing as a close call when you're a professional burglar. Because you've always got somebody inside the house watching. They've got a police radio and they're on a walkie-talkie and they got men outside the house on both sides of the street with a walkie-talkie. So, should the people come home unexpectedly, should they not follow their pattern, should some neighbour spot something and call the police . . . well, you've got your man with the walkie-talkie to spot them as they are coming up the street and you're long gone.

Q: When you're in there are you pretty nervous?

A: You're under pressure. A tremendous amount of pressure. You can't make any mistakes because time is of the essence. You've got to get the goodies and get out as quickly as you can and you can't leave anything behind.

Q: You're working pretty fast?

A: Absolutely. Never more than four or five minutes from the time you go in, get the merchandise and out.

Q: How about arsons – are they a common activity of organized crime?

A: That's a big money-maker for organized crime. People who are in business for themselves, they usually don't have the guts it takes to do something like that, number one. Number two, when you want something done professionally you go to the experts, and the mob is always known to provide any service that'll fit your needs for the right price. I would say that most of the arson work is supplied by legitimate businessmen: mobsters themselves who buy an old building . . . they'll sell it several times, six or seven times, and each corporation will pay more and more for it until finally it's insured for half a million dollars – they might have bought it for $50,000. Then they pop it. And they have no respect for life. None whatsoever. I went on an arson trick one time out-of-town and when I got there there was a house very close to this particular place that had to be burned. There was a family in that house, so I made a call back to Buffalo and I told them, 'There's a family here. If I blow this building they're liable to get killed.' The people I was

taking orders from, they were screaming and ranting and rav-
ing. They said, 'I don't give a shit who has to die. Do what
you're told and do it now.' So that's the type of people that
we're talking about. Their reputation is at stake. If they promise
a guy that a place will be burned, it's going to be burned no
matter who dies. It makes no difference to them. As long as they
get the money. That's the bottom line. Cash . . .

Q: How about fraudulent bankruptcies?

A: That's a pretty common practice.

Q: How does it work?

A: Well let's say for example that you're a businessman who's
having problems with your business, your cash flow. You've
already overextended yourself at the local bank but you need
ten, fifteen, twenty thousand to make ends meet to keep your
doors open. Well it always seems that you'll approach a friend
of yours and speak of your problem. Sometimes it's a bank
official. They make certain recommendations: they may re-
commend that you go and see so-and-so. This man will lend you
whatever you need. The interest is a little high but you need the
money. So you meet so-and-so and you borrow the money,
everybody's happy, everybody's chummy chummy. This is
step one for them. They've done this a hundred times. Now
they'll make it so that you don't do a lucrative business. See,
they don't want you to pay back the loan. They want the
vig – that's the interest – to build up, understand? To a point
where you can't possibly pay it back, which only means one
thing. You got to turn over about fifty-one percent of your
business, or possibly all of it. They might start off with ten percent and then fifteen and then twenty, and graduate to that
figure, but eventually they'll wind up with the joint. Now, mind
you, your name is on all the certificates, all the business papers,
so it appears perfectly legitimate and that's where they have the
edge. They can't get these licences. They can't function in
society so they need you, and they use you and by the time they
get through with you, you're penniless. You're destroyed.
Your life is destroyed and there's nothing you can do about it.

Q: They want you still in the business, though, do they?

A: Yes. They have to have you there because they'll order merchandise, hundreds of thousands of dollars worth of merchandise, you see, and then they'll sell it at half the legitimate
wholesale price and you'll declare bankruptcy. How you going

to pay your bills? Now you face fraud. And if you look like you're going to be a problem to them, they'll kill you.

Q: Okay, we've talked about bankruptcies, we've talked about the various activities, but . . . what about the mob's involvement in murder?

A: Let me clarify something for you. You don't go to a made guy and say, 'Listen, I want so-and-so bumped off, here's five, ten thousand dollars,' cuz he'll tell you, 'Yeah, sure we'll take care of it.' He'll take your money, and when you come around a short time thereafter he'll give you a slap on the face and tell you to get lost. What are you going to do about it? But they'll murder their own people or people who are on the fringe. People that they deal with daily. Armed robbers, burglars, arsonists, gamblers – even soldiers. Once in a while a lieutenant, a cappo. When they murder a guy they murder him in a certain way, to send a message to other people.

Q: What way?

A: Well in the case of a stoolpigeon, they might cut your penis off and stick it in your mouth. Maybe you thought you was a tough guy – they're liable to put a rope around your neck and tie it to your feet. When they let go of your feet you slowly choke yourself to death, and they pull your pants down and leave you laying there somewhere on the street to show that you're a punk. Sometimes they'll kill you with an icepick, too. Certain guys, that's their favourite weapon, an icepick. They like to take a guy and hang him on a meathook and then just stick him with the icepick. One guy made a crack one time – he said, 'When I get through with this guy we'll shove the hose in his mouth. He'll make a beautiful lawn fixture, be sprinkling all over.' You know what I mean? And they laugh about it. They like to see you squirm. They like fear. They thrive on it. They like to prove to themselves what men they are.

Q: Have you ever seen any of these atrocities?

A: No comment . . .

Q: Are there other examples that you can think of?

A: It used to be they'd go to work on you. Get a baseball bat and break your legs, or your arms – you know, break some fingers, that kind of stuff. That's a warning. But they don't do that any more because it doesn't pay off to do that. In the old days with the *moustachios,* if a guy got worked on or worked over, he'd keep his mouth shut. It was a question of pride to him. He took his beating and he kept his mouth shut. Today, with the FBI and the Witness Protection Program and all the things that are available to criminals who are being exploited or extorted, they don't keep their mouth shut. You go to work on a guy with a baseball bat, chances are he's going to run to the FBI because he knows he can live happily ever after someplace else. He don't have to take that abuse from you. So they no longer break your arms and legs. They just kill you . . .

Q: How many murderers have you known?

A: Well listen. You know, people in the mob or outside the mob, they don't talk about how many guys they've killed, you know what I mean? You might hear that so-and-so's got two under his belt or so-and-so's got four under his belt, or that so-and-so when he got mad he used a knife to cut the guy all up or he broke a gun on his skull, or whatever. So, how many murderers? How many made guys are there in the mob? That's how many murderers.

Q: When these people have to kill, does it work on them – do they have nightmares, or do they have regrets? . . .

A: Nightmares? What, are you crazy? Regrets? What are they gong to regret? If you even show the slightest weakness when it comes time to kill a guy, when you go on the score to kill that guy, they'll kill you. So what regrets?

Q: The first time someone murders it must be difficult, though?

A: Well you're asking me a question that only a murderer could answer. I'm not a murderer. I can't answer it.

Q: No, no. I'm saying that the first time a kid or a made man goes to shoot somebody, that must be a pretty difficult thing.

A: Well how could you say that? If it was so difficult, you wouldn't do it in the first place. What's the greatest gift in this world? It's life isn't it? Who gave you the right to take it? Then why do they kill time and again and again and again?

Q: You don't think there's any . . .

A: Well how could they have a conscience? What conscience could you have? . . . Naturally there's a reason. They like to kill and perform a ritual, if you know what I mean. It's a technique. They've mastered the art of murder. For example, a guy by the name of Johnny Cameleri – there was a split in the outfit in Buffalo and he was behind it all. So on his way to a place that he frequented – it was his birthday as a matter of fact and they were having a little party for him – they shot him to pieces, you know, right at the door, just as he went to walk in.

And then one time there was a kid by the name of Richie Falice – a rough-and-tumble kid. He had given one of the mob's sons a rough time, so they called him in on the carpet. They had a sit-down and the kid didn't realise what he was playing with. He thought these guys were honourable guys. He told them right out, he said, 'Listen, I'll fight any of you man-for-man, toe-to-toe.' But the mob don't have any men. They don't work that way. So they got somebody who was close to this kid, another made guy naturally, another member, and one night this kid was bowling and this guy whispers something in his ear. Something like, 'Hey, Richie, so-and-so wants to see you. They're going to make that score tonight.' The kid was a knock-around guy. He was a burglar, an armed robber, fooled around with junk, whatever. He stepped outside of the door of the bowling alley. They found him a few hours later one block away. They had kicked in his ribs, his face, broke all his bones. They tied a rope around his neck and they bound his hands behind his back and then they tied the rope around his feet – his ankles – and they put the rope from the feet to the neck and they held his feet back towards his neck, so when they let go the rope pulled on his neck. You understand? And he strangled himself to death. And that's the way they killed him. I think he was nineteen years old, maybe twenty. He was just a baby. He had a wife that was pregnant, was going to give birth. But you see they're men of honour. They have compassion and feelings. That's why they killed him because they're so compassionate.

Q: Does it happen a lot?

A: It happens as often as necessary. For whatever reasons that they feel it's justified. No-one in the mob can make a hit without permission from the top. There has to be a sit down. It has to be okay. So when a guy is murdered, it comes from the top on down. Certain people in the circle know . . .

Q: Can I ask you what a typical day might have been like for you?

A: Well the day was determined by how the night ended. You start off your day like everybody else. You shower, you shave, you have breakfast, sometimes just a cup of coffee at home because you like to eat out all the time, you're used to eating out a lot. You go for breakfast and you run into so-and-so and so-and-so and you might talk about this and talk about that. You got a few things on your mind. You want to check this out or check that out and the day passes and you go home and have your dinner or you go out and have your dinner. Or you come home and freshen up, get a little more dapper, meet your girl or meet some of the guys at a local cabaret spot where certain people congregate: wiseguys, rounders, burglars, stick-up men, arson men, guys like that. And you talk, you just kibbitz, and sometimes out of small conversations come big things. Things happen.

Q: What about the family in all this?

A: Well, you're talking about me personally or you're talking in general?

Q: In general.

A: In general, wiseguys make a big thing out of their family. They say you got to respect your wife and respect your kids, but that's bullshit. How're you respecting your wife and your kids when you're never home? How do you respect your wife and kids when you're out committing crimes all the time? How do your wife and kids benefit by you being in the can doing time, or having your name in the paper?

Q: How about you yourself with your wife and kids?

A: I was like the rest of them – a bum. That's all they are. Glorified bums. Just that simple. Selfish.

Q: So the family isn't a major part of a mobster's life – his personal family?

A: Well he makes it appear that way. That's part of the con. After all, anybody that's respectable does well by their family, isn't that right? Well they always *appear* to do well by their family. 'Look at the beautiful dresses I bought for my wife, the nice shoes I bought for my kids.' Takes the family on vacations. But where did they get the money from? What about girlfriends!

Q: Do they know what you were doing for a living?

A: They have an idea, but they don't really know and they aren't allowed to ask any questions. It's a little different in a wiseguy's family. [The wife] doesn't ask any questions. And she doesn't have a sweet life either. She's got a miserable life as a matter of fact. She's forced to socialize with other wiseguys' wives and she's not allowed to move about freely as people in other families do where the wife has a say. The wiseguy's wife has no say. Nothing. Just take care of the kids and the house and shut up.

Q: Okay, you're through with it all now – what made you get out?

A: Conscience, I guess. It's . . . seeing all the deceit and trea-chery around me and being part of it. Realizing that you spend most of your life making an art out of beating people out of things. I didn't go to work every day, let's put it that way, so how did I make my money? I made it through scheming, treachery, crime and here I have four children and I'm raising them in this atmosphere. My friends, my associates – so-called friends . . . they're not my friends . . . they're all the same calibre of people so that's all my children were exposed to and that's all life would have to offer them if I didn't break away from this, you understand? I had to break away at all cost . . . It's difficult for me to preach one thing to my children and in fact I'm doing just the opposite . . . As an intelligent human being it got so I just couldn't justify my actions.When I couldn't justify it in my own mind the way the rest of them do. They have to justify these things on a daily basis. They have to. Otherwise they couldn't function. They couldn't live with themselves. But I reached the point when I could no longer justify it. As an intelligent human being I couldn't justify my actions.

Q: You couldn't justify continuing on in the mob. It came – it was starting to get to you?

A: That's right. If – if I was a selfish person and thought only of myself and had only myself to take care of, then it's a different story. Then maybe I would have continued – I don't know. I'll never be able to answer that question. But I had four children and I had to make a life for them, so I did what I had to do.

Q: Was it a pretty difficult decision to make?

A: Well it took me two or three years to make it. I thought about it for a long time. I didn't know how I was going to do it. I knew I was going to do it but I didn't know how. I didn't know by which means.

Q: What would the mob do if they knew you were sitting here talking to me now?

A: What would they do? Well if they could get their hands on me they'd kill me nice and slow. Just that simple, but who cares? What's the difference? I could tell you to walk off a curb and you would get hit by a car. I'm not afraid of them. That I'll tell you right off. If I was afraid I wouldn't have done what I did . . .

Q: Why won't mobsters talk after they've been sent to prison?

A: Well I'll tell you what. If you ask a guy why he won't open up, he'll tell you it's a question of honour, it's a question of self-respect. That's bullshit. That's all bullshit. It boils down to two things. One is fear and the second and more important one is that you're born and raised in one neighbourhood and all you know how to do is to take 'action'. Maybe you're a bookmaker, maybe you're an arson man, maybe you're a burglar or a stick up man, maybe you're an all-round athlete . . . but all your connections stem from that neighbourhood, you understand? All the people that you earn with, that you make money with, they're all criminals. So if you can't be trusted, if you're a stoolpigeon, how are you going to earn? And not only can't you earn, but you can lose your life. So that's why they keep their mouth shut. There's no honour. What honour? You mean to tell me there's honour with people that rob and steal and murder? What honour? They don't even respect their own families – how are you going to respect somebody else? Where's the honour?

Q: It's called the Honoured Society.

A: Yeah. Honoured by whom? Do you honour it? You want to socialize with murderers, extortionists, arsonists, burglars? Is that the kind of people you mix with? Well it's an honoured society, right? Honoured by whom and for what?

Appendix II
Program Synopses.

Connections I, June 12, 1977

The first program opened with several definitions of organized crime as presented during interviews with several acknowledged experts – on both sides of the law. It was followed by *The Montreal Connection*, which sketched the history of the Cotroni/Violi Mafia family in that city, and its long-standing ties with the New York Mafia family of Joe Bonanno, who had been recently deposed and replaced by Carmine Galente.

The *October Crisis Connection* explained the links between Quebec cabinet minister Pierre Laporte (murdered in 1970 by his FLQ kidnappers) and Montreal Mafia figures. Featured was an interview with a former executive assistant to Laporte, who said he had looked for campaign financing from Nicola Dilorio, a key lieutenant in the Montreal mob. He also disclosed that the Mafia had offered its assistance in trying to locate Laporte after his kidnapping.

The Loan Shark Connection was a chillingly authentic examination of one of organized crime's major money-making enterprises. As with the rest of the series, it derived much of its impact from the fact that many of the people involved were shown on the screen, and some were even interviewed. It had the added dimension of a taped telephone conversation between a victim of a Montreal loanshark and the loanshark himself. As the camera zoomed slowly in on the revolving reels of a tape recorder, the voice track presented an unfolding life-and-death confrontation in which the victim argued that he was unable to pay the exorbitant interest being demanded, and the loanshark threatened to bomb the victim's home and have his wife and children shot.

The Toronto-Buffalo Connection began by taking the government of Ontario to task for refusing to admit to the existence of organized crime in Toronto. It then proceeded to systematically demonstrate that in the Toronto area there was not just one Mafia family, but a thriving confederation of four led, respectively, by Paul Volpe, John Papalia, Natale and Jimmy Luppino, and Mike Racco. It pointed out along the way that while Racco's son Domenic was serving time in prison for shooting another youth, representations on his behalf were made to members of the Penitentiary Service and the Minister of Justice in Ottawa by Federal Liberal MP Charles Caccia. (Caccia was later to report he had dropped the case on learning of Racco's background and current activities.)

Next came *Portrait of a Mobster,* a thumbnail profile of Toronto Mafia boss Paul Volpe, which included film of Volpe in the back yard of his home talking with Macadam and excerpts from an "interview" Macadam had recorded secretly on his body-pack tape machine in the kitchen of Volpe's house. Volpe's wife, it was disclosed, was a buyer for one of the country's most fashionable women's clothing stores and his brother Albert owned a chic antiques boutique in Toronto's crypto-Bohemian Yorkville district. Another brother, Frank, helped run the family's huge loansharking operation.

"I'm not ashamed of anything I do," Volpe was heard saying. "I'm not a pimp. I'm respectful to my wife, I don't molest young girls, I don't go out and booze and look to beat up girls – I don't do none of that stuff. I don't go and hit my wife across the face. I've never touched my wife . . . and I guess that bothers them [the police] . . ."

The Union Connection detailed the attempts by members of the Luppino Mafia family to take control of an Ottawa plasterers' and cement masons' union, and the courageous efforts of union official Jean-Guy Denis to resist them. Denis explained on camera how he had been threatened with violence several times by Natale Luppino, and his son described how he had been beaten by two Luppino thugs after they had come to the door of his house looking for his father.

Denis recalled his reactions to the threats and violence in a way that lent justification to the whole *Connections* effort to put the names and faces of organized crime before the public:

"I couldn't believe it, myself. I felt, you know, this can't happen here. It's Canada, and everything should be peaceful. When I realized that these people were actually members of organized crime, I decided I had to stand up and fight . . ." It was one of the series' most moving moments.

The *Chemical Drug Connection* described Toronto as the illicit "speed" capital of the world. It was built around film of the United States DEA Washington operations room – the so-called "war room" and film shot by a *Connections* crew shortly after an RCMP raid on an illicit speed factory in Toronto.

The final item on the first program, *The Family Connection*, was the shortest of the show, but also the most significant. In it were detailed for the first time in public the elaborate blood ties that bind together the various Mafia families across the nation. It was a revelation to even the most experienced Mafia-watchers, and it represented the culmination of the project's research effort. It began with a wedding, and the narrator's script read:

"In the world of organized crime, weddings can be more than just the union of bride and groom. They can also be the formation of alliances or a renewing of old underworld acquaintances. So it was in 1972 at the wedding that united the Luppino family of Hamilton and the Commissos of Toronto.

"There was the proud father of the groom, old Giacomo Luppino.

"There were the brothers of the groom, Jimmy and Natale Luppino.

"And among those from the bride's family was her cousin Rocco "Remo" Commisso.

"And from Montreal came Pietro Sciarra, later murdered, just after seeing the movie, *The Godfather*.

"Another relative in attendance was Paolo Violi, the head of the Montreal Mafia.

"And from Toronto there were the Volpes – Paul and Frank. And John Papalia from Hamilton.

"From Guelph, Ontario, came Frank Sylvestro. And the godfather of the Montreal Mafia, Vic Cotroni was present.

"And if one wedding can bring together most of the criminal power of the country it becomes useful to look at the family ties that have evolved over the years. At the centre there is Paolo Violi, the leader of the Montreal Mafia. And Violi's best man and also godfather to one of his children – Vic Cotroni. And Violi's father-in-law Giacomo Luppino of Hamilton . . . and his sons Natale and Jim . . . who thus become Violi's brothers-in-law. And Paul

Volpe of Toronto, who is godfather to one of Natale Luppino's sons.

"It is Volpe who arranged the lawyer for Violi when he was arrested in Toronto.

"And then there is John Papalia of Hamilton who is godfather to Violi's son.

"And among the sons of old Giacomo Luppino is Domenic who, as well as being a brother-in-law of Violi is a son-in-law of "Remo" Commisso who, it has become clear from wiretaps, is one of Paolo Violi's key Toronto associates.

"But the ties are not limited to the East. For in Vancouver there is Carlo Gallo. One of his children has Paolo Violi of Montreal for a godfather. And Carlo Gallo has recently been implicated with "Remo" Commisso of Toronto.

"And then there is Joe Gentile, Gallo's boss and a key figure in the Vancouver underworld. He is godfather of one of Violi's children."

Connections II, June 13, 1977

This program opened with *The Financial Connection*, an attempt to answer the question, "What do these hoods do with all their money?" It described how former contract killer Meyer Lansky had diverted his considerable talents into the world of finance and had invented a series of methods for "laundering" the mob's dirty money so that it could be channelled back into legitimate business-es. It introduced his Toronto associate and the man who had done much of his banking in Switzerland and elsewhere – John Pullman. It also introduced an associate of Pullman's and detailed a launder-ing operation undertaken by that associate Burnett for a Detroit man.

Next came *The French Connection*, a description of the origins of the notorious Marseilles-New York heroin pipeline, and of the largely unknown role played in the operation by Montreal gangs-ters. As a French-speaking city, Montreal provided a comfortable working environment for the Corsican drug dealers and couriers; one that was just a few minutes' air time from New York City, where they made frequent visits to collect money, make deals and settle disputes. The item included interviews with two Canadians who were former French Connection couriers and who had been located by researcher Michel Auger. There was also a taped tele-phone conversation between Montreal drug dealer Frank Dasti (a member of the Cotroni/Violi operation) and a New York customer eager to buy cocaine from him. The chat between the crooks provided some low humour with its simple-minded code ("suits" was used to represent pounds of cocaine) and the customer's complaints about the merchandise: "It's gummy. I don't know what the hell it was. It's like, gummy – you know? And all that hard gummy part they've got to cut away . . . ." The tapes had been obtained by *Connections* from an American source, and provided a complete and startlingly candid record of a major cocaine transaction from beginning to end.

The French-Canadian Connection was structured around the sensational interviews with Claude Dubois and one-time rival gang leader Pierre McSween. It detailed the rise to underworld power of the Dubois brothers and the challenge they had recently presented to the established Mafia organization for criminal supremacy in the city. It was not a new story but, once again, the impact of seeing the principals involved chatting casually with interviewers or going about their business under surveillance by *Connections* cameras, was enormous.

The Political Connection was a straightforward presentation of the story of Pasquale "Paddy" Calabrese's encounters with Vancouver MP John Reynolds.

Calabrese was interviewed, using the cover name – Pat Cala – from his Vancouver undercover role. Reynolds was also given an opportunity to tell his side of the story.

The final hour of the second program was devoted to what was perhaps the most ambitious investigation undertaken by *Connections:* an exploration of the role which five former Hong Kong policemen known as the Five Dragons might be playing in the Canadian West Coast drug scene. It was an extremely complex story to try to tell on television, and one in which even police intelligence units had been able to supply relatively little useful support, since they themselves had only recently begun to investigate these men.

The Hong Kong police force was described as among the world's most corrupt, a charge supported by former Hong Kong police department officer Walter Easey:

". . . the force was about eight or nine thousand strong and I know definitely of two people who weren't [being paid off by criminals]. One was a religious nut – he was a Plymouth Brethren or something – the other was just crazy and no-one could trust him, so . . . he never got anything and he was thrown off the force shortly afterward . . . he was too unreliable to pay."

Royal Commissions into the situation had uncovered the fact that the police in Hong Kong ran most of the night life and the crime that fed on it. And the five police sergeants who were reputed to be the richest, most corrupt and most powerful on the force, the item disclosed, had all recently moved to the Vancouver area. The men were called "The Five Dragons."

The question was raised of how and why these men – each worth a fortune in money obtained in Hong Kong bribery and corruption – had been allowed to move to Canada. The program documented substantial real estate holdings in Vancouver and Toronto controlled by members of the Five Dragons.

The story was then extended into the realm of the Five Dragons' connections with police, in Canada. Walter Easey described how, at a dinner in Vancouver with some old Hong Kong police buddies, he had asked about the Vancouver law enforcement situation, and he had been told there was no problem: that they had the police situation under control.

This was followed by an interview with an unidentified man who had been one of the biggest drug exporters operating out of Thailand. He stated that he had refused to testify in a Vancouver drug trial because he believed that the Vancouver RCMP was infiltrated by informants who were known to have leaked information to traffickers. Such a police force, he felt, could not offer him adequate protection.

Connections: The Second Series

This series of three programs opened with a general update on what had happened in the lives of some of the principal players in the first two shows. From there it moved into a profile of Paolo Violi, examining the reasons for his rise to power in the Montreal Mafia and the conflicts that led to his murder in 1978. Then came *The Godfather Connection*, a look at the "leadership race" taking place in the wake of Violi's murder and featuring the Burke-Macadam interviews with Vic Cotroni, Vincenzo Randizi, Nicolo DiIorio and Joe DiMaulo.

A brief item on the new a phisticated techniques being used in organized crime robberies provided a transition from the Montreal items into the story of the Vancouver stock scam, in which Calabrese was shown discussing the sale of "stolen" securities with Vancouver mob figure Joe Romano.

Two more items filled out the first ninety-minute program. One was *A Visit from the Mob*, which looked at the mob's extortion techniques and featured a Montreal Police Department videotape of an actual extortion attempt against a local notary. Complete with sound, it had been made with a concealed police camera, and had all the drama of real life. The second portion, *Death in the Mob*, dealt with the mob's ultimate source of power – murder. Leaning heavily on excerpts from interviews with Vincent Teresa and Chuck Carlo, it described some of the techniques and rituals of organized crime killings.

Program Two began with Burke's interview with an oily Montreal promoter and pimp named Ziggy Wiseman. As with the other interviews with confirmed criminals, this one provided little hard information, but simply by letting the man state his own case conveyed volumes about his way of life. And in so doing it went a long

way toward dispelling any romantic illusions about a mob composed of tough, wily, honourable men in the Al Pacino mould.

The Toronto Connection, which followed, was a sequel to a
portion from the first series in which all the main Toronto mob
figures were introduced. It served as a set-up for *Toronto Update*,
which described the changes in the lives of these men over the past
two years. Notable was the release from prison of Domenic Racco,
the extension of the Luppino operations into the trucking industry
and the blossoming of the real estate empire of Paul Volpe associate
Angelo Pucci. From Toronto, the program jumped briefly to Haiti,
to establish Paul Volpe's long-standing connection there with casino gambling.

Then came *The Casino Connection*, the story of the search for
"Bonnie's Canadians" in Atlantic City, New Jersey and Toronto.
As with the Vancouver stock scam, the item worked extremely well
as television, thanks to the careful planning and the courage and
resourcefulness of Paddy Calabrese.

Macadam's essay on the Hell's Angels, *The Biker Connection*,
opened the final program, which then moved through a repeat of the
Family Ties section of the first series (showing the blood links
between the nation's various Mafia families), the item on the Getty
kidnapping and the other Italian story, the *Calabrian Connection*,
and to the concluding item called *Life in the Mob*. This last section
relied heavily, once again, on material from the interviews with
Vincent Teresa and Chuck Carlo. Given that it was composed
entirely of what television producers derisively refer to as "talking
heads," it had a dramatic potency that was breathtaking due to the
material's authenticity. On television, as in other media, the truth is
a powerful attention-grabber.